Iain Sinclair

Noise, Neoliberalism and the Matter of London

Niall Martin

Bloomsbury Academic
An imprint of Bloomsbury Publishing Plc

B L O O M S B U R Y
LONDON · OXFORD · NEW YORK · NEW DELHI · SYDNEY

Bloomsbury Academic
An imprint of Bloomsbury Publishing Plc

50 Bedford Square	1385 Broadway
London	New York
WC1B 3DP	NY 10018
UK	USA

www.bloomsbury.com

BLOOMSBURY and the Diana logo are trademarks of Bloomsbury Publishing Plc

First published 2015
Paperback edition first published 2017

© Niall Martin, 2015

Niall Martin has asserted his right under the Copyright, Designs and Patents Act, 1988, to be identified as Author of this work.

British Library Cataloguing-in-Publication Data
A catalogue record for this book is available from the British Library.

ISBN: HB: 978-1-4725-7484-8
PB: 978-1-3500-2847-0
ePDF: 978-1-4725-7486-2
ePub: 978-1-4725-7485-5

Library of Congress Cataloging-in-Publication Data
A catalog record for this book is available from the Library of Congress.

Series: Bloomsbury Studies in the City

Typeset by Integra Software Services Pvt. Ltd.

Iain Sinclair

Bloomsbury Studies in the City

Series Editors: Lawrence Phillips, Regent's University London, UK; Matthew Beaumont, Senior Lecturer in English, University College London, UK.

Editorial Board: Professor Rachel Bowlby (University College London, UK); Professor Brycchan Carey (Kingston University London, UK); Professor Susan Alice Fischer (City University of New York, USA); Professor Pamela Gilbert (University of Florida, USA); Professor Richard Lehan (University of California, USA); Professor John McLeod (University of Leeds, UK); Alex Murray, Lecturer (University of Exeter, UK); Professor Deborah Epstein Nord (Princeton University, USA); Professor Douglas Tallack (University of Leicester, UK); Professor Philip Tew (Brunel University, UK); Professor David Trotter (University of Cambridge, UK); Professor Judith Walkowitz (Johns Hopkins University, USA); Professor Julian Wolfreys (Loughborough University, UK).

The history of literature is tied to the city. From Aeschylus to Addison, Baudelaire to Balzac, Conrad to Coetzee and Dickens to Dostoevsky, writers make sense of the city and shape modern understandings through their reflections and depictions. The urban is a fundamental aspect of a substantial part of the literary canon that is frequently not considered in and of itself because it is so prevalent.

Bloomsbury Studies in the City captures the best contemporary criticism on urban literature and culture. Reading literature, film, drama and poetry in their historical and social context and alongside urban and spatial theory, this series explores the impact of the city on writers and their work.

Titles in the Series:

New Suburban Stories
Edited by Martin Dines and Timotheus Vermeulen

Irish Writing London: Volumes 1 and 2
Edited by Tom Herron

London in Contemporary British Literature
Edited by Nick Hubble, Philip Tew and Lynn Wells

Salman Rushdie's Cities
Vassilena Parashkevova

G.K. Chesterton, London and Modernity
Edited by Matthew Beaumont and Matthew Ingleby

Brooklyn Fictions: The Contemporary Urban Community in a Global Age
James Peacock

Contents

Abbreviations   vii

Introduction - 'Doctored maps, speculative alignments':
    Iain Sinclair and the Matter of London   1
    Noise and Iain Sinclair   10
    The return of the unselected   14
    Noise as parasite   18
    Staging and the locative effect of noise   20

1   Reforgotten Cities: Noise and the Politics of Method   27
    Finding form   27
    The locked shutter   29
    Walking the city: Psychogeography as cut-up   38
    The 'John Bull printing set' and small-press politics   47
    Reforgetting: Forms of complicity   51
    The walk as spatial collage   54

2   Parasitic Poetics: *Lud Heat* and the noise of genre   59
    Background noise: *Lud Heat* and its contexts   60
    The 'charting instinct': Long poems, big cities   64
    'These facts fade. The big traffic slams by':
    Art in absolute and abstract space   72
    '[I]n there for the duration': Poetry as workplace   77

3   The Vessels of Wrath: Noise and Form in *Downriver*   87
    The empty vessel   87
    '[N]o female sound': Noise and narrativity in *Downriver* 92
    The locked room   98
    '[No] sides to take': The fiction of disorientation   104
    Opposition in a world without sides   108
    The 'vessels of wrath': Satire and cynicism   116

4   Between Archive and Ash: *Rodinsky's Room*   121
     The solemn mystery of the reappearing room   121
     Noise as *lieu de mémoire*   123
     Room as archive   125
     Lichtenstein and noise as redemption   128
     Sinclair and the production of absence   132
     Ghost storage   138

5   Roadworks: Orbiting the Orison   141
     The politics of bus stops   143
     The road as parasite   149
     An unpeopled country: Misrecognition and
     reforgetting on the Great North Road   160

Conclusion - *Ghost Milk*: Calling Time on the Grand Project   179

Works Cited   188
Index   199

Abbreviations

AA   Sinclair, I. (2013), *Austerlitz & After: Tracking Sebald*, London: Test Centre.

AS   Sinclair, I. and Klinkert, R. (2007), *Ah! Sunflower*, The Picture Press, DVD.

CC   Sinclair, I. (1996), *Conductors of Chaos: A Poetry Anthology*, London: Picador.

D   Sinclair, I. (1991), *Downriver*, London: Paladin.

DB   Sinclair, I. (2007), *Debriefing*, The Picture Press, DVD.

DD   Sinclair, I. (2007), 'Diving Into Dirt', in S. Gill *Archaeology in Reverse*, London: Nobody in Association with the Archive of Modern Conflict.

DS   Sinclair, I. (2004), *Dining on Stones*, London: Hamish Hamilton.

EO   Sinclair, I. (2005), *Edge of the Orison*, London: Penguin.

GM   Sinclair, I. (2011), *Ghost Milk*, London: Hamish Hamilton.

HRE   Sinclair, I. (2009), *Hackney, That Rose-Red Empire*, London: Hamish Hamilton.

KMD   Sinclair, I. (1971), *The Kodak Mantra Diaries*, London: Albion Village Press.

LCD   Sinclair, I. (2006), *London City of Disappearances*, London: Hamish Hamilton.

LH   Sinclair, I. (1998), *Lud Heat and Suicide Bridge*, London: Granta.

LO   Sinclair, I. (2002), *London Orbital*, London: Granta.

LOf   Sinclair, I. and Petit, C. (2002), *London Orbital*, Illuminations, DVD.

LOT   Sinclair, I. (1997), *Lights Out for the Territory*, London: Granta.

LT   Sinclair, I. (2001), *Landor's Tower*, London: Granta.

RD   Sinclair, I. (1994), *Radon Daughters*, London: Cape.

RR   Lichtenstein, R. and Sinclair, I. (2000), *Rodinsky's Room*, London: Granta.

SD   Sinclair, I. (2013), *Silenic Drift*, London: Strange Attractors.

SM   Sinclair, I. (1999), *Sorry Meniscus*, London: Profile Books.

WG   Sinclair, I. (2002), *White Goods*, Uppingham: Goldmark.

WST   Sinclair, I. (1995), *White Chappell, Scarlet Tracings*, London: Vintage.

Introduction

'Doctored maps, speculative alignments':
Iain Sinclair and the Matter of London

Assembled over forty years of charting London's 'unresolved' and 'reforgotten' spaces, Iain Sinclair's account of the city where he lives and works is simultaneously one of the most distinctive visions of the urban condition at the dawn of the twenty-first century and, this study will argue, one of the most compelling. As a writer and film-maker, Sinclair has chronicled London's transformation from a down-at-heel former imperial metropolis into a node in what sociologist Saskia Sassen has dubbed the network of 'global cities' (2005). In so doing, he has described the peculiar and often paradoxical spaces that emerge when the lived reality of urban life seems incompatible with inherited ideas of national identity and civic function. Visually, his work presents us with a city of decaying Victorian asylums and motorway hotels, allotments and shopping malls, 'retail landfill' and pop-up art spaces in former synagogues. As such, it is a London characterized by its familiar unfamiliarity – an uncanny London that in its particularity reflects a world where cities are both the same all over and places of encounter with cultural strangeness.

The tools he has used to explore this city reflect the peculiarity of its topology. 'The matter of London', he writes, 'is exposed by doctored maps, speculative alignments, black propaganda. The revenge of the disenfranchised' (LOT: 26). Although applied to the operations of the mysterious London Psychogeographical Association, it is an inventory which provides a checklist of the devices deployed in Sinclair's own poetry, fiction, essays and films. Maps derived from the world of nation states that first emerged in Medieval Europe, the world that found its literary expression in the Matters of Britain and France, are of little use in getting your bearings in Millennial London. For, where the Matters of Britain and France, the legends of Arthur and Charlemagne, are stories of aggregation and political and imaginative enfranchisement, the 'matter of London' in an era of globalization involves stories of disaggregation and dissolution. Its stories require new cartographies organized around seemingly *ad hoc* constellations or 'speculative alignments'. Thus, the topoi around which Sinclair elaborates his London mythography include, for example, the former engine shed that in 1967 hosted the Congress on the Dialectics of Liberation, the occult significance of Nicholas Hawksmoor's eighteenth-century churches, the gangland pubs of Whitechapel and Spitalfields, the slagheaps of the former Beckton gasworks and the amnesiac landscapes bisected and produced by the A13 and M25 motorway.

Despite its apparent idiosyncrasy, however, Sinclair's matter of London provides a compelling account of one of the most important chapters in contemporary urban history. For, as Marxist geographer David Harvey reminds us, the London described by Sinclair is the capital of a country which was, along with Augusto Pinochet's Chile and Deng Xiaoping's China, one of the first places in the world to experience, or be subjected to, that collection of economic and social doctrines that has come to be known as neoliberalism (2005: 7). As Harvey also points out, the consequences of the neoliberal argument that the market, not the state, is the most efficient mechanism for solving economic and social problems are experienced with particular intensity in the city. Whether in de-industrialization and the creative destruction of no-longer profitable industries, the breakdown of welfare systems that sustain large sections of the urban population, the deregulation of the financial sector, or simply in the privatization of public facilities, the philosophy of Friedrich Hayek as implemented by Margaret Thatcher and rebranded by New Labour under Tony Blair has been a major force in the shaping and reshaping of London since the late 1970s. Sinclair's matter of London is thus the story of neoliberalism in one of its earliest and most doctrinaire manifestations.

As well as reshaping the urban space of the city in which he lives, the impact of neoliberalism is an insistent presence in any narrative of Sinclair's life. A doctor's son born in Cardiff in 1943 and raised in Maestog, Wales, Sinclair took a degree in English and Fine Arts at Trinity College, Dublin, where he also met his future wife Anna, discovered the work of the Black Mountain Poets, made films, wrote poetry and edited the university literary magazine, *Icarus*. After four years in this 'timeless Dublin bohemia' (Jackson 2003: 45), he moved to London where he took further courses in art and film-making at the Courtauld Institute (University of London) and the London School of Film Technique, before settling down to life as a writer, film-maker and casual labourer in the East London borough of Hackney. Opening his own small press, The Albion Village Press, in 1970, he quickly established a life of creative and economic self-sufficiency:

> unlike now, I knew that if I got down to only having a fiver left, I could go out that day to the Manpower agency and there's a job. That's it. So what's to worry about? The whole garden was planted up with vegetables. In 1972 our first child was born, and it was really very nice. It was all that stuff of the previous era – making your own bread, and yoghourt, and living very simply, in a pleasant area where things were cheap, and producing your own books, and walking into the Whitechapel gallery and putting on an exhibition .... (Jackson 2003: 67–8)

This life spent writing, publishing his own and his friends'[1] poetry and making 8 mm film 'diaries' (Jackson 2003: 85) was financed by casual labour and remained sustainable, he recalls, until 1975, when 'suddenly and noticeably [London] became a harsher environment, moving towards the beginning of that Thatcher period which was on the horizon' (Jackson 2003: 86). The deteriorating economy coincided with the scaling-back of his small-press poetry activities, a move into second-hand book trading and the final demise of the Albion Village Press in 1979. However, with the publication of the novels *White Chappell, Scarlet Tracings* in 1987 and the James Tait Black Memorial Prize winning *Downriver* in 1992, he attracted the attention of a much larger and more mainstream public. Since then, as a small-press poet whose prose writing is published by major international houses including Paladin, Granta and Hamish Hamilton, Sinclair has occupied a unique position within the British cultural landscape. As a writer of neo-Modernist poetry who is also a regular contributor to the *London Review of Books* and occasional presence on national broadcast media, including that bastion of 'middle-brow' England, BBC Radio 4 (*Hackney, That Rose-Red Empire* (2009) was the BBC Radio 4 'Book of the Week'), he straddles two apparently antithetical worlds of cultural production. Consequently, as Robert Bond and Jenny Bavidge point out, his career 'trajectory' cannot be reduced to a linear journey from 'small press

---

[1]   These included Renchi Bicknell, Brian Catling, J.H. Prynne, Peter Riley and Chris Torrance.

obscurity' into 'metropolitan visibility' (Bavidge and Bond 2005: 2) but rather, as Kirsten Seale suggests, is better seen as a 'series of negotiations that refuse to conform to standard narratives regarding literary production and success' (Seale 2008: 5). As such his text is always concerned with its relation to the wider economic life of the city, with the ways in which ideas of poetry and the aesthetic are bound up with and complicit in the forms of economic practice which shape and reshape urban space. Rather than unacknowledged legislators, Sinclair's artists typically act as unacknowledged speculators. They are the visionaries who do the necessary preparatory work for the developers and money-men, for the business of imagining the city, he insists, cannot be separated from the business of selling the city.

A similarly ambiguous narrative runs through his accounts of his life as a casual labourer. Where writers' alternative *curricula vitae* typically furnish material for the dust-jacket biography, Sinclair's is integral to his text. His employment record as described in his writings performs a shadow dance with the economic and social doctrines of the Chicago school. As an employee of the soon-to-be disbanded Tower Hamlets' parks department (*Lud Heat*) and ullage man in the last days of the Truman brewery on Brick Lane, he worked the final shifts in an economy where the sometimes absurd bureaucracy of local government described in *Lud Heat* (LH: 39) complemented the 'benevolent paternalism' of long-established industries in the post-War consensus that Harvey terms 'embedded liberalism' (Harvey 2005: 11). As a dock-worker at the Chobham Farm container depot (*Ghost Milk*), he played a semi-witting part in the de-industrialization of the London riverside, thereby helping to produce the derelict landscape that is integral to his fiction of the 1990s (*Downriver*). As a second-hand book dealer scouring provincial bookshops for unrecognized treasures to be sold on to a network of international collectors (*White Chappell*), he performed a parody of the Thatcherite small-time entrepreneur, contributing to the burgeoning heritage industry by turning culture into commodities. A professional writer since the 1990s, unlike many of his contemporaries, Sinclair has not sought support either from academia or the Arts Council but has instead remained very much in the city with the result that the city and its cultural economies are constantly foregrounded in his texts. Making your living as a writer, his work shows, cannot be separated from the wider economic context that shapes the city about which he writes. The day-to-day business of letters, the need to constantly recycle texts, is an integral part of his practice of letters. As Seale points out, his novel *Dining on Stones* recycles passages from at least six earlier works (Seale 2008: 182–3). In his work as a writer and film-maker, consequently, he investigates the implications of London's transformation not only for the city and its denizens but also for the languages in which he seeks to understand and represent the changing forms of urban life. Sinclair's matter of London is thus materialist in the familiar Marxist sense of incorporating pointers to the conditions that circumscribe and inform the arenas of cultural production including its own.

The materialism evident in this concern with the conditions of cultural production is also reflected in his cast of characters. An assortment of misfits and marginals, they are drawn from the ranks of the 'out patients' of mental health institutes, book-runners, 'white goods' traders, Vietnam draft-dodgers, Ripperologists, commissioning editors, conceptual artists, memorabilia collectors, blues guitarists, freelance documentary film-makers and literary tourist guides, that, as an unbounded class, closely resembles the 'indefinite, disintegrated mass thrown hither and thither' that in nineteenth-century Paris Marx labelled the 'lumpenproletariat' (1977: 63). Like Marx's *lumpenproletariat* or Parisian *bohème*, Sinclair's characters are emanations of the city. Typical in this respect are the 'out patients' working as 'runners' for second-hand book dealers in *Downriver*. Their parlous existence in a marginal economy and on the fringes of institutionalized care epitomizes the situation of the denizens of a city where social support for the poor and vulnerable is 'out-sourced' – in this case, to the second-hand book trade. Like Marx's 'indefinite, disintegrated mass' too, Sinclair's characters have no identifiable relation to an obvious mode of production. In part at least, a 'creative class' their typically subversive and invisible modes of creation bear little resemblance to those posited by Richard Florida as the regenerative motor of the post-industrial city (Florida 2003). Rather, with no visible support they represent the class that Guy Standing terms the global precariat (Standing 2011).

Sinclair's 'matter of London' is distinguished above all, however, by its faith in the legibility of the city's own matter: by its belief that 'the spites and spasms of an increasingly deranged population' can be read from 'its walls, lampposts, doorjambs' (LOT: 1). Reprising the famous Situationist slogan, in a recent outing he even turns 'psychogeologist' to trace 'the beach beneath the pavement' through an exploration of the minerals of London architecture (SD: 5). More generally, his texts find their cues in the incidents and particularities of location in what at times seems to be a compulsive stenography of place, they appear to be dictated or summoned by a city which demands inscription: which manifests itself in '[a] delirium of coded information, hot text: cancer grey lampposts frantic to declare their allegiances. Scribbles stacked like battle honours' (LOT: 49).

In *London Orbital*, he coins the term 'eye-swiping' (LO: 91) to describe this process of decoding the material detritus of the environment, and in the same text he provides this example of the procedure:

> The distance to the roundabout was calculable by reading the debris left at the side of the road. Single cans of Foster's ('Official beer of Sydney Olympics'), Stella Artois, Carlsberg Special Brew and Tango. Two packets of Walkers Crisps (Cheese & Onion), one of Salt & Vinegar. Five McDonald's/Coca-Cola cans. One Lambert and Butler (King Size) cigarette packet. Two Marlboro. One Silk Cut. A Cocoanut Bar. Smilers. Four cans of Red Bull ('a carbonated taurine drink with caffeine'). Three burger cartons; one milk carton (2pc fat). Diet Cola. Dr Pepper. Orange peel. Knotted condoms. One stainless steel watch (LB417, Japan). One burnt-out car: POLICE AWARE. One motorcycle engine. These are the contour rings of civilization as they spread out from the Old Orleans ('A Taste of the Deep South') Roadhouse. (LO: 417)

Here, the insistent focus on the grainy particularity of London delivers a double message about space: the specificity of an English roadside is constituted through the listing of global brands. It is a double message that rehearses a more general tension in Sinclair's depiction of the matter of London as the site of a struggle between the global and the local which in turn reflects a tension within his text between, on the one side, a demand for the sort of universal intelligibility which brings with it an international readership and, on the other, a resolute refusal to translate the idiosyncrasies of culture and place into a language suitable for export. It is encountered again, for example, in his portrait of the literary tourist guide – a 'shifty unshaven polymath nebbish' – who, in *Downriver*, lectures a Californian couple on the 'arcane ritual' of Thameside executions: 'in spate, and lying outrageously [the guide] appeared to be rehearsing for an occasional column in *The Times Literary Supplement*, that would get up everybody's nose with its preening erudition' (D: 53–5). It is a sketch in which it is easy to hear an ironic comment on his own text's fraught relationship with ideas of 'world literature'. With its freight of local reference and delight in topics as recondite as Hawksmoor churches and gangland pubs, it too seems to revel in a 'preening erudition' calculated to disrupt a cultural economy predicated on communication across borders, to resolutely set its face against the cosmopolitan. Tellingly, after listening to this 'nebbish' the Californian couple resolve to abandon London at the earliest opportunity for a Hemingway conference in Venice. A Sinclair conference in Venice seems a remote prospect.

In Sinclair's various strategies for materializing London it is possible to recognize a similar tension between the global and the local, or rather the paradoxes that arise when we attempt to make sense of space through an appeal to these binaries. His matter of London is constituted through attention to the ways in which the city is produced through its own historical specificities and the detritus of globalization; how it becomes readable because of its differences – and unreadable insofar as it is constituted through signifiers of the global. His matter of London, in other words, displays a careful attention to the turbulence and paradoxes generated by the forces of globalization as they are registered in a formerly imperial culture and in particular the complexities of memory and history involved in this encounter. Significantly, the subject of the argument between the local guide and his cosmopolitan clients concerns the local's expertise in global culture, the film roles played by Randolph Scott. Sinclair's London is a city with a similarly complex entanglement in global space: it is a city adjusting to its status as a client state of the United States within a new imperial system but a city which is also eager to forget the stain of its imperial past and its histories of colonial and domestic violence. As such it is also a city which constantly challenges the adequacy of personal and cultural memory as systems of orientation and navigation, a city where memory and the places of memory seem increasingly unreliable, where knowing where you are today is no guarantee that you will wake up in the same place tomorrow. As Stephen Gill, Sinclair's companion on a visit to the Olympic Park, tells him on seeing the erasure of his beloved wasteland under the Olympic development, 'I had a kind of territorial feeling, everything had been taken away. I almost cried in the back of the car, it is such a political experience' (GM: 70).

Matter, communication theory tells us, is noisy. It is the material through which information is transmitted that makes its presence felt as noise. Whether as the copper of the telephone wire or the thickness of the fibre-optic cable, matter speaks as noise. As interference, noise reminds us that any message is always dependent in someway on some act of forgetting. Sinclair's matter of London is no exception. His fidelity to the clamour of forgotten voices emanating from its margins and materials produce a city in which the conditions of communication and resistance can never be ignored: a London which is both global city and myth-saturated locale. To more fully explore the ways in which his text produces and reflects upon this tension, this study consequently turns to the concept of noise as it is formulated in communication theory. Sinclair's texts are noisy, I argue, not because of their attention to the city as an acoustic environment, nor because of the visual style of the collaborative works with, for example, Marc Atkins, Emma Matthews or Dave McKean, nor because of their 'difficulty' or 'inaccessibility', nor yet the 'voices' that are so important in his account of cultural production (Jackson 2003: 76). They are noisy I argue because they are consistently drawn to the spatial and cultural regions where the tensions between order and disorder, communication and resistance are most acute. It is in these turbulent or stochastic zones where interpretation is constantly threatened by excesses of disorder and order that the concept of noise becomes most pertinent. For, as it has been developed in communication theory, the idea of noise encompasses precisely the forms of interdependence between order and disorder, the intelligible and the chaotic, that characterize the global city and which are emphasized in Sinclair's concern with the textual and spatial politics of cities which are familiarly unfamiliar.

Although given a variety of formulations by thinkers such as Claude Shannon, Norbert Wiener, Gregory Bateson and Michel Serres, accounts of noise share a fascination with its paradoxical status as both an obstacle to, and an absolute precondition of, successful communication. Too much noise or disorder, communication theory tells us, and information is lost to the operations of chance, but too much order, and a message loses its information content by becoming wholly predictable. As such, noise theory furnishes us with a concept usefully qualified to bring into focus the dynamics at play in the relationship between the local and the global in terms of the tension between transmission and resistance, the tensions which structure Sinclair's account of London as a global city.

In a formulation this abstract, however, the concept of noise is clearly too general to provide detailed insight into the various facets of Sinclair's text. All literary texts are, after all, 'noisy' to the extent that they are polysemous and thus have the capacity to sustain multiple and competing interpretations. Every poem is noisy insofar as it illustrates the potential of indeterminacy to generate meaning. Similarly, every city is 'noisy' in the sense that it threatens us with a constant data overload, requiring citizens to adopt protective filters to go about their daily business. My aim here consequently is to show how the concept of noise can produce reading strategies that will allow us to better explore specific aspects of Sinclair's account of the global city. Through this 'noisy' reading of his text, I want to show that Sinclair's work is particularly attuned to a noise endemic within the ideology of neoliberalism itself. Sinclair's account of London, I will argue, is distinguished by its attention to the forms of noise generated in the contradiction between neoliberalism's avowed commitment to the promotion of the free and frictionless circulation of information and the neoliberal subject's increasing sense of surveillance and restraint; the contradiction that is between an avowed ideological commitment to mobility and liberty and the experience of lost liberties and increased carceralization that is the lived reality of the neoliberal city. Or as Sinclair puts it:

> [o]nly by erecting secure fences, surveillance hedges, can they assert their championship of liberty. The threat of terrorism, self-inflicted, underwrites the seriousness of the measures required to repel it. Headline arrests in the Olympic hinterland followed by small print retractions. (GM: 71)

To this end, I want to first fill out some of the implications of the idea of noise as simultaneously an obstacle to and prerequisite of communication and to indicate their relevance to aspects of Sinclair's text which will be more fully explored in subsequent chapters.

Noise and Iain Sinclair

Noise's doubled status as simultaneously something abhorred and desired has been given numerous formulations. It is signalled as early as 1943 in Norbert Wiener's demonstration that errors provide the feedback necessary to improve control. An insight which Mark Nunes points out is the founding principle of the time and motion studies that underpin the Taylorized production of Fordist economies: 'Error, in effect, serves its purpose as a corrective – what keeps purpose on purpose and tasks on goal' (Nunes 2011: 7). In his 1948 paper, 'A Mathematical Theory of Communication', Claude Shannon gives this understanding of the desirability of error a further theoretical twist in his argument that the successful transmission of information is always dependent on a degree of uncertainty with the apparent corollary that the more improbable a message, the more information it contains. After Shannon, as Colin Grant observes, we have learned to recognize that all communication is dependent upon a 'penumbra of uncertainty' (2007: 1): that uncertainty is in fact a condition of communication. Gregory Bateson gave this principle of informatics an ecological turn in his cybernetic hypothesis that what is noise at one point in a system is information elsewhere in the system, thereby shifting the domain for the analysis of noise away from mathematical information systems to the realm of organisms and ultimately to the environment itself.

Bateson's views on systems theory and the principle of homeostasis, while revolutionary in the 1960s, once applied to markets become, as Sinclair points out in his satire of Thatcherism in *Downriver*, a key component of Silicon Valley capitalism and the neoliberal economic orthodoxy of the 1990s. Thus Bateson, star of the Congress on the Dialectics of Liberation, makes a cameo appearance in *Downriver* as an item on 'The Widow' or Margaret Thatcher's reading list:

> Another impassioned bull on matters ecological? She'd already worked her way yards into the lectures of Gregory Bateson (as delivered to the Fellows of Lindisfarne). Time has, she discovered, this marvelous facility for civilizing the most recalcitrant material. Stuff that would have put you at the head of the Prevention of Terrorism Index in the 1960s, when it was still prophetic and active, could now be broadcast from St Anne's Cathedral, Limehouse in a safely retrospective form. (D: 221)

The broader implication of noise as a marker and producer of paradigm shifts within language and culture are explored by Michel Serres in his analysis of the parasite. In French, he points out, where '*parasite*' also means 'interference', the word identifies a 'somewhat fuzzy spot' in language: 'a parasite is an abusive guest, an unavoidable animal, a break in a message' (2007: 8). What is named 'parasite', he argues, depends on the perspective we adopt. As such, noise situates and locates us as subjects but always contains the information which can disorientate and relocate us – which can transform the radicalism of the 1960s into the standard business procedures of the millennium.

Serres also points out the close association of noise with the city: 'The town makes noise, but noise makes the town' (2007: 14). His chiasmus reminds us that, from at least the legend of Babel onwards, stories of cities have been intimately connected with ideas of noise. For the most part those stories use noise to portray cities as places of confusion, disorder, threat or simply annoyance, but noise is also surprisingly frequently numbered among the distinctive pleasures of the city. Thus René Descartes wrote to a friend extolling the advantages of foreign cities over the countryside as places of meditation. Surrounded by people whose language he does not speak, he writes, he has discovered the perfect location to pursue his meditations:

> I take a walk each day among the bustle of the crowd with as much freedom and repose as you could obtain in your leafy groves, and I pay no more attention to the people that I meet than I would to the trees in your woods or the animals that browse there. The bustle of the city no more disturbs my daydreams than does the ripple of a stream. (1991: 31)

Similarly, proto-*flâneur* Thomas de Quincey records that his pleasure in listening to people speak Italian at the London opera lay in the fact that he could not understand a word of the language (2009: 79). More generally, as Elizabeth Wilson (1992) has argued, it is the association of cities with noise and disorder that has allowed them to act as places of refuge and liberation for those wishing to escape overly oppressive systems of order and control. Michael Hardt and Antoni Negri also place the aleatory at the heart of metropolitan life. Cities, they write, are about

> the unpredictable, aleatory encounter or, rather, the encounter with alterity. The great European Modernist literary representations of the metropolis,

from Charles Baudelaire to Virginia Woolf and from James Joyce to Robert Musil and Fyodor Dostoyevsky, emphasize this relation between the common and the encounter. Village life is portrayed as a monotonous repetition of the same. You know everyone in your village, and the arrival of a stranger is a startling event. The metropolis, in contrast, is a place of unpredictable encounters among singularities, with not only those you do not know but also those who come from elsewhere, with different cultures, languages, knowledges, mentalities. (2009: 252)

For Hardt and Negri, this noise is not just one of the benefits of the city; it marks the emergence of the city as a productive force that replaces the factory in the post-industrial economy. For, whereas the forces of production of industrial capitalism were located within the factory, post-industrial capital seeks to extract value from the wider forms of sociality which find their richest expressions within the city. The noise of the city is thus the source of 'the "artificial Common" that resides in languages, images, knowledges, affects, codes, habits, and practices' (2009: 250) from which post-industrial capital draws its surplus value.

The constitutive relationship between noise and the city thus becomes even more important in the context of the 'global' city. As the cities, we inhabit come increasingly to be understood in terms of their participation, or non-participation, in transnational communication economies and in terms of their interconnectedness (Castells 1989, 1996; Harvey 1989; Sassen 2001, 2006), so ideas of noise as that which is both an obstacle to and a prerequisite of successful communication acquires an increasingly strategic position in thinking the urban. Thus, Bill Gates' dream of 'frictionless capitalism' (Schirato 2003: 10) requires ever-increasing standardization: the assurance that the same protocols and codes will be used across the global network. Insofar as that process of standardization becomes cultural, it produces cities which are themselves correspondingly standardized and indistinguishable. As such our cities are noisy not just because, as places of strangers and strangeness, they stage encounters between mutually incomprehensible languages, but they are noisy also because they have become banal, unremarkable. Global cities are, in other words, noisy both as places of heterogeneity and homogeneity.

Sinclair's text deploys a number of techniques to reveal and comment on this tension including the use of the noise inherent in 'literary' language. The title *flesh eggs & scalp metal* (given first to a volume of poetry in 1983 and then recycled for a 1989 poetry collection) provides a convenient example. Here the introduction of linguistic noise through the substitution of 'l' for 'r' gives the sign 'fresh eggs and scrap metal', familiar from the fringes of many British towns and cities, a new and grotesquely vivid life. The technique has of course been extensively theorized. Literature as 'organized violence committed on ordinary speech' (Jakobson qtd. Erlich 1980: 219) or the conscious deployment of ambiguity and equivocation in order to privilege connotative over denotative meaning has been examined by, amongst others, Roman Jakobson, Viktor Schlovsky and Jurij Lotman and informs such venerable theoretical concepts as defamiliarization and the alienation effect. Lotman gives the correlation between noise, literature and environment one of its most ambitious formulations when he writes that art is Art because, like life, it 'is capable of transforming noise into information', because, uniquely '[i]t complicates its own structure owing to its correlation with its environment (in all other systems the clash with the environment can only lead to the fade-out of information)' (1977: 75). Some years later, William Paulson further elaborated this meta-linguistic thesis to argue for literature as 'the noise of culture' (1988). For Paulson, literature as a 'noisy channel' is a marginal activity in a communicative economy dominated by instrumental forms of language use, and, as such, 'creates meaning by putting meaning in jeopardy' (1991: 269). In a move which, as we will see, anticipates Jacques Rancière's formulation of the political, Paulson argues that '[b]y perturbing existing systems of meaning [noise] enables the creation of new ideas and ultimately new domains of knowledge' (1991: 269).

In '*flesh eggs & scalp metal*' the noisy defamiliarization of the familiar sign precisely identifies Sinclair's topographic concern with the hybridity of edgelands – with spaces that are neither rural nor urban, country nor city, agricultural nor industrial. It identifies these edgelands as areas of contamination and of transmutation, as zones of instability within imaginary topographies of the city. Simultaneously, it invokes his thematic concern with marginal economies and with poetry as a marginal economy concerned with the production of value from waste – the flesh eggs and scalp metal advertised are, after all, poems. As such it also suggests the place of small-press poetry production within a self-sustaining cottage economy in which reader and producer are as interchangeable as chicken and egg. Noise as organized violence to language thus works here to locate Sinclair's subject with the precision of a geotag.

However, while his poetics exploit the resources of noise at the level of technique, the operation of noise within Sinclair's text is not restricted to the opacity of his neo-Modernist lyric. Insofar as noise constitutes the necessary excess or waste, without which a system, whether linguistic or economic, will not function, Sinclair's work is 'noisy' in a number of ways that are not purely linguistic. He is, for example, particularly attentive to the importance of the 'unresolved' as it manifests itself in the psycho-political geography of the city's edgelands. He is drawn to those waste spaces, such as Beckton Alp, the slag heap of the former Beckton Gasworks, which seemingly shrug off attempts to reincorporate them within a productive economy. It is from the perspective of its refuse, he writes, that 'London makes sense' (WG: 22; DOS: 190).

The return of the unselected

In this sensitivity to the 'unresolved' and the 'reforgotten' Sinclair's aesthetic and political vision registers a perception of what noise theory encourages us to term *the return of the unselected*. Claude Shannon identifies the basic mechanism of this form of return in his argument that the information carried by a message has nothing to do with its content but is due rather to the fact that every message represents a number of selections from a range of possible alternatives (1948: 379). A message informs, he suggests, not because it carries information as a kind of cargo but because the message itself represents a series of choices which could have been otherwise, and it is these unselected alternatives whose return constitutes noise (MacKay 1969: 11; Botting 2004: 229). Noise, we might say, arises from the fact that in order to arrive, a message must have been able to go astray.

From this perspective Roman Jakobson's classic account of the six functions of language provides a useful schematization of the elements which can return as noise within the semantics of communication. According to Jakobson's schema, any message will display an orientation to at least one of the following functions:

1. Referential   context
2. Emotive   addressor

3. Conative	addressee
4. Phatic	contact
5. Metalingual	code
6. Poetic	message

That is, a given message can be a statement about the world (referential), about the attitude of the speaker (emotive) or person spoken to (addressee); it can function simply to check the condition of the channel (phatic) or be a statement about the language of the message (metalingual) or about the message itself (poetic). We can make statements about the world, communication theory suggests, only because we can also make statements about the code: we can't say 'the grass is green' unless we can also say what 'green' means, and because we can also say what green means, a statement about the world can be mistaken for (or become) a statement about the code and vice versa. As we will see much of the noise that distinguishes the poetics of *Lud Heat* is generated through a radical uncertainty about the status, or in Jakobson's terms, the 'set', of different sections of the text which confuse referential, emotive and poetic elements.

Equally, the identification of noise with the return of the unselected draws our attention to the place of noise in other theorizations of return. Most pertinently, given Sinclair's use of psychogeographical techniques, it encourages us to consider the critical role of ideas of return in Sigmund Freud's account of the psyche. The idea of noise as the return of the unselected, for example, finds an obvious expression in *The Psychopathology of Everyday Life* (1901) insofar as its subject is precisely the errors, glitches, mistakes and accidents which, while appearing to represent a loss of information, actually constitute the trace of what could not otherwise be expressed. In hypothesizing the insistent presence of the unselected in a variety of forms ranging from the hysterical symptom to dream logic, to parapraxis and the uncanny, psychoanalysis has given us a range of terms for reading discourse as spoken and unspoken, for recognizing in noise, the boundary of the sayable and the unsayable.

Within Sinclair's text this form of return is primarily focused on the idea that walking activates and provides access to voices and stories that cannot be articulated in other more fully sanctioned configurations of urban space. This correlation between walking cure and talking cure is a constant theme within his work but is given a particularly forceful statement by Norton, the protagonist of *Dining on Stones*:

> I started to embark on monumental walks; do it that way, I thought, work the gap between *personal* psychosis and psychosis of the city: the crisis of consciousness lives in faulty synchronisation. Sometimes the city was crazier, sometimes my fugues leapt ahead: fire visions, sunsets over King's Cross gas holders. We are part of the madness. Monitor everything: weeds, green paint on a wooden fence in Maryon Park, swans hooked by Kosovans on the River Lea, the way an Irish barman in Kentish Town stubs out his Sweet Afton and scratches a cut that never heals on his right wrist. (DOS: 287)

Of even greater importance to Sinclair's mapping of London, however, is Freud's second model of return which he elaborates in *Beyond the Pleasure Principle* (1920). Here, Freud shifts from a content-based notion of return – the return of something from somewhere – to a notion of return which, in the concept of *Nachträglichkeit*, notes the generative role of returning in producing its own 'content'. Glossing this move in Freud's thought, Jacques Derrida suggests that his reconceptualization of the idea of return allows us to see that 'the present in general is not primal but, rather, reconstituted, that it is not the absolute, wholly living form which constitutes experience, that there is no purity of the living present' (1978: 210). In addition to forcing Freud to abandon his 'topographic' model of the psyche for a dynamic model based on flows and drives, Derrida notes that the perception that the present is never present has dramatic implications for Freud's model of interpretation and reading. Specifically, it forces Freud to discount the idea that dreams are the distorted expression of an original text 'hidden' in the locked box of the unconscious which can be decoded through the use of a formal schema, code or key. As Derrida notes, the 'conscious text is … not a transcription because there is no text present elsewhere as an unconscious one to be transposed or transported' (1978: 211). Instead, in pursuing this theme he comes to recognize that in dream logic the sign exists as a trace: that it is not the content, but the context and relation that is critical. As such, dream logic operates with the materiality or noise of the sign – the sound of a word, or, the shape of a letter, the place of the signifiers within a network of associations which are entirely singular, and which cannot, consequently, be translated or transcoded:

> The materiality of a word cannot be translated or carried over into another language. Materiality is precisely that which translation relinquishes. To relinquish materiality: such is the driving force of translation. And when that materiality is reinstated, translation becomes poetry. In this sense, since the materiality of the signifier constitutes the idiom of the dream scene, dreams are untranslatable. (1978: 210)

The concept of *Nachträglichkeit* thus marks the recognition that every dream exhibits its own noisy logic, smuggling a private meaning through a web of particular associations on the back of its public message or 'manifest content'. In this respect the dream discovers the noisy element in every sign, and reveals that this lies in the materiality which is defined as 'precisely that which translation relinquishes'.

In *White Chappell, Scarlet Tracings*, Sinclair effectively deploys this insight as the basis of a critique of empiricist historiography. As Wilhelm Emilsson observes, taking the unresolved question 'who was Jack the Ripper?' as emblematic of the historian's desire to recover an original identity or event, his novel suggests that there can be no single answer to the question of who committed what came to be known as the Whitechapel murders, for, like the unconscious, the locked box of the past is always either empty or overfull. The women murdered in Whitechapel in 1888 were, in one sense, sacrifices to the compulsion to discover the identity of their murderer. As the narrator tells his accomplice, Joblard, the idea of the detective produces the idea of the crime, and hence, the aim of their investigations must be to overcome their own obsessions, 'otherwise they will be doomed not to relive the past but to die into it' (WST: 198).

According to the logic of *Nachträglichkeit*, the crime is always constructed after the event which becomes thereby its impossible origin. At this level, the real perpetrator of the Whitechapel murders was Sherlock Holmes, for as Emilsson writes '[a]n enigma of this magnitude in the period when Holmes, the greatest detective in the world, reigned supreme can be seen as Iain Sinclair's challenge to the ultrarational world view symbolised by Doyle's hero' (2002: 276). As the product of the impulses repressed by the Victorian valorization of rationality and science, Whitechapel's 'scarlet tracings' figure the past as the present's other and as such invite a deconstructive hermeneutic. As Emilsson notes, Sinclair's novel 'may be viewed as a noir version of Derrida's deconstruction of phallogocentrism' (2002: 278): his detectives 'deconstruct the present in order to get to the past' (2002: 282) but this is of course impossible 'for the events of Whitechapel are "under erasure"…one sign leads to another along the infinite twisted strings of signification' (2002: 282).

Noise as parasite

As the enterprise of writing a novel about Jack the Ripper that denounces a cultural obsession with Jack the Ripper suggests, Sinclair's work is noisy too in its intimate relation to that idea of noise that Serres calls 'the parasite' (2007). Through a reading of Jean de La Fontaine's version of Aesop's fable 'The Town Mouse and the Country Mouse', Serres shows that the naming of the parasite, deciding what gets called noise, is a strategy for stabilizing a system around a given set of values, but the presence of the parasite, like the presence of noise, reveals the provisional character of those values. It is a reminder that other configurations of the system are always possible and thus produces the theorem: 'noise gives rise to a new system, an order that is more complex than the simple chain. The parasite interrupts at first glance, consolidates when you look again' (2007: 14). Sinclair's text is distinguished by its consciousness of its own parasitic relationship to the wider economies it critiques. Whether in the deconstruction of 'Ripperology' or satires of Thatcherism, it is acutely aware of its complicity in that which it denounces: that its celebration of waste in itself constitutes the kind of excess necessary for the functioning of the neoliberal economy. Sinclair's satire is conscious that satire always derives its energy from its targets. As the narrator of *Downriver* quips, '[t]he worse it got the more we rubbed our hands' (D: 72).

It is this acute sensitivity to the parasitic logic at work in his text and wider society that, for many readers, renders Sinclair's politics ambiguous. Ben Watson gives this worry an apothegmatic expression in his article 'Iain Sinclair: Revolutionary Novelist or Revolting Nihilist?' (2005). Several years later Sinclair, parsing Watson's question as an accusation that he promotes 'no values in the contemporary world beyond a belief in poetry' declared simply that he was 'right' (GM: 145). His rejoinder is of course wholly ambiguous. It can be read as a confession that he does indeed privilege the values of poetry over politics but equally as an invitation to explore their equivalence.

Read as an assertion of the political value of poetry as the language of excess and of noise, Sinclair finds powerful support in Rancière's argument that in a globalized arena organized around a communicative economy which demands absolute fungibility, or translatability, poetry is indeed the only form of politics. For, in the face of the demand for absolute translatability, Rancière argues, politics as usually understood has been reduced to a simple naming and enumeration of parts. In its belief that it has resolved all antinomies and put an end to history itself, the neoliberal insistence on the sovereignty of the market has effectively instituted a logic of the 'police' in the place of politics – a concern with defending the way things are, or the existing 'partition of the sensible', through an insistence on the proper meaning of words (Rancière 1999, 2009, 2010). Politics today means determining what is perceptible and what is sensible – who has a voice and who is relegated to the position of noise: 'Political activity is whatever shifts a body from the place assigned to it or changes a place's destination. It makes visible what had no business being seen, and makes heard a discourse where once there was only place for noise' (Rancière 1999: 30).

For Rancière, consequently, true politics involves making sensible what is excluded from the technocratic and consensual model of society. Rather than a dispute about the meaning of words, true politics occurs in the kind of 'disagreement' where one party does not even recognize that the other is speaking a language: 'An extreme form of disagreement is where X cannot see the common object Y is presenting because X cannot comprehend that the sounds uttered by Y form words and chains of words similar to X's own' (1999: xii). As we will see in the discussion of *Lud Heat* in Chapter 2, Sinclair's work provides powerful examples of this form of disagreement both in his refusal to subordinate the occult to the aesthetic and in his concerns with poetry in, and as, a workplace.

More generally, one of the most important examples of this 'disagreement' over the nature of a 'common object', I argue, concerns the notion of the common itself. This concern with the common is partly spatial. It relates to the common as a form of space occluded in the division of the world into the private and the public (with their corresponding political persona, the individual and the state) and equally as the form of space occluded in the antinomy of the local and the global. But, as Michael Hardt and Antoni Negri point out, the common is also exemplified in language itself (2009: ix) and specifically within language's refusal of ownership and definition. The commonness of the common tongue, in other words, lies in the noise that is generated by the errancy of the signifier, its refusal to be put in its proper place (Panagia and Rancière 2000: 116). It is this noisy quality of language which Rancière terms 'literarity':

> This excess of words that I call literarity disrupts the relation between an order of discourse and its social function. That is, literarity refers at once to the excess of words available in relation to the thing named; to that excess relating to the requirement for the production of life; and finally, to an excess of words vis-à-vis the modes of communication that function to legitimate 'the proper' itself. (Panagia and Rancière 2000: 115)

Within the context of the post-political, noise as the marker of the unsignifiable or untranslatable, marks a site of resistance to the imperative to reduce form to function, to extract a sense which can then be put into circulation.

Staging and the locative effect of noise

Making the common object visible, Rancière suggests, involves a staging, and staging is possible only through use of the excesses of signification inherent in language. Sinclair's engagement with this problem of staging can be seen most clearly when we consider his work as not exclusively textual but as exploring the boundaries which reveal new possible spaces of articulation between the political and the aesthetic. In this respect, his matter of London effectively constitutes a spatial performance which works to re-partition the sensible through problematizing the boundaries of genre, media and authorship. For example, his simultaneous membership of the avant-garde and the mainstream illustrates his ability to problematize the relationship between map and territory by being both and neither. Elsewhere this staging takes the form of collaborations with other artists and writers, and with the promotion of lost and 'reforgotten' precursors who are presented within his work less as avatars of alternative traditions than as means of exploring what is meant by the terms 'alternative' and 'tradition'.

One such staging that brings together the themes discussed above takes place in 'Diving Into Dirt', Sinclair's introductory essay to the photographer Stephen Gill's *Archaeology in Reverse* (2007), an otherwise textless collection of Polaroids charting the site of the 2012 London Olympics immediately prior to its redevelopment. The production of space as 'wasteland' as a necessary preliminary to its 'regeneration' is, as Erik Swyngedouw (2007: 61) and Merijn Oudenampsen (2007: 121) observe, an integral aspect of neoliberal urban policy, and as Sinclair's essay makes clear, *Archaeology in Reverse* thus makes visible the fundamental dystopian/utopian dynamic that is seemingly integral to contemporary constructions of the urban. Articulating Gill's work with respect to that dynamic, Sinclair concentrates on its temporal implications:

> if you don't have a version of the past that will stand up in court – Jacobean manor house, Augustinian monastery, brutalist powerstation – you will be provided with a new script: future impossible. The glittering city that is always just over the horizon. That twitch you feel in the soles of your feet, the hot earth, is the first tremor, a tsunami intimation of system-built structures waiting to climb out of the turf. (DD: 3)

Like Gill's, Sinclair's work insists upon the necessity of wasteland; 'the old grungy Arcadia of the marshes' (DD: 10) is a vital area within the city's emotional topography, which, as Gill's photos reveal, is far from empty but rather fulfils a spectrum of cultural and ecological needs which cannot be accommodated elsewhere, and certainly not in the 'system-built structures' waiting to displace it. In this attention to the temporality of the globalization of space, Sinclair shares with Rancière a perception that the institution of equality as an ever-deferred *telos*, effectively institutionalizes and promotes inequality. The promise of the glittering city becomes a justification for turning the present into a state of exception that links urban regeneration with regime change:

> These vast development sites, in their prolonged phase as exclusion zones, reduce Lammas lands to a state of occupation. War newsreels with everything except the land mines.

It's like the road to Basra this endless convoy of trucks....Dirty
wheels....The Virtual City supplied by a Real-world transport. (DD: 9–10)

Without a culturally sanctioned claim to an environment, a space that is
already *recognized*, as a neoliberal citizen you are condemned to a life of
'occupation' – of living in a permanent state of exception. To make sensible
the world that is excluded in this articulation of civic space and hence reveal
its political dimensions involves an act of perception in which the ethical is
inseparable from the aesthetic. It is not just that the presentation of the future
Olympic site as a waste space ripe for redevelopment ignores the thousands of
uses to which it is put by local people but rather that its identity as a common
space can only be made visible by virtue of the excess literarity of art, by virtue
of art's refusal of closure. The common is thus a form of space that is lost in
redevelopment, but it is also an awareness of shared space that can be made
sensible only through the excessive signification of photography, in Gill's
photographs of, for example, empty lager cans.

In *Archaeology in Reverse* this perception of the interrelation of noise with
the political and the aesthetic is registered in Sinclair's attention to Gill's camera,
a '1960s family model Coronet rescued from the Wick market' (DD: 5). This
'sentimental totem salvaged from ruin' which 'operates as a filtering device,
imposing a slight softness on the terrain' is the source of the noise which
distinguishes Gill's stylistic and ethical vision. Its images characterized by their
'cataract vision: milkiness, unpredictable focus, collusion with place' (DD: 5)
are emblematic of Gill's refusal of 'that mendacious deceit, closure' (DD: 3) and
of his respect for the Other as ethically unknowable: 'Loving retrieval, like a
letter to a friend, never possession. Nothing Gill brings back to his studio for
processing or playful arrangement is concluded' (DD: 3).

However, Sinclair's introduction is also informed by his sense that Gill's
landscape only becomes visible as a 'wake': 'a wake, not for a lost zone, but
for a city that has not yet been built' (DD: 6). This city whose loss is to be
read in the surveyor's marks announcing the advent of the Olympic village is
the antithesis of the glittering city which never arrives. It is in effect a vision
of the polis grounded in a Rancièrean conception of noise: a city founded on
the radical proposition that equality must be recognized as the expression of
a dissensus in the present rather than as the yet to be realized: the recognition

of the garden within the wasteland and that the right to the city includes its empty lager cans.

This study explores the forms of noise at work in Sinclair's distinctive vision of the matter of London and as such it does not aspire to present a comprehensive account of his work. In addition to Robert Bond's (2005) Adorno-inspired reading of Sinclair's earlier works, there are more recent and fuller guides to his oeuvre by Robert Sheppard and Brian Baker. Instead, working in accordance with its own 'doctored maps' and 'speculative alignments', it examines the operation of noise in Sinclair's work through noisy readings of texts which are selected to reveal different aspects of his account of the matter of London.

The first chapter examines the relationship between Sinclair's politics and his use of techniques which accentuate accident and contingency. Beginning with his account of the Congress on the Dialectics of Liberation, it shows how an emphasis on contingency allows him to navigate between the unsatisfactory alternatives presented at the Congress: the New Left authoritarianism of those advocating the revolutionary overthrow of the capitalist system or the personal transformation of consciousness advocated by Allen Ginsberg. Sinclair's emphasis on the contingent and the aleatory is seen in his adaptation of the Situationist practice of psychogeography. Instead of an associative engagement with the city, his investigation of arbitrarily chosen routes works to reveal hidden or repressed urban narratives. Following him on an early walk, we see how his practice as an urban walker is contrasted to the purism of former Angry Brigade member and small-press poet, Anna Mendelssohn. Whereas Mendelssohn's political and poetic practice is organized initially around the revolutionary overthrow of society and then a withdrawal from society, Sinclair's political praxis is implicated within the politics of urban space and seeks its rationale in an ethics of complicity and in a consciousness of 'failing to fail'.

The second chapter examines the relationship between Sinclair's poetics and the production of dissensual space through attention to the ways in which his long, occult, poem *Lud Heat* problematizes the notion of an interpretative community by refusing to relegate its occult elements to the status of metaphor. This disruption of the poetic reflects the poem's concern with the incommensurability of the two kinds of space that Henri Lefebvre terms absolute and abstract or sacred and commercial. The result is the production of a noisy or dissensual space which also renders Sinclair's inclusion in an alternative 'tradition' of British poetry problematic. *Lud Heat* also introduces the idea of the parasite through the theme of the artist – the 'narrator' and Hawksmoor – as vessels for messages they cannot understand, extending the idea of a dissensual space from the city to the subject and to the text.

In Chapter 3, the investigation of dissensual space shifts to the relationship between noise and form in the novel *Downriver*. Read as a post-historical novel – as a novel, that is, which is conscious of the implications for the novel form of Francis Fukuyama's declaration that the dissolution of the Soviet bloc marked the end of history, it explores the different meanings of Sinclair's description of the work as a 'vessel of wrath' and gesture of 'atonement'. In describing *Downriver* as a 'vessel of wrath', Sinclair suggests a concern with the novel as a form that communicates its own containment. In the wider context of a postmodernist fiction which has foreclosed the possibility of bearing witness to historical events, *Downriver* gives voice to the wrath born out of its inability to speak the truth from which its narrative springs. As such, *Downriver* is concerned primarily with noise as the return of the unselected and with what narrative must leave out in order for it to work as a form of cognition.

Understood as his attempt to include the 'female sound' missing from his earlier fiction, *Downriver* becomes a meditation on the impossibility of giving voice to that which is excluded by the logic of narrative itself. This is marked most clearly in the novel's concern with the ways in which the identities of the women killed by Jack the Ripper will always be constructed by their role as victims within his story. Jack the Ripper as such serves as an emblem of the violence of narrative which transforms all of its subjects into victims of its logic.

The role of dissensual space in 1990s London is then discussed through the novel's response to the fatwa on Salman Rushdie and the consequent promotion of the novelist to the ideological front line separating an enlightened West from a fundamentalist Other. Rather than promoting the novel as a dialogical form for the representation of a multicultural society Sinclair's fiction maps a space of dissensus where secular and sacred constitute constantly shifting boundaries within a malleable landscape.

This problematization of community through noise extends to the novel's satirical mode insofar as satire is presented as a parasitic language that draws its energy from what it denounces and hence combines wrath with pleasure.

Chapter 4 considers the relationship between dissensual space and memory through an account of Sinclair's frequent returns to 'Rodinsky's room' – a room in an East End synagogue whose last occupant, David Rodinsky, had apparently disappeared without trace in the 1960s. Examining *Rodinsky's Room*, the collaborative work written together with Rachel Lichtenstein, the chapter shows how this space serves as a locus for two kinds of noise. For Lichtenstein, the room marks a breakdown of the tradition that separates herself from her ancestors and has to be preserved as an archive in which nothing is potentially without significance. For Sinclair, by contrast, Rodinsky's story is generated by the needs of the city. Legends are necessary to produce a marketable identity – to reinvent Spitalfields imaginatively prior to its commercial development, it is simply one of the stories of absence that the city constantly produces in its efforts to reinvent itself. Whereas Lichtenstein's account of Rodinsky's room is informed by the redemptive logic evident in Walter Benjamin's theses on the philosophy of history, Sinclair's reflects a more Rancièrean understanding of Benjamin's tradition of the oppressed – suggesting that its implied teleology of redemption can be used to shore up the identity of the living.

Chapter 5 examines the critical place of the road as simultaneously a conduit and an obstacle within Sinclair's engagements with neoliberalism through readings of his *London Orbital* project and his account of following the Great North Road from London to Northampton in the footsteps of the nineteenth-century poet John Clare in *Edge of the Orison*. As an emblem of personal mobility but also the locus of anxieties generated by the free circulation of information, the road occupies a chiasmic place within the topography of globalization and Sinclair's text is alert to the way in which roads function as expressions of wider paradoxes within neoliberal thought.

In his M25 walks, Sinclair engages with one of the flagship engineering projects of the Thatcher administrations which promoted motorway building as an emblem of its commitment to personal mobility and individual freedom. Implicit in this idea of the road as a channel of communication is the suppression of its existence as a medium or place. Sinclair's task in the *London*

Orbital project is to make the road visible – and this means locating it at the juncture of two paradigms of representation – between film (the medium of the road movie) and surveillance tape with its associated transformation of the gaze. In investigating the M25 as place, Sinclair reverses the ideological project of liberalism which seeks to mask the noise of mediality and create the road as a place that is neither local nor global.

Where the M25 orbital motorway suggests the transformation of freedom into stasis, the Great North Road explored in *Edge of the Orison* is the emblematic road of modernity leading from the country to the city. In walking away from the city back to the landscape of rural enclosure, Sinclair reverses the narrative of freedom to return to the traumatic event of enclosure that produces both liberalism and the metropolis. In following the route taken by the peasant poet John Clare from an Epping Forest mental asylum back to his home village in Northamptonshire, Sinclair's exploration of the Great North Road returns to the issue of the unnarratable. As a peasant poet and an escapee from an asylum, Clare's confrontation with his lack of permission to narrate is twofold. As a peasant poet his relation to the ideologically charged category of Nature renders his poetic testimony suspect within Marxist readings of the Romantic canon, while as the hallucinatory narrator of 'The Journey out of Essex' his powers of self-observation are similarly compromised. Sinclair's reading of Clare as a member of the reforgotten shows him as a man seeing himself not seeing. Clare uses the road as an alibi to stage the drama of representation, to tell the story of a man who cannot tell his story. In this emphasis on Clare, Sinclair shows us a poet who in his sensitivity to his own objectification and silencing is sensitized to the silences in the world around him.

The study concludes by reviewing the recurrence of noisy tropes within Sinclair's *Ghost Milk* (2011) which extends his concerns towards the different forms of locality constructed by the forces of globalization expressed in 'Grand Projects' such as the London 2012 Olympics.

1

Reforgotten Cities: Noise and the Politics of Method

Finding form

'Iain Sinclair: revolutionary novelist or revolting nihilist?' Ben Watson's question addressed to fellow travellers in the British Socialist Worker's Party in 1997,[1] positions Sinclair within the maws of a familiar binary. Revolution or nihilism, political engagement or philosophical resignation, action or reaction: which side are you on? The aesthetic, once again, stands arraigned in the court of the political and the critic alternating between prosecutor and defence attorney delivers a verdict rather than a reading. Does Sinclair's obsessive logging of the cultural contours of neoliberalism constitute a form of resistance to the inscrutability of power in 'Mogadon Britain' (SM: 19) or do his meanderings through its 'edgelands' amount to nothing more than a 'document of nostalgic radicalism' (Macfarlane 2005: 4)?

Although given a particularly tendentious expression by Watson, it is a question that reflects a clear duality within Sinclair's work which shows him to be at one and the same time a sharp-eyed commentator on the production and circulation of cultural capital, including his own, and a late-late-Romantic who appears to subscribe to a view of artistic production as a compulsive, even occult, activity. Clearly, a writer who despite his acute

---

[1] The question was addressed but never posed: Watson's essay 'composed after the election of new Labour' was only published, online, in 2005. After calling on expert witnesses V.I. Lenin and Leon Trotsky and dutifully denouncing the aestheticism of Derrida, Watson eventually gives Sinclair a conditional discharge, concluding that he may be a revolutionary novelist but cautions that: 'He may be tempted by a future of saleable London-guidebook gothickry, Auberon Waugh-style oddball cynicism and promotion of artists in his circle. In the political conflicts ahead, his conviction that all working-class politics is a charade may become an excuse to dally with the right or even with fascism ....' (Watson: 2005).

sensitivity to capital's ability to commercialize critique and turn a profit on dissent nevertheless continues to affirm the power of the imagination as an agent of emancipation presents the reader with problems which are more than purely interpretative. MacFarlane, for example, notices the presence in Sinclair's work of a sensibility more 'usually associated with the *Daily Telegraph* [rather] than with avant-garde psychogeographers', and goes on to categorize Sinclair's approach as 'nostalgic radicalism' (2005: 4). Similarly, John Heartfield has denounced Sinclair for his 'Londonostalgia' and obsession with the 'arcane and archaic'. This Londonostalgia, he claims, is a form of romanticism and as such, as 'bogus' as earlier romanticizations of the countryside (Heartfield, n.d.).

In a more measured assessment of Sinclair's politics, Brian Baker suggests that he 'exemplifies the utopian aspirations of the late-1960s counter-culture, disillusionment with its failure, and the subsequent realignment of critiques of contemporary conditions of life from an explicitly Marxian politics to an oppositional stance concerned with the configuration of urban space' (2007: 2–3). Against those who, like Heartfield, would dismiss Sinclair as one of a new breed of 'Londonostalgics', Alastair Bonnett in an equally careful account of his politics seeks to explain Sinclair's apparently wayward antiquarianism in terms of the ambivalent place of nostalgia within British radicalism in general. Unlike continental theorists of scientific socialism, he argues, British radicals have historically retained an idea of the past as a site of authenticity and unalienated labour, and hence it has provided a point from which to critique the condition of modernity. Sinclair, he argues, is able to reappropriate nostalgia as the basis of a new radicalism precisely because of its marginalization within the tradition of mainstream, progressive and scientific socialism. Sinclair thus provides 'a double mapping of modernity and loss [which] is narrated as an engagement with alienating and often brutally instrumental landscapes' (2009: 54).

In this chapter, I want to explore the issues raised by and concealed in Watson's question by returning to Sinclair's earliest published work – his accounts of the Congress on the Dialectics of Liberation in the late 1960s. I will argue that in his accounts of the Congress, Sinclair reveals the limitations of the political alternatives represented by Stokely Carmichael and Allen Ginsberg and discovers in the principle of the contingent and the accidental, a means of negotiating their apparent contradictions. This emphasis on the political potential of the aleatory and the contingent, I argue, distinguishes his practice of psychogeography from its earlier incarnations as *dérive* within the urban theory of the Situationist International and provides a ground for the formulation of a political position which attempts to maintain the possibility of critique while recognizing the inevitability of complicity and capital's powers of recuperation.

The locked shutter

Intoning lines from his poem 'TV was a Baby Crawling Towards That Death Chamber', Allen Ginsberg sits cross-legged on Primrose Hill. Behind him the city stretching out into the distance has, thanks to the distinctive silhouette of the recently opened Post Office Tower, screen left, suddenly become legible as London. When they were filmed in July 1967, the opening scenes of Sinclair's and Robert Klinkert's made-for-TV documentary, *Ah! Sunflower*, presented a study in the iconicity of the modern that directly reflected the young film-makers' conviction that 'film was the future ... that we all should be making movies and that those movies should go out into the streets and engage with the social themes of the moment' (DB).

In London to attend the Congress on the Dialectics of Liberation at the Roundhouse in nearby Chalk Farm, Ginsberg was, as Amy Hungerford notes, the face of the counterculture, 'an instantly recognizable figure in "our whole political life"' (2005: 270), and personified aspirations for the radical transformation of politics. Poet had become politician: the author of *Howl* (1956) was now the spokesman for the hippies, a new force in global politics that commanded the attention of Western media. The Congress itself, attended by such counterculture luminaries as R.D. Laing, Herbert Marcuse, Stokely Carmichael and Gregory Bateson embodied the belief that, in Sinclair's words, 'the rockstars could get together with the existential psychiatrists and politicians to thrash out a new culture' (DB). The revolutionary transformation not only of culture, but politics itself seemed to be imminent.

Equally of its moment, the Post Office Tower, was at 177 metres, on its completion, the tallest building in London and the first construction to break with the height restriction on new London buildings imposed after the Second World War – the first sign of a skyline to come. Built to house the new microwave transmitters that would connect London with the rest of the country, Postmaster General Tony Benn described it on its opening as a symbol of the technical and architectural skills of Britain's second industrial revolution.

Conjoined in Sinclair and Klinkert's frame then, tower and poet together constitute a chronotope of a revolutionary modernity whose advent is heralded in Ginsberg's address to camera:

> Six thousand movie theatres, 100,000,000 television sets, wires and wireless crisscrossing hemispheres, semaphore lights and morse, all telephones ringing at once connect every mind by its ears to one vast consciousness This Time Apocalypse – everybody waiting for one mind to break through. (AS; KMD: 41)

The ambivalence of Ginsberg's attitude to this moment of revolutionary transformation is, however, evident. It is a moment, he makes clear, which is both utopian and dystopian. The 'vast consciousness' which is about to become manifest through the technology of communication and connection, he indicates, holds the very real danger of turning all communication into noise. Cutting from the park to a garden, the poet addresses the camera on the dangers of cameras:

> If you will keep your mind on the image in front of you which is my face in the camera or in the TV tube or screen and realise now that I am looking from the other side directly into a little black hole imagining that you are there and also imagining what would be possible to say that would actually communicate through all the electricity and all the glass and all the dots on the electric screen so that you are not deceived by the image seen but that we are both on the same beam which is that you are sitting in your room surrounded by your body looking at a screen and I am sitting in my garden with my body with the noise of cars outside so that we are at least conscious of where we are and don't get hypnotised into some false universe of just pure imagery so that, in other words, you are taking the film in front of you [Iain Sinclair 'yes'] as an image with a grain of salt as an image rather than as a final reality so that you don't get deceived either by my projections or the projections of the newscaster who will follow me. (AS)

In foregrounding the tensions between medium and message, this address to cameras rehearses anxieties about the ambivalent relationship of private person and public figure which reflect in part wider tensions about the role of technology in mediating the relationship between the personal and the political. The apocalyptic breakthrough of a collective consciousness, it seems, may simply be the final realization of Guy Debord's society of the spectacle: a world in which the (broadcast) medium subsumes any possible message. With its opposition of voice as the token of truth and presence to the image as the agent of mystification (hypnosis) and the amnesia of false consciousness, it encodes Ginsberg's own anxieties about his personal transition from poet to spokesperson, from speaker to mouthpiece, for, as Eric Mottram notes, Ginsberg was, in 1965, 'a media man, fearful of global electronic communications networks but trying to employ them for his own ends of humane communication' (1972: 19). In the opening scene of Sinclair and Klinkenberg's film Ginsberg is, in other words, a man engaged in the wholly paradoxical endeavour of attempting to deploy his own celebrity as a means of negating the effect of celebrity.

This paradoxical venture is the first of numerous ironies presented in the film, including Ginsberg's own novel and noisy solution to the problem. Attempting to circumvent the logic of spectacle inherent in broadcast media, he tries to exploit the medium's dual capacity to transmit both signal and noise or semantic and affective messages by replacing verbal communication with the resonance of mantras. Mantra as resonance, he hopes, will connect bodies with bodies at a purely somatic level. Inevitably however, the lengthy section devoted to Ginsberg's chanting in the garden becomes a dead spot in the film which only serves to reinforce the ironies of the film-makers' relation to celebrity and its use to denounce celebrity. For, given Ginsberg's general anxiety about the possibilities and perils of electronic broadcast communications, Sinclair and Klinkert's project cannot help but register the ambivalence of its own situation in staging that tension.

Sinclair's appreciation of the dangers inherent in the mobilization of Ginsberg's image and of his own complicity in the economies of representation are made explicit in *The Kodak Mantra Diaries*, the chapbook he compiled to document the experience of making *Ah! Sunflower*. Here he explains that the film owed its existence to the interest of a national broadcaster attracted by Ginsberg's growing celebrity. West German TV company West Deutsche Radiofunk (WDR) 'were amused by the thought of Ginsberg & said that they would put up the marks for a small movie. That was the pillowcase we had got our heads into' (KMD: [4]). The pillowcase image suggests an ambivalence not only about this particular deal but about the activity of reporting in general, echoing the epigraph to the chapbook taken from the *New York Times* reporter Jane Kramer's account of Ginsberg in America, *Paterfamilias*: ' "It's a bad bag, reporting," Snyder mused. "Somehow I don't think it's possible to be in that bag and get anywhere spiritually speaking" ' (KMD: [1]).

Reporting is an ideologically suspect activity insofar as its material is always presented as a mediation between presence and absence. Whether it sets out to describe an event to those who were not present (as news) or are no longer present (as archive), it purports to represent an inside to an outside and thereby always threatens to transform the 'truth' of experience into the alienation of spectacle. In a politics which emphasizes being, experience, spontaneity and authenticity, broadcast media is understood as enemy terrain for, notes Sinclair:

> TV will have endless programmes on Ginsberg, on [Stokely] Carmichael, even on [Emmett] Grogan. Turn them into faces. Into more brand names. They won't have programmes BY them. And they won't have programmes FOR them. And nobody is clear-sighted enough to see it. (KMD: [15])

Even though Sinclair and Klinkert's film essay provides Ginsberg with the opportunity to warn against the dangers of amnesia attendant on broadcast media, the project is set up in such a way as to force upon Ginsberg the 'responsibility' of the 'central image' which he is determined to evade.

The resulting tensions, more fully detailed in *The Kodak Mantra Diaries*, come to a head when after two days' filming, the novice cameramen discover that they have forgotten to release the shutter-lock leaving them with '5000 feet of black film'. The error means reshooting several scenes, including the reading on Primrose Hill. Although Ginsberg is gracious about their request to reshoot, time has moved on and the mood has changed. Ginsberg is distracted, having heard from New York that his partner Peter Orlovsky has been committed to Bellevue following a psychotic episode during which he had broken all the windows in their apartment. The accident of the locked shutter, thus inadvertently produces one of the film's most revealing moments, a tetchy interview where the strains of the counterculture project are enacted in miniature.

> *Sinclair*: Negroes rioting in Newark, Detroit. Guerrilla activity in South America, China – wherever it is, it is just all part of the same global eruption, is this true do you think?
>
> *Ginsberg*: Well you said so, I don't know. How the fuck would I know? I got a letter that all the windows in my house were smashed and he's in Bellevue, that's why I'm not really in a mood to make movies. (AS)

Given that the political function of madness is one of the key issues of debate within the Congress, Ginsberg's anxiety about his partner's psychosis has a wider significance that, in the context of the film, seems to signal the limitations of the countercultural project as a whole. The Congress was, David Cooper notes, organized by himself and three other psychiatrists who, as a result of their clinical work on schizophrenia, had come to believe that '[m]ost people who are called mad … come from family situations where there is a desperate need to find some scapegoat, someone who will consent … to take on the disturbance of each of the others and, in some sense, suffer for them' (1968: 7). Having identified madness as the form of scapegoating practised within the 'family system', Cooper extends the concept of the scapegoat from the family to explain 'certain political facts in the world around us', namely the production of 'the enemy' in the Vietnam war:

> After the conversion … of man into the 'inhuman', there is a further subtle metamorphosis. The 'inhuman' become 'non-human'. At this point they become the ultimate projected versions of ourselves, those bits of ourselves that we wish most finally to destroy in order to become Pure Being. (1968: 8)

The aim of the congress as identified in its full title – *The Congress on the Dialectics of Liberation (for the Demystification of violence)* – was to identify the forms of hidden violence exercised by existing political systems; to debate the appropriate forms of response to this 'scapegoating'; and to discuss the possibilities for a non-violent politics. The Congress was, in other words, expressly concerned with the forms of violence involved in the production of order, in sense-making as a form of epistemological violence that produces madness as its absolute Other. In this context, Ginsberg's inability to shift his attention from the fate of his lover inevitably takes on an ironic resonance, suggesting implicitly the limitations of his political project.

As rehearsed in *Ah! Sunflower* and *The Kodak Mantra Diaries*, the implications of this concern with forms of violence involved in the production of order are made explicit in the open-forum confrontation between Stokely Carmichael in his advocacy of Black Power and Ginsberg in his advocacy of non-violent resistance and the transformation of society through the transformation of individual consciousness. For Carmichael, violence is racial and is visited on black people by white people. Fighting such violence requires direct action against the fact of racial oppression, a message which, Sinclair notes, is well received by the predominantly white liberal audience (KMD: 24). Ginsberg, on the evidence of his visit to Russia, argues that violence 'falls' on black and white alike and should be resisted through non-violent means. Hence,

> all happenings should be propositional rather than oppositional. Proposals and constructions rather than negations & bring-downs. One of the difficulties with finding a symbolic action language has been the tendency to repeat the old forms of criticism, rather than to shift the scene entirely & enter into a new universe which might be Play, Pleasure, Fun. Honey catches more flies than vinegar. (KMD: 34–5)

The exchange between Carmichael and Ginsberg rehearses a recurrent argument within left-wing discussions of violence and, on this occasion, seems to articulate the limitations of the countercultural project to transform the terms of politics, suggesting this is a luxury that is available only to those who are not subjected to the forms of direct and manifest violence experienced by African Americans.

Seeking to refine the terms of this debate, Slajov Žižek has more recently distinguished between 'subjective' violence which is 'performed by an identifiable agent' and two forms of objective violence: 'symbolic' violence which is 'embedded in our language and in its forms' and 'systemic' violence which arises from the 'smooth functioning of our economic and political systems' (2008: 1). According to Žižek,

> subjective and objective violence cannot be perceived from the same standpoint: subjective violence is experienced as such against the

background of a non-violent zero level. It is seen as a perturbation of the 'normal', peaceful state of things. However, objective violence is precisely the violence inherent to this 'normal' state of things. Objective violence is invisible since it sustains the very zero-level standard against which we perceive something as subjectively violent. (2008b: 2)

The difficulty in perceiving objective violence, Sinclair's account suggests, is partly due to the visibility of subjective violence. Confronted with the spectacle of racial violence in the United States, Ginsberg's plea for non-violent strategies which will transform the terms of political struggle inevitably appears divorced from the reality of political struggle as it is experienced by those subjected to overt violence. In part, as Žižek's account of objective violence makes plain, this is because the violence to which Ginsberg addresses his argument is encoded within the terms of political debate itself. In this respect, the aim of the congress, to examine the forms of violence encoded within the articulation of political subjects, is self-defeating as it seeks to bring into the arena of adversarial debate and arena-form discussion the forms of violence that are encoded within the staging of that discussion.

Žižek's formulation allows us to identify Ginsberg's problem in this debate as an example of the problem that Michel Serres addresses through the figure of the *tiers exclu*, or excluded third. The *tiers exclu*, Serres explains, occupies a discursive position which is necessarily excluded from discursive articulation: 'To hold a dialogue is to suppose a third man and to seek to exclude him: a successful communication is the exclusion of the third man' and as such, communication or dialogue is always a 'game played by two interlocutors considered united against the phenomena of interference ... tied together by mutual interest: they battle together against noise' (1982: 66–7). In his debate with Carmichael, Ginsberg is trying to make a space for the *tiers exclu* – to make visible the violence of exclusion in the production of political subjects.

Drawing on the vocabulary used by Herbert Marcuse during the Congress, Cooper formulates this distinction in terms of the difference between quantitative and qualitative revolutionary situations. Quantitative change is 'a response to intolerable conditions of existence' but may simply replace one system of domination and repression with another, whereas '[q]ualitative change is a change of the system as a whole' (1968: 179). It is this perception that informs fellow delegate, Gregory Bateson's, formulation of the cybernetic hypothesis, that what is noise at one point in a system is information elsewhere, for as Serres shows in his reading of 'The Town Mouse and the Country Mouse', the *tiers exclu* marks the points of vulnerability where any system of meaning is open to transformation. Qualitative change is achieved precisely through the recognition of the ways that struggle produces the *tiers exclu* and the construction of strategies to incorporate the excluded.

The problem confronted separately by Ginsberg at the Congress and Sinclair's film of Ginsberg then is how to reveal the *tiers exclu*. For Ginsberg, as we have seen, chanting mantras is a strategy which can achieve only limited success, rapidly becoming a further element within the spectacle. Within the film, it is Sinclair's struggle against the mechanical 'noise' of the locked shutter rather than the mantra that reveals the transformative potential of the *tiers exclu* insofar as it is the locked shutter that produces the film's narrative crisis. In revealing Ginsberg's inability to politicize the personal, it suggests too that the direct confrontation with madness overwhelms its theorization.

Re-narrativized by Sinclair first in *The Kodak Mantra Diaries* and then in *Debriefing* (the 'extra' that is included on the film's fortieth-anniversary DVD release) the purely mechanical noise of the locked shutter, gathers symbolic force coming to stand for the failure of the film and of the countercultural project more generally. In *The Kodak Mantra Diaries* Sinclair describes how after having initially sold the project to WDR on the strength of Paul McCartney's involvement and having failed to contact the Beatle, they are unexpectedly presented with his phone number; '[b]ut by then it was too late' (KMD: 63). The project which was born out of being at the right place at the right time succumbs to a sense of its belatedness: the hippies queuing to see Ginsberg read the poems of William Blake at the Roundhouse have become 'extras', who 'waited to get into the Roundhouse as if they were going to view Lenin's corpse' (KMD: 66). The revolutionary potential of the counterculture has already succumbed to the 'money spiral' (KMD: 66), the optimism of 1967 is already overlaid with the disillusion of 1968.

In *Debriefing*, Sinclair writes the film off to experience and then redeems it as a necessary false beginning: 'Doing the film was a way of finding out this isn't how you work' (DB). Its failure prompts him to discover in *The Kodak Mantra Diaries* the method he was to use for the next forty years.

[T]he lesson that I learned was the form I used in this first book, by accident, which was a diary form of short, sort of Polaroids of my own life, transcripts of long tapes, photographs, documentary evidence that would appear randomly, found footage, letters, telegrams – put in the whole lot and that kind of gives you the structure of a whole book and I'm kind of using exactly the same techniques forty years later. (DB)

In turning his lost footage into a lesson about found material, Sinclair's work discovers its characteristic dynamic: the central principle that the proliferation of accounts and points of view serves to illustrate the absence of any authoritative referent and thereby foregrounds the presence or noise of the medium in the construction of the message. At the same time, this shift away from a documentary project structured around a central responsible image towards a more immersive form of reporting effectively establishes the assemblage of fragments and varying points of view – including, notably, two accounts of an LSD trip – as the core of Sinclair's artistic practice. In the chapbook and 'camera passed from hand to hand' (DB) he discovers his own version of the key Modernist technique of collage, the technique in which Budd Hopkins suggests 'the philosophical core of modernism received its most literal expression' (1997: 5).

Collage, Hopkins argues, owes its methodological centrality in Modernist aesthetic practice to its refusal of a fixed perspective and its dissolution of existing antinomies between representation and abstraction, sign and object, and, in its inaugural instance – Picasso's *Still Life with Chair Caning* (1911) – photography and painting. In its emphasis on media at the expense of message, collage presents an obvious example of the Modernist investment in that which communication theory terms noise. Collage enables Modernism to be read as a turn in a variety of arts away from representation towards their proper media and is the emblem of a general Modernist investment in noise as the sign of the material.

Collage, in Hopkins' view, is thus a 'complex new hybrid' in that it not only dissolves the antinomies of the artificial and the real, but as a 'philosophical attitude, an aesthetic position that can suffuse virtually any expressive medium', it eliminates any identification of medium and subject, providing the 'sole methodological link between such Modernist masterpieces as T.S. Eliot's *The Waste Land*, Joyce's *Ulysses*, the music of Igor Stravinsky, and the architecture of Frank Lloyd Wright, and it lies, of course, at the very heart of the century's most important new art medium – the motion picture' (1997: 5).

As such, Hopkins effectively points us to two different sources of noise within the collage. In addition to its noisy insistence on the presence of the medium in the message, the noise which works to problematize assumptions about representation, collage can also be read as a peculiarly urban form whose juxtapositions of discrete and heterogeneous elements mimics the centrality of fragmentation and collision to the Modernist urban experience. As such, collage is a form which, in it is collisions, mimics the noise of the city.

It is in relation to collage as a device for allowing space to the aleatory that we should understand the politics of Sinclair's emphasis on urban walking and psychogeography as creative resources within his text. Walking within Sinclair's work is a form of spatial collage that emphasizes and foregrounds the accidental and contingent. It gives space to the chance encounters that reveal the obscured or occult connections that produce alternative narratives of space. Simultaneously, walking as a social practice which is tolerated, prohibited or regarded with suspicion serves as a useful device to reveal a material politics of space that would otherwise remain invisible to those who remain within sanctioned precincts. Walking, in other words, is a device which materializes the city through an emphasis on the aleatory.

Rather than a simple disillusionment with the politics of the counterculture, it seems more appropriate to characterize Sinclair's politics as a working through of the contradictions presented by that politics – an attempt to resolve the problems of representation posed by the technologization of communication or the society of the spectacle through an investigation of the possibilities of noise, or contingency, in a variety of forms.

Walking the city: Psychogeography as cut-up

'If there is one person who, more than any other, is responsible for the current popularity that psychogeography enjoys, then it is Iain Sinclair', writes Merlin Coverley (2006: 119). As Coverley notes, psychogeography's elevation from the obscurity of the *Internationale Situationist # 1*, 1957, to a weekly column in a UK broadsheet is intimately associated with the work and influence of

Sinclair. However, Sinclair's own commentary on the term and concept suggest his attitude to psychogeography is rather more equivocal than Coverley's attribution implies. In conversation with Kevin Jackson in 2003, for example, Sinclair emphasizes the opportunism involved in his use of the term: 'I thought psychogeography could be adapted quite conveniently to forge a franchise – which is what happened, more than I could have imagined! [Laughs] It took off!' (Jackson 2003: 75)[2] He strikes a similarly ambivalent note in conversation with Stuart Jeffries:

> For me, [psychogeography] is a way of psychoanalysing the psychosis of the place in which I happen to live. I'm just exploiting it because I think it's a canny way to write about London. Now it's become the name of a column by Will Self in which he seems to walk about the South Downs with a pipe, which has got absolutely nothing to do with psychogeography. There's an awful sense that you have created a monster. In a way I've allowed myself to become this London brand. I've become a hack on my own mythology, which fascinates me. From there on in you can either go with it or subvert it. (Jeffries 2004)

The nature of the ambivalences informing Sinclair's psychogeography and of his nuanced understanding of the praxis becomes apparent from his most explicitly psychogeographical text, the prose collection *Lights Out for the Territory: 9 Excursions in the Secret History of London* (1997). Here, the opening essay of the collection, 'Skating on Thin Eyes: The First Walk', provides one of Sinclair's clearest statements of psychogeographical intent. The essay begins:

> The notion was to cut a crude V into the sprawl of the city, to vandalise dormant energies by an act of ambulant signmaking. To walk out from Hackney to Greenwich Hill, and back along the River Lea to Chingford Mount, recording and retrieving the messages on walls, lampposts, doorjambs: the spites and spasms of an increasingly deranged populace. (LOT: 1)

---

[2] In full: 'I think the word first crossed my path in the 1960s, but it didn't really take. The Situationist Era drifted through me, and I didn't think I was practising anything which resembled it, until it kicked in as a term employed by Stewart Home and his associates, who were reworking cultural history, and using Situationist terms to parody the National Front's activities in Limehouse. I mean, they weren't seriously interested in where things fell on the map, they were just using those forms, but I seriously was interested in where things fell on the map. I thought psychogeography could be adapted quite conveniently to forge a franchise – which is what happened, more than I could have imagined! [Laughs] It took off!' (Jackson 2003: 75).

The emphasis on cutting immediately marks the distance between Sinclair's psychogeographical practice and that described by Guy Debord.[3]

> In a *dérive* one or more persons during a certain period drop their relations, their work and leisure activities, and all their other usual motives for movement and action, and let themselves be drawn by the attractions of the terrain and the encounters they find there. Chance is a less important factor in this activity than one might think: from a *dérive* point of view cities have psychogeographical contours, with constant currents, fixed points and vortexes that strongly discourage entry into or exit from certain zones.
>
> But the *dérive* includes both this letting-go and its necessary contradiction: the domination of psychogeographical variations by the knowledge and calculation of their possibilities. In this latter regard, ecological science, despite the narrow social space to which it limits itself, provides psychogeography with abundant data. (Knabb 1994: 50)

Where Debord advocates a practice of submission and drift, Sinclair invokes psychogeography as an active practice which in its hinted anti-social inclinations – 'to vandalize dormant energies' – mirrors the psychosis attributed to the wider population.

In this emphasis on cutting as opposed to drift, Sinclair also alerts us to the presence within the traditional repertoire of the avant-garde of two techniques whose differences although apparently minimal are of critical significance. With its emphasis on drift and the suspension of volition, the *dérive* closely resembles other techniques for accessing the unconscious by evading the mediation of consciousness such as the free association exemplified by automatic writing. Sinclair's conceit of the walk as a mark inscribed upon or incised within the city, however, is more readily identified with an other equally well-established avant-garde genre typified by the technique of the cut-up, a technique which can be traced back to Tristan Tzara but which achieved its greatest prominence in the work of William Burroughs and Brion Gysin (who serves as an important link between the European avant-garde and the North American counterculture). As earlier practitioners of the technique had discovered, the power of cut-up lies in its ability to release images and energies

---

[3]   Debord's description here, however, does not accurately reflect the broad range of psychogeographic techniques practiced by the SI, some of which, such as using a map of London to navigate the Harz mountains, more closely resemble Sinclair's psychogeographic practice.

whose affective power would otherwise have been contained and rationalized by the cognitive structure of narrative or other forms of conscious patterning. Just as cutting up and reassembling existing texts reveals imagery contained within, but not articulated by, the original, in carving a crude V into the sprawl of the city, Sinclair in effect marks out an itinerary which will conjoin, or constellate, within the space of his text, figures and events whose connections are initially topographical. Here, the V-shaped walk is intended to reveal the presence of a city which cannot be articulated within more structured or more rationally motivated encounters with urban space. The fragility of the mechanisms through which we normalize the city, the assumption of the stable subject denoted by the first person pronoun and its attendant scopic regime, are suggested in the title, 'Skating on Thin Eyes'. Sinclair's text gestures towards the chaos of a space unstructured by the grammar of capital and the eyes/ 'I's that sustain subjectivity.

Where the notion of *dérive* as drift is easily associated with the endless play of the signifier celebrated in post-structural accounts of textuality and hence invites us to read the notion of *dérive* as symbolic of the radical homelessness of the Freudian subject, a cut-based psychogeographic praxis invites other constructions of the relationship between the city and the subject. In terms of the classical structuralist distinction between syntagmatic and paradigmatic linguistic operations, Sinclair's use of the *dérive*-as-cut represents a form of radical syntagmatism in that it elevates pure contiguity to the primary principle of textual organization. Critically, this methodological insistence on the syntagm transforms the city itself into a place of encounter rather than the site of self-encounter implied by the *dérive*-as-drift. Whereas the *dérive*-as-drift produces a city which reflects the operations of the *dériviste*'s unconscious, the *dérive*-as-cut shifts the focus away from the unconscious of the *dériviste* towards the population as a whole and a wider cultural unconscious so that psychogeography becomes in Sinclair's formula, 'a way of psychoanalysing the psychosis of the place in which I happen to live' (Jeffries 2004).

It is this concern with minimizing the role of the *dériviste* that informs Sinclair's anxiety that, as originally conceived, the 'proposed walk was far too neat' (LOT: 5) and his hope 'for an accident to bring about a final revision' (LOT: 5). The desired accident which he 'finds' in an 'invitation six months out of date' to the opening of a site-specific installation at the University of

Greenwich, entitled 'the curve of forgetting' constitutes the sort of 'arbitrary revision' which can authorize his walk precisely because, as a message from the city to the walker, it seems to provide a motive which, paradoxically, will eliminate any residual shred of intentionality.

Crucially, the discovery of an accidental motive also transforms the V from a sign imposed upon the city (a letter) into the trace of a gesture (an incision), which will release the energies and voices harboured by the city as text. This sense of the V as a mark which hovers somewhere between a signifier and a purely graphic form is also strongly indicated in his account of his inspiration for his V-shaped route:

> I had developed this curious conceit while working on my novel *Radon Daughters*: that the physical movements of the characters across their territory might spell out the letters of a secret alphabet. Dynamic shapes, with ambitions to achieve a life of their own, quite independent of their supposed author. (LOT: 1)

The revision of Paul Auster's similar conceit in *City of Glass* is subtle but important. Where the apparently arbitrary movements of Auster's character around the streets of New York spell out the name of the mythical city of noise – 'OWER OF BABEL' – a message which becomes visible only from the elevated perspective of the cartographer, Sinclair's 'secret alphabet' will be composed of characters which, even from a cartographic perspective, may not be recognized as letters but are rather 'dynamic shapes'.

One such dynamic shape is 'LAING' (LOT: 10) – the sign simultaneously of the construction company responsible for much of the redevelopment of the city and of R.D. Laing the anti-psychiatrist whose theories of the social construction of mental illness provide an alternative model for understanding the 'psychosis' attendant upon that redevelopment. Where a Freudian inspired psychogeography would find an expression of its own constitutive lack within the material environment, a psychogeography drawing on Laing's account of mental illness as visited upon the individual by her social environment can be expected to provide a far less individual-oriented version of the psyche. Where the notion of drift points us to a Freudian subject and a politics of loss, the notion of cut, consequently, encourages us to attend to the social and material aspects in the construction of psychosis.

The way in which the distinction between cut and drift serves as a figure for the distance between Paris and London is again registered when Sinclair writes:

> Drifting purposefully is the recommended mode, trampling asphalted earth in alert reverie, allowing the fiction of an underlying pattern to reveal itself. To the no-bullshit materialist this sounds suspiciously like *fin-de-siècle* decadence, a poetic of entropy – but the born-again *flâneur* is a stubborn creature, less interested in texture and fabric, eavesdropping on philosophical conversation pieces, than in noticing *everything*. (LOT: 4)

In locating his psychogeographic investigation at the point where letters hover between sign and shape, Sinclair quite literally opens his text to 'everything', refusing even the meta-selection that distinguishes the sign from its noisy material substrate. In this concern with the tension between the material and the semiotic, we glimpse the more general ambiguity that informs Sinclair's depiction of the 'matter of London' as it combines the materialist with the archaic sense of the mythography of London, 'the refleshing of Lud's withered hyde' (LOT: 26).

The concern with the matter of London as simultaneously material and mythical is evident in the lengthy meditation on 'tagging' that opens the first essay. As the poor relation of graffiti and street art, tagging constitutes a sort of background noise which, Sinclair suggests, approaches the condition of phatic communion within the streetscape – 'the only constant on these fantastic journeys' (LOT: 4). As background noise, graffiti's unselected, Sinclair is attentive to the ways in which the instability of sign and form evident in tagging carry messages about the wider culture:

> Urban graffiti is all too often a signature without a document, an anonymous autograph. The tag is everything, as jealously defended as the Coke or Disney decals. Tags are the marginalia of corporate tribalism. Their offence is to parody the most visible aspect of high capitalist black magic...The name, unnoticed except by fellow taggers, is a gesture, an assertion: it stands in place of the individual artist who, in giving up his freedom, becomes free. (LOT: 1)

Tagging as a compulsive assertion of identity which dissolves identity in noise effectively marks the *reductio ad absurdum* of liberal principles of freedom of expression: 'The public autograph is an announcement of nothingness, abdication, the swift erasure of the envelope of identity' (LOT: 1–2). Tagging as a form of psychosis and as a form of logo in this sense can be read as mirroring the mystery of commodity fetishism itself and, in identifying the tag as a parodic commentary on the language of capital, Sinclair alludes to Theodor Adorno's dictum that Modernist art in its refusal of function – its insistence on form and materiality – apparently scandalizes the utilitarian rationale of a culture where value is associated with the instrumental but actually reveals the concealed truth of that economy: the principle of commodity fetishism.

The constant presence of these jealously defended but semantically empty marks – tags and logos – within the margins of our culture act as a suture of seemingly opposed categories: the individual and the corporate, the aesthetic and the commercial, but above all, of the material and the 'black magic' that produces capitalist value. In choosing to open his essay with this meditation on the relationship between the tag and the logo, the similarity between the marginalized script at the edge of culture, a form of cultural production which seems almost uniquely resistant to commodification and the heavily policed signs that drive an economy based largely on the operation of 'signs, affects and code' (Hardt and Negri 2009: 299), Sinclair also prepares us to read his walk as exploring the city as the expression of a particular kind of space produced by the various forms of immaterial labour. And, as the conjunction of the tag and logo indicate, it is a space in which the post-Fordist economy is understood in terms of the identity of value and waste.

In the juxtaposition of the tag and the logo, two signs whose outward similarity serves to highlight the polarities of value and waste within the immaterial economy, Sinclair allows us to glimpse the space that is occluded in the articulation of experience around the binary categories of the public and the private. As we have seen, for Hardt and Negri, language serves as an important example of the cultural commons upon which capital relies in order to produce value. Language is neither public nor private but, precisely and necessarily, common, for 'if large portions of our words, phrases or parts of speech were subject to private ownership or public authority – then language would lose its powers of expression, creativity, and communication' (2009: ix). As a paradigmatic form of the common, the tag and the logo as linguistic operations provide a useful demonstration of the dynamics of appropriation upon which capitalist value is produced through immaterial labour. If the logo is emblematic of the strategy through which capitalized value is generated through the privatization of a common resource, in its juxtaposition with the tag, it is evident that this privatization is achieved not simply through the parcelling off of a particular area of language or sign but that it involves a more general process of eviction. Brand identity is, in effect, achieved at the expense of individual identity. The corporate body materializes itself through the appropriation of a graphic form as the marker of individual identity, while the taggers in their parody of that model of individual identity as a form of private property, perform their own dispossession and in so doing provide that surplus required for the production of value in an immaterial economy.

For Hardt and Negri, language thus serves an important heuristic purpose in that it can 'help readers retrain their vision, recognizing the common that exists and what it can do' (2009: ix). Sinclair, in his insistence that his project should be seen as an act of 'ambulant signmaking' and devotion to 'recording and retrieving' the language of the city, effectively describes a project which is positioned to explore the relationship between the language of the common – language which is neither public nor private and its corresponding dimension in urban space.

The nature of this project becomes clearer as Sinclair continues his account of London's graffiti. If tagging presents us with a graphic instance of the ways in which matter emerges through semantic exhaustion and points to the operation of this process at the heart of the liberal economy, his account of the writing on East London walls goes on to reveal another inversion of sign and matter insofar as these walls provide the material substrate for voices which have no other place within the rapidly privatizing media ecology of what is, in 1997, still a proto-digital period: 'As newspapers have atrophied into the playthings of grotesque megalomaniacs, uselessly shrill exercises in mind control, so disenfranchised authors have been forced to adapt the walls to playful collages of argument and invective' (LOT: 3). These 'disenfranchised authors' include creative voices that have matched their message to the precarious, 'here-today, gone-tomorrow' ecology of the wall but also voices who find in the wall an opportunity to deliver messages which would otherwise be unheard:

> My own patch in Hackney has been mercilessly colonised by competing voices from elsewhere: Kurds, Peruvians, Irish, Russians, Africans. Contour

lines of shorthand rhetoric asserting the borders between different areas of
influence. Graffiti could, I hoped, be read like a tidemark. In the course of
our walk we'd find precisely where the 'Freedom' of Dursan Karatas gave way
to the 'Innocence' of George Davis – OK. (LOT: 3)

In this account, the walls of the neoliberal city provide the material substrate for
voices whose physical and discursive locations have been erased or are under
threat of erasure by the forces of globalization. The walls mediate messages
that emanate from regions which are unrecognized on other maps or which
cannot survive in an increasingly privatized mainstream media ecology. The
walls of Hackney, in other words, present the psychogeographer with a space
that provides a map of spaces which could not otherwise be mapped.

As such, rather than a vision of the metropolis as an endless drift which
mirrors the psyche's homelessness, attention to the graffiti on a walk through
Hackney allows us to see the metropolis as a home to those voices that it has
itself 'disenfranchised': a city which is the home of the homeless, of parts with
no part. This homelessness can be territorial as in the case of the displaced
Kurdish 'mountain people ... queuing politely for their turn at the photocopier'
(LOT: 13–14) or temporal, as in the legend 'George Davis Is Innocent' which
persists as an echo of an otherwise forgotten crime. The persistence of
messages long beyond their topicality – such as George Davis and the Angry
Brigade graffiti – points to the ways in which the history of the district has
been made up of successive communities of the displaced who have in turn
been displaced from the locality. These communities include the successive
waves of immigrant populations – Huguenot, Irish, Jewish, Cypriots and
Bangladeshi – but also historical and sociocultural groups such as hippies, 70s
radicals and East End gangsters. In this place of the displaced, even attempts
to thematize transience produce their own exclusions: elsewhere, Sinclair
notes that the plans to turn the Princelet Street synagogue into a 'Museum of
Immigration' refused to feature the room of the Jewish caretaker also in the
building as it was 'too gothic' (Sinclair 2011a).

Informing this vision of East London as a place of radical homelessness,
a place where even the exclusions of a rhetoric organized around exclusion
become visible, is an understanding of the city's peculiar relation to the
logic of enclosure. If the metropolis is historically the product of the wealth
generated by the ongoing processes of appropriation exemplified by the

enclosure of the English commons – as Sinclair will explore through the figure of John Clare in *Edge of the Orison* (2001) – it is also produced as a new commons by those dispossessed in that process: a new commons which then becomes available for the new acts of appropriation and enclosure that define the cityscape of London in the 1990s. It is this double process which produces London as simultaneously a new common and the site of a new enclosure that generates the ambivalence in the title, *Lights Out for the Territory*. In one sense, through its allusion to Mark Twain's 'Territories' and the yet-to-be-appropriated lands beyond the American frontier, it identifies the space explored in Sinclair's texts with a form of commons, a realm of freedom beyond the spatial categories of the public and the private. At the same time, it provides an unequivocal message about the fate of this space for which it will soon be 'lights out'.

The 'John Bull printing set' and small-press politics

This concern comes into sharper focus when Sinclair's itinerary takes him to Amhurst Road in Stoke Newington, which, in the 1970s, was the home both of the poet Tom Raworth's Matrix press (one of the most significant publishers of small-press verse) and, at no 359, the 'John Bull printing set' used by the 'supposed members' of the direct action anarchist faction, the Angry Brigade. Here, the principle of topographic contiguity established by the cut enables Sinclair to elaborate on the connections between politics and poetics in what, from the perspective of the 1990s, might seem to be a lost era of British radicalism. Quoting one of the Angry Brigade dispatches composed by Anna Mendelson [*sic*][4] (who went on to write poetry as Grace Lake) he remarks its resemblance to the 'suppressed urban poetry of the Thatcher years' (LOT: 27) and notes with irony that the 'Angry Brigade communiqués were the only small-press publications to be thoroughly reviewed and debated in the nationals' (LOT: 28). The textual resemblances of poetic and political texts, he suggests, constitute a

---

[4] Anna was born Mendleson and her obituaries are in the name Mendelssohn, as she is named in Sinclair's *Ghost Milk*.

hybrid form [which] prophetically alludes to the coming state of English poetry, when the technical language of psychoanalysis and political rhetoric (plus Walter Benjamin and Theodor Adorno) would respond to the crisis in our cultural and social lives by striking a spectacular treaty with the imperatives of the gutter. (LOT: 28)

Again, as in the tag and the logo, similarities of form and material are juxtaposed to reveal the resemblance of apparently antithetical cultural forms. Just as the hand-printed political communiqué resembles small-press poetry, so the headlines of the tabloid – the 'imperatives of the gutter' – provide the stuff for the poetry of, for example Peter Reading, while Sinclair himself explores their potential as a resource for dystopian imagery in *Downriver*.

'SEX CHANGE WIFE' MURDERED AFTER WITCH'S WEDDING. *Husband wanted affair with another man, court told.* DERANGED KILLER IS LOCKED AWAY FOR EVER – *54-year-old man's fingernails were ripped off with pliers – Mr Berman was a loner.* CLASS WAR DENY ATTACK. DRUGS DOCTOR BACK ON REGISTER. WOMAN RAPED BY GANG WHO LACED DRINK ... (D: 100)

The formal similarity of these small-press publications are not superficial: both poetry and politics, he notes, are marked by their distinction between the communal and the popular. As he observes: 'So selfless and communally based was the spirit of this poetic that it was universally denounced as elitist and resistant to ordinary intelligence' (LOT: 28). The irony here marks the recognition that just as the territorial and ideological enclosures that constitute the logic of neoliberalism have produced the metropolis as the home of the disenfranchised, so the continuing processes of cultural enclosure mean that it is now almost impossible to articulate any notion of the communal or the collective outside of that recognized by the market in the form of popular culture.

To further unpack the ironies condensed in this observation, however, it is necessary to look more closely at the perspective in his account of the 'conjunctions of Amhurst road' (LOT: 30). Initially, this seems to be a simple rehearsal of the familiar narrative of the 1990s that presents the radicalism of the 1960s and 1970s as the product of an era whose final demise was signalled by the almost total collapse of state communism in the late 1980s.

In his account of Amhurst Road, Sinclair seems to view the moment of British radicalism represented by the Angry Brigade as a mistake from which it is now possible to move on. His remarks on Anna Mendelson's life after the Angry Brigade convey a sense of this sense of leave-taking. The real meaning of Mendelson's political actions, he suggests, cannot be recovered from the official history presented in the national press. They are only revealed subsequently in her poetry: '*This* is what was always true, the courage of her attack, the intelligence operating with and through her stress: the achievement in her transcribed internal monologues ... The rest, the tabloid stuff, was an accidental apprenticeship' (LOT: 29).

This suggestion that radical politics was simply an 'accidental apprenticeship' to the real business of writing poetry, seems to provide *prima facie* evidence of that 'withdrawal from political commitment' which Brian Baker discerns in Sinclair's work. However, in his depiction of Mendelson's life in terms of a move from terrorism to quietism and in his eulogy on Mendelson's poetry, Sinclair also provides a pen portrait of something like Hegel's beautiful soul – or *belle ame* (Morton 2009: 13): of a figure that preserves the illusion of its own innocence by projecting its disorder onto the world from whose corruption it believes itself to be radically detached.

In this respect, Mendelson's narrative stands in stark contrast to the autobiographical thread worked into the essay. While Mendelson was hand-printing communiqués for the Angry Brigade, we learn that Sinclair was supporting his own small-press aesthetic and communitarian politics by taking casual work from the Manpower Commission. Elsewhere, he notes that this provided him with privileged access to the hidden spaces and scenes of the 'endgame of industrialism' (Sinclair and Boal 2011).[5] Here he records how, as a casual labourer in an economy undergoing the traumatic transition from Fordism to post-Fordism, he inevitably found himself caught up in the industrial disputes that marked the end of organized labour and which

---

[5] 'This is how it worked – when I was down to my last ten pounds in the world I would take whatever the Manpower Agency had to offer, employment on the day for the day ... introducing opt-out causal to endangered industries desperate enough to hire unskilled dope-smoking day-labourers who would vanish before the first frost or the first wrong word from the foreman. Everybody knew on both sides of the deal – it was 1971 – knew that it was all over the places we were dispatched by the unemployment agency were by definition doomed – the excitement of being parachuted into areas I'd never visited' (Sinclair and Boal 2011).

gave birth to the landscape of deserted factories and docks explored in his subsequent writings. Recalling his time as '[c]heap scab labour ... brought in to circumvent the union stranglehold on the docks' (LOT: 50), Sinclair duly annotates his place in the city's wider historical and topographical transformations: 'The docks were finished. Chobham Farm was the final dispute ... The Chobham speculators, hard-hats and pinstripe suits, were the forerunners of the LDDC pirates, the cardinals of the Isle of Dogs' (LOT: 50). The death of the Port of London and his early entry in to the precariat, however, does not diminish the lyricism of his reminiscence:

> Heartbreaking sunrises as we drove to work, chill autumnal mists over the Lea Valley. Lunchhour picnics among the sunflowers, effluent-fed weeds. Trains shunting in the background. Talk of travel, gossip with the drivers. Letters from Tony Lowes in Kabul. (LOT: 50)

The elegiac tone of the passage is achieved not simply through the recollection of a vanished London but because Sinclair acknowledges his part in bringing about that disappearance. Where Mendelson retreats from radical politics into an even more radical poetics, the form in which the beautiful soul finds its truest expression, Sinclair discovers his subject in his recognition of his complicity with the processes of destruction. At the same time as he charts the London that is vanishing before the forces unleashed by the liberalization of the financial markets in 1986 and the subsequent expansion of the City, he is also describing the London that gave birth to these forces. Similarly, even as his text presents an auratic vision of culture as a counter to the commodified version presented by city branders, by authenticating and sanctifying places and figures that are on the point of erasure – the disappearing city of his 2006 anthology, *London City of Disappearances* – the auratic city he describes is simultaneously created and destroyed by the forces unleashed by neoliberalism.

Thus, if Mendelson's trajectory from radical politics to radical poetics represents one iteration of the radical, it has to be distinguished from Sinclair's indication of his own complicity in the disasters he describes, and it is in light of this complicity that we can read Sinclair's concern 'with the configuration of urban space' (Baker 2007: 2) as exploring the possibilities of politics and the notion of the radical in the wake of the countercultural moment. Critical to his exploration of this axis of the spatial and the radical is the temporal notion of the 'reforgotten' which, as noted above, constitutes one of the principal forms through which Sinclair engages with the return of the unselected.

Reforgetting: Forms of complicity

In its most straightforward articulation, the notion of the 'reforgotten' points to the operations of forgetting in historiography. In place of an historiography which constructs a past out of the materials which enable us to narrativize the present as the culmination of what has gone before, it alerts us to the critical role of 'forgetting' in the construction of history as the narrative of community – a process discussed at length by Benedict Anderson (2006). From this perspective, history as the story of a community is regarded as a discourse fashioned as much by what is forgotten, or unselected, as by what is remembered and consecrated in, for example, the blue plaques attached to the houses of the notable.

It is by concentrating on the unselected, Sinclair shows, that we see the metropolis as the city of the disenfranchised. This is particularly true in an area so steeped in Walter Benjamin's 'tradition of the oppressed' (1969: 257) as Hackney and London's East End with its successive waves of immigrant populations. In his depiction of the 'the conjunctions of Amhurst Road', however, the reforgotten does not point simply to the unselected within the dominant narrative of history (the defeat of radicalism, the failure of utopian politics), it also alerts us to the ways in which the counterculture has been incorporated within enterprise culture.

Thus Sinclair recalls that, as a young film-maker interviewing two fringe members of the Angry Brigade, 'what struck [him] the most was the Habitat domesticity, polished mugs on hooks, cut flowers in jars', while their paranoia about being under surveillance and constantly checking the road for suspicious vehicles resulted in a 'twitchy net-curtain syndrome that would not have been out of place in Carshalton or Purley' (LOT: 30). In pointing to the middle-class trappings of the Angry Brigade, Sinclair alerts us to the more general complicity of the political radicalism of the 1970s with the economic radicalism of the 1990s – a point reinforced by his suggestion that if the fusion of radical politics and radical poetics is marked textually, the same is also true commercially:

This material [evidence from the Angry Brigade trial] is of enormous
interest to wealthy nostalgics (those who *were* there and can't remember,
and those who like to play dangerously in retrospect). Counter-culture
ephemera, throwaways, psychedelic posters, the 'School Kids' issue of
Oz, the Burroughs toy in *IT*, *Sigma* papers, Situationist durables: all have
their price-tag, their accountants and their archivists. Mimeo'd single issue
chapbooks of free verse, or anarchist bulletins, they are fused in second
generation meltdown. (LOT: 28)

As such, the reforgotten denotes not simply that which is repressed and
denied by blue plaque history – already ironized in the mock plaque
commemorating artist Jane Gifford (LOT: 37) – it also points to that which
the supposedly lost history of radicalism wishes to forget about itself: its
complicity with the order it wishes to displace, the precorporation of
counterculture within enterprise culture.

The Habitat domesticity of the fringe members of the Angry Brigade
invites us to speculate on what the counterculture shares with enterprise
culture, to read the neoliberalism of the1990s not as the defeat of radicalism
but as already latent within its radical aesthetic. Sinclair's indication of the
Angry Brigade's Habitat domesticity serves as a reminder of the more general
point that the Left 'has never recovered from being wrong-footed by Capital's
mobilization and metabolization of the desire for emancipation from Fordist
routine' (Fisher 2009: 34). It reminds us of the ease with which Thatcherism
co-opted the anti-establishment rhetoric and beliefs of the counterculture in
order to present itself as a radical force within politics.

However, if Sinclair's portrayal of the Angry Brigade points towards the
operation of the reforgotten in radicalism's forgetting of its own complicity
in the order it wishes to overthrow, Sinclair's text also reveals the operation
of other forms of reforgetting at work in neoliberal London which concern
capital's own reforgetting of, and reliance upon, the notion of the common
occluded in the contest between private and public space.

For Hardt and Negri, as we have seen, the transition from Fordism to post-
Fordism takes the form of a shift from 'material to immaterial production'
in that the value of those material goods that are produced is 'increasingly
dependent on immaterial factors and goods' (2009: 132), that is, on factors

external to the process of production. This process is particularly evident in the city where property values are determined not by the intrinsic value of a property but by the neighbourhood, a fact registered in the estate agent's adage 'location, location, location' (2009: 156). For Hardt and Negri, consequently, the metropolis has a critical role in the production of the common insofar as '*the metropolis is to the multitude what the factory was to the industrial working class*' (2009: 250). Immaterial value, in other words, is increasingly located in forms of production and ownership outside the capitalist system of private property, in the realm of the common: 'the "externalities" are no longer external to the site of production that valorizes them. Workers produce throughout the metropolis, in its every crack and crevice. In fact production of the common is becoming nothing but the life of the city itself' (2009: 251).

As we have seen in the Introduction, according to Hardt and Negri, an important part of the way in which the metropolis produces the common is by facilitating aleatory or chance encounters. In their vision of the Modernist city as a place that emphasizes the relationship 'between the common and the encounter' (2009: 252), they distinguish between the metropolis as the site of a common comprised through the contact of singularities or difference, and the village as the site of community, understood as a group articulated around the repetition of the same. An important part of the common, in other words, is located precisely in the noise endemic to the metropolis, and just as language can maintain its communicative function only through the operation of noise, so noise, the return of the unselected, the possibility of going astray, is necessary to constantly recreate the common (without the tag, no logo; without the tabloid, no experimental verse). Noise as the language I do not speak becomes the condition of the common which is itself predicated on the possibility of encounter. Cities become pathological, consequently, insofar as they prevent the production of a commons by reducing the opportunities for aleatory encounter. 'All contemporary metropolises are pathological in the sense that their hierarchies and division corrupt the common and block beneficial encounters through institutionalized racisms, segregations of rich and poor, and various other structures of exclusion and subordination' (Hardt and Negri 2009: 257).

The walk as spatial collage

Sinclair's insistence on the city as encounter, in other words, is readable in terms of a production of the commons, a reassertion of the space that is occluded by the division of the world into the public and the private. The nature of that occlusion becomes apparent if we map the itinerary of his walk schematically in terms of the type of space it figures as formed by encounter. The walk is conceived within the domestic space of Sinclair's home on Albion Drive in Hackney. This is presented, however, less as a domestic space than as an interface with the public world. It is a place of address in that it is the place where messages addressed to the writer as writer (eventually) reach him. These messages include the invitation 'six months out of date, to attend the inauguration, in Seminar Room 178, Technology Faculty, University of Greenwich, of *seminarium*, "a permanent site-specific installation" by Richard Makin' (LOT: 5) and the call inviting him to the site of the anti-road protest at Claremont Road from 'an audibly distressed woman, a writer, enraged by a sense of her own powerlessness in the face of near-demonic forces' (LOT: 7). The domestic as public interface is further suggested through his depiction of home in terms of 'the chaos of my desk, the bills, unanswered letters, unsolicited typescripts, fliers for last season's poetry readings' (LOT: 5). It is a desk which is, in other words, less a scene of writing than of noise, and home is home it seems by virtue of being the address of a particular kind of (mis)communication.

This domestic space seems to have its antithesis in the walk's 'arbitrary revision' (LOT: 7), the visit to Makin's *seminarium*. This piece of institutional art is nominally public but in fact reveals the labyrinthine character of public space. The 'bureaucratic comedy' in which the department secretary denies all knowledge of Makin's work and the existence of room 178 only to discover that it adjoins her own office mirrors the chaos of Sinclair's own desk while Sinclair's extensive quotation of the text accompanying the invitation serves as a silent commentary on its own reflections on the relationship of word and place:

> Makin was given complete freedom regarding the site and the nature of the piece .... The piece is textual and is condensed from the site's appellation, the artist working with the constraints of synonyms, associations and the etymology of the compounded words seminar room. These served to

focus heterogeneous responses to the subject environment and its broader surroundings and were instrumental in producing a poetic constellation evoking various motifs correlational to the function of that environment. The yield is an equivocal conjunction intended to instigate a pondering and contemplation of simultaneously the presented semantic arrangement and the functions of the host space, the receiver situated within this weave of locus and stream of words that have emerged from the nominative of a particular physical domain: a transparent and resonant superimposition of word and place. (LOT: 5–6)

The monstrous language of explication, we recognize, is the price of admitting Makin's text into its chosen location, the academic context of the seminar room and becomes in turn metonymic for the interface between art and public space and specifically the wider academic context of 'difficult' verse and serious art. The suspicion that the third person of the opening sentence is just a flimsy guise, for Makin's own voice adds uncertainty about the text's ironic intent to the general discomfort of the reader/viewer encountering his 'sponsored graffiti of the most elevated kind' (LOT: 6):

germinal   storm

(driving towards the harbour)

empty   chamber (LOT: 46)

The juxtaposition of text and exposition suggests that public language operates according to a basic economy in which excessive reticence has to be countered by excessive prolixity in order to restore some form of semantic equilibrium. It suggests that public space is articulated around a sign that delivers a public meaning. As a space of encounter, it seems particularly unsatisfactory: 'My take on the affair was over with the nod of acknowledgement. If the poet hadn't been around, we've [*sic*] have been back in the corridor in seconds. Fine, got it, nice plot; check out the photo at home' (LOT: 46).

Confronted with Makin's 'uplifting tags', Sinclair registers the demands of this semantic economy as forms of anxiety: first of interpretation, 'I muttered something about Ian Hamilton Finlay. Which was clearly a mistake' (LOT: 46) and then of self-justification: '[w]e are the ones forced to come up with an explanation, to defend our presence, as we stalk the table, dripping puddles across the floor. Spoke aloud, put into words, our journey sounds insane. It *is* insane' (LOT: 46).

The walk's second destination, Claremont Road and 'the barricaded remnant of the M11 motorway extension protest' (LOT: 46) presents an alternative account of the relationship between art and public space. At this site, Sinclair's conceit of the cut is literalized by planners forcing a motorway extension through a residential area and the violence latent in the contested boundary between public and private is actualized in compulsory purchase orders. Claremont Road represents a fault line in the articulation of public and private where the private has become public in the most literal of senses: 'Clusters of communards sit in the middle of the road on battered sofas. Furniture that was once private, kept for best in front parlours, is left to the mercy of the weather. Outside is inside. There are no secrets' (LOT: 53). In response to this focus on the boundary of the private and the public as a zone of contest, the forms of protest have also evolved to become a negotiation between the expression of a particular grievance and a dramatization of the metropolis as the scene of conflict between the different spatial orders of the private and the public: 'The encampment has evolved to the point where it looks staged, a forum for bored journalists, But it's real enough for the people who live here in a state of semi-public siege' (LOT: 54).

The significance of the protest, Sinclair suggests, lies in the fact that it cannot succeed: the construction of the motorway cannot be resisted, the residents cannot prevail over the city's imperative to modernize and improve its efficiency as a system. As such, the caller's 'sense of her own powerlessness in the face of near-demonic forces' (LOT: 7) is emblematic of the more general sense of powerlessness in the face of capitalist realism: 'The situation would be insupportable if it wasn't finite.' Sinclair, however, recognizes that this powerlessness fundamentally alters the function of protest in that it is undertaken not to prevent something but to bring about a redistribution of the forces that existed before the protest, to effect, in other words, what Rancière terms the 'redistribution of the sensible'. This redistribution of the sensible includes the realignment of social groups such as residents and activists (and those who find their homes in protests), but it also involves a new perception of the environment which is generated by the familiar psychogeographical trope of love at last glance: 'Alliances have been struck between ancestral enemies. They are no longer opposing motorways, they're celebrating a forgotten parade of houses that would otherwise not be worth a glimpse out of the car window' (LOT: 53).

Claremont Road, in other words, is an art of the faultline between public and private realms but itself points to the realm of the common.[6] The activists' understanding that this protest is finite but that the eviction of the residents from the houses provides a temporary home for a larger protest movement who can in this interstice, between eviction and demolition, find a means of producing a new common which temporarily dissolves the entrenched lines between communities. A new collection of techniques and vocabularies and expertise in the medium of protest that will enter the national vocabulary is a means of producing a new space in the interstices of the public and the private.

This exercise in the redistribution of the sensible chimes with Sinclair's depiction of the walk's discovery of its own 'comfortable' space in Silvertown and 'the unselfconscious ordinariness' of Prince Regent's Lane:

> These streets...are operational, with no hidden agenda. They are content with disaffection. Resigned to something less than mediocrity. The shops don't make much profit, but they survive...Mechanics prepared to take things to pieces...You can walk here without appearing freakish. The streets don't give a damn. (LOT: 49)

In this celebration of the spaces in which it is still possible to walk without feeling 'freakish', Sinclair's practice of psychogeography identifies walking as a form of practicing the common, of tracing a space which is neither public (where presence requires justification) nor private in that it is articulated against the public. In this his psychogeography provides a rationale for the recovery of the space that would otherwise be occluded in the intensified conflicts between public and private attendant on neoliberalism. His text provides a site for the joyful encounters that prevent the city becoming pathological, that act as a form of exorcism, by reacquainting the reader with a spatial order that would otherwise be occluded in the imperative to forget.

---

[6]   In fact in that the threatened destruction of the chestnut tree on George Green, Wanstead became a focal point and a symbol for the protestors: 'A chestnut tree (later capitalized and given a definite article) suddenly became the focus for protestors and increasing numbers of locals... The protection of the Chestnut Tree came quickly to symbolize what was under threat from the road' (McKay 1996: 149).

2

Parasitic Poetics: *Lud Heat* and the noise of genre

Bristling with scare quotes, Allen Fisher's review of *Lud Heat*, Sinclair's long poetic mythography of East London, published as a letter to Sinclair in *Place* (2005), Fisher's even longer poetic mythography of South London, provides an exemplary instance of a noisy reading:

> Your symbolic attachment to place is not merely that place given meaning by inherent attraction, by 'magic', or by unaccountable attachment to soil. Nor is it solely the pyramidic structure of any of your 'key' buildings ... Your concern is energetic and about energy where the place becomes symbol of ourselves ... (2005: 153)

Punctuation here signals a fear of contamination. Fisher deploys his quotation marks to quarantine terms and ideas from which he wants to defend his own text: the notion of 'magic' the idea that 'key' buildings can actually 'generate' energy. Sinclair's terminology is allowed into his text on sufferance: he acknowledges the existence of this other language but hurries on as quickly as possible to the comfort and safety, the presumed common ground, of abstraction: 'your concern is energetic and about energy'. The quotation marks register, in other words, a break of communication and of community between the two poets: they mean something like 'I think I know what you are saying but I hope what you really mean is ...'. In this insistence on translation, Fisher identifies a resistance experienced by many readers of Sinclair's poem – namely a sense that within this late-Modernist exploration of metropolitan life, there lurks a pre-modern commitment to magic and the occult; that *Lud Heat*'s fascination with systems of arcane knowledge is intended not as conceit or commentary but as an expression of the poet's genuine conviction.

As the noisy signifiers of a break in community, these quotation marks have a double reading. Whereas other readers may be able to sit back and enjoy Sinclair's occult speculations, Fisher cannot do this because in other respects Sinclair's language is Fisher's own. Both *Lud Heat* and *Place* are the products of what has come to be known, thanks largely to the efforts of Eric Mottram, Ken Edwards and Barry MacSweeney, as the 'British Poetry Revival' – to the tradition of experimental poetry, that is, which represents a continuation of Modernist technique in opposition to the consensual language of the verse associated with the Movement. For Fisher consequently the language of *Lud Heat* represents a form of return of the excluded, of that which he cannot speak because it represents a worldview which is incompatible with his own poeisis. It is the nature and consequences of this rupture that I want to explore in this chapter.

Background noise: *Lud Heat* and its contexts

Punctured by the spires and towers of Hawksmoor churches, the skyline of *Lud Heat* serves as the signature of a Gothic imaginary which has since the 1980s come to seem almost ubiquitous in the representation of London. The idea, first developed in Sinclair's poem, that the churches built by Nicholas Hawksmoor (c1661–1736) between 1712 and 1730 form the focus of a system of occult energy at work in the heart of the modern metropolis was taken over directly by Peter Ackroyd in his 1985 novel *Hawksmoor*, and forms an important visual and thematic element in Alan Moore and Eddie Campbell's graphic serial *From Hell* (1991–8, 1999), from where it travels into the film of the same title directed by Albert and Allen Hughes in 2001. More generally, the poem's preoccupation with the place of the occult in contemporary London, of the secret causalities connecting its monuments and thoroughfares, has been echoed in novels as diverse as Alan Moorcock's *Mother London* (1988), China Miéville's *King Rat* (1998), Will Self's *How the Dead Live* (2000), Michele Roberts' *In the Red House* (1990), Geoff Nicholson's *Bleeding London* (1997), Nicholas Royle's *Director's Cut* (2001) and, from a different perspective, Neal Stephenson's Baroque cycle. Consequently when Roger Luckhurst asks '[w]hat is it about contemporary London that apparently defeats cognitive languages or proves resistant to Realist representation and thus encourages the occult imagination to flower?' (2003: 336), *Lud Heat* is a good place to go for answers.

As a product of the 'British Poetry Revival', *Lud Heat* slots easily into a history that seems all too susceptible to analysis in terms of the locative effect of noise. It is, in literary historical terms, a product of the battle for the meaning of Britain which raged across numerous anthologies, little magazines and poetry journals from the mid-1950s onwards.[1] The critical role of noise in that battle and the construction of corresponding notions of Britishness is heard in Al Alvarez's sniffy dismissal of experimental poetry in his introduction to *The New Poetry* where he writes that 'the experimental techniques of Eliot and the rest never really took on in England because they were an essentially American concern' (1973: 21). In response, Michael Horovitz's *Children of Albion: Poetry of the 'Underground' in Britain* (1969) gathered some sixty poets who, while rejecting the 'baleful Shadow' (1969: 316) of Eliot's influence, gleefully embraced the lessons of 'the rest' – Pound, Williams and Olson – to demonstrate not only that experimental techniques were flourishing in British poetry, but that they could be used as tools to dismantle the restricted notions of Britishness that the Movement sought to naturalize.

Despite its ebullience, however, Horovitz's counter-blast did little to contest the Movement's ownership of what constituted poetry or what constituted Britishness and Alvarez's gesture of denial was repeated with contemptuous ease by Blake Morrison and Andrew Motion's assertion in the introduction to *The Penguin Book of Contemporary British Poetry* (1982) that their anthology marks 'a shift of sensibility' which 'follows a stretch, occupying much of the 1960s and 70s, when very little – in England at any rate – seemed to be happening...' (1982: 11).

Given the transparently exclusionary logic through which the 'Movement Orthodoxy' sought to normalize its own aesthetic by dismissing any 'vaster range of poetry, with a wider range of poetic practices' (Sheppard 2005: 2) as un-British, un-interesting, or simply invisible, it is tempting to produce a counter-history that is defined by that exclusion. Thus, as Peter Barry writes, '[u]ntil the 1980s contemporary British poetry was usually mapped as a stark oppositional polarity, with a conservative (that is, anti-Modernist) *mainstream*,

---

[1] For a detailed account see Peter Barry's *Poetry Wars* and Robert Sheppard's review, 'Poets Behaving Badly' (2006) at http://jacketmagazine.com/31/sheppard-barry.html [accessed 20 October 2014].

which is implacably opposed to the excluded, embattled and experimental *margins*' (2000: 11).

The construction of this oppositional polarity, however, even as it produces the excluded as the noise which sustains the identity and coherence of the Movement, produces the Movement as the noise that endows the excluded with an (illusory) identity in difference. Thus, where 'that alimentary spasm, the Movement' (CC: xv) is constituted in the first instance through its exclusion (or evacuation) of Modernist techniques, then Robert Sheppard's 'vaster range of poetic expression' only becomes available as an object of discourse, or for marketing anthologies, through its rejection of the orthodoxy – the 'past metrics, self-satisfied irony, the self-regarding ego and its iambic thuds' (Mottram, in Alnutt 1988: 131) – represented by the Movement.

To place *Lud Heat* within an oppositional narrative that ranges the Movement against the poets of the British Poetry Revival, effectively replicates the polarization of space which, I will argue, is interrogated by the poem itself. Thus while historically *Lud Heat* may belong to the moment of the British Poetry Revival, and indeed may be one of its key texts, we should also recognize its critical stance towards that (op)position – its sensitivity to the ambiguities involved in the construction of any identity. As Sinclair suggests in the introduction to his anthology of 'elective outsiders' (CC: xvi), *Conductors of Chaos* (1996) the history of contemporary British poetry can be all too easily recuperated as the plot of a bad feel-good movie: the story of the 'pick-'n'-mix shambles of has-beens, headcases and emerging chancers who will put one over on the All Blacks' (CC: xiii). This ambiguity must be born in mind as we consider the construction of place in *Lud Heat* which in this reading will be considered both as a British Poetry Revival text, but one where the dynamic of noise and signal is not limited to the articulation of its difference from the centre ground of the Movement.

The politics of noise are less convoluted at the level of technique. As Alvarez makes clear, mainstream post-war British poetry defines itself through the rejection of any poetic technique which focuses attention on the noise of its medium. The result is a post-war poetic orthodoxy which 'privileges a poetry of closure, narrative coherence and grammatical and syntactic cohesion, which colludes with the process of naturalization' (Sheppard 2005: 2), or as Andrew Crozier puts it:

the poets who altered taste in the 1950s did so by means of a common rhetoric that foreclosed the possibilities of poetic language within its own devices: varieties of tone, rhythm, of form, of image, were narrowly limited, as were the conceptions of the scope and character of poetic discourse, its relation to the self, to knowledge, to history, and to the world. Poetry was seen as an art in relation to its own conventions – and a pusillanimous set of conventions at that. It was not to be ambitious, or to seek to articulate ambition through the complex deployment of its technical means: imagery was either suspect or merely clinched an argument; the verse line should not, by the pressure its energy or shape might exert on syntax, intervene in meaning; language was always to be grounded in the presence of a legitimating voice – and that voice took on an impersonally collective tone. To its owners' satisfaction the signs of art had been subsumed within a closed cultural programme. (1990: 12)

The techniques excluded from this common rhetoric are united variously in their tendency to disturb the communicative function of poetry; they are techniques which privilege, in one way or another, principles of resistance. Sheppard supplies a useful inventory when he writes that non-Movement poetry is characterized by 'techniques of indeterminacy and discontinuity, of collage and creative linkage, of poetic artifice and defamiliarization' (2005: 1).

Sheppard also illustrates the direct correlation between technique and the production of space when he notes that almost half of the poems in *New Lines*, the first Movement anthology, used the first person plural (2005: 22): invoking therewith an implied community of poet and reader, a world of shared assumptions which is at once specifically that of English middle-class men but is extended through the 'moral embrace' of the third person plural to include humanity in general. A poetry so dependent on the production of assent cannot risk the deployment of techniques which problematize or disturb that assumption of communication grounded in a shared, or common, sense.

But again, a simple oppositional account of the techniques deployed in non-Movement poetry can obscure productive tensions between different elements within the repertoire of indeterminacy gathered under the name of Modernism. If the third person plural underpins the moral rhetoric of community in Movement poetics, Modernist poetics may also be susceptible to similar rhetorical strategies. Before examining how Sinclair deploys specific techniques of resistance in order to figure the relationship between textual and topographical space in *Lud Heat*, however, it is useful to consider the more general relationship between noise and place in Modernist poetics.

The 'charting instinct': Long poems, big cities

Emphasizing literature's social function as a form of cognitive mapping, Steven Johnson suggests that, for their original readers, the urban novels of Dickens, Balzac and Zola formed an important 'interface' with the new and disorientating complexity of the nineteenth-century city: 'The Victorians had writers like Dickens to ease them through the technological revolutions of the industrial age, writers who built novelistic maps of the threatening new territory and the social relations it produced' (1997: 19). Extending Johnson's concern with the cognitive aspect of the relation between text and social context to the encounters with the urban found in the canonic texts of literary modernism, it is evident that coherence and any concomitant affect of readerly reassurance have been largely abandoned. Instead of trying to make sense of the complex reality of late nineteenth- and early twenty-first century urban environments, the Modernist text seems rather to mimic in its own structure and practices of signification the uncertainties and complexities found in the urban environment. On a first encounter texts such as *The Waste Land* (1922), *Ulysses* (1922), *Mrs Dalloway* (1925), *USA* (1938), *Paterson* (1946–58), and even Ezra Pound's 'In a station of the metro' (1913), exhibit the same bewildering semiotic complexity as the world they describe. Their organizing principles are obscure, and even when their general structure has been apprehended, there are still countless points of local detail which remain more or less impenetrable. If, as Peter Barry notes, the city as a topic in British poetry is more or less exclusively the preserve of Modernism, this is testimony to the homology of text and subject (2000: 5). Reflecting its defining concern with the (im)possibility of knowledge, Modernism figures the city as an epistemological problem, as ultimately unknowable, or, as an arena in which knowledge has to be actively produced by the reader.

Formally at least, *Lud Heat* is a typical example of the Modernist paradigm. At 141 pages and composed from meditative free-verse lyrics, journal entries, essay sections, maps, diagrams and a scattering of Egyptian hieroglyphs, *Lud Heat* falls naturally into a tradition which stretches back to *The Waste Land* and *Paterson*, while its more direct predecessors include Roy Fisher's *City* (1962) and Allen Fisher's *Place* sequence begun in 1970, with Lee Harwood's rather shorter *Cable Street* (1968) forming an even closer geographical neighbour. As Sheppard notes, the 'poetic inheritance of the work is largely American': it takes from William Carlos Williams and from Pound not only the perception that poetry has the permission to include blocks of prose, but the recognition that this 'ragbag approach is arguably well suited to capturing the cluttered physical collage of urban space' (Sheppard 2005a). As we will see, that suitability is due in part to the text's manipulation of the degrees of noise inherent in different linguistic modes: the juxtaposition of prose with its emphasis on communication, and free verse, with its hermeneutic of indeterminacy, replicate within the text the idea of an environment which is variably accessible and resistant. The poem, in other words, uses communicative noise to replicate an urban environment experienced in terms of channelled movement and areas which are more, or less, readable. Similarly the mixture of pronominal stance typical of lyric and essay reflects the multiplicity of the urban environment, in contrast to the third person plural that typically defines and stabilizes the space of Movement verse.

However, it is in its relationship with Charles Olson and the Black Mountain credo of open field poetics that the poem most clearly displays the ambiguity of its affiliation to its Modernist and American inheritance. As formulated in Olson's 'Projective Verse' manifesto of 1950, open verse involves the rejection of ' "closed" verse, that verse which print bred and which is pretty much what we have had in English & American, and have still got despite the work of Pound & Williams' (1994: 613) in favour of poetry based on 'the kinetics of the thing' (1994: 614), the belief that '[a] poem is energy transferred from where the poet got it (he will have some several causations), by way of the poem itself to, all the way over to, the reader' (1994: 614).

In the manifesto, Olson maps the form of this verse through a series of binary oppositions: open verse is a poetry of the breath rather than the word, of sound rather than intellect, of direct perception and affect rather than intellection; its unit is the syllable, it is the poetry of man in an environment; poetry as practice rather than commodity; poetry fully integrated into life as a distinctive form of perception or a deroutinization of response rather than a verse produced for a social purpose or as a commodity. As Sheppard notes, Olson had a profound effect on British poetry's thinking of place outside the national consensual rhetoric practiced by movement poets: his 'local universalism' offering poets a way 'to define themselves against geographical structures...as a way both larger and intimate [*sic*] than concerns with nationality' (2005: 59). It is this ethos that informs Allen Fisher's monumental *Place* project with its identification of an 'I, not Maximus, but a citizen of Lambeth' (11) and the characterization of his work as

> an essay
>
> in fragments   that brought together
>
> bring about their own symmetry
>
> their own chaos. (2005: 9)

Olson is certainly a presence in *Lud Heat*; he provides an epigraph – 'life, /with a capital F' suggesting a poetry immersed in life – and is name-checked in the essay on Stan Brakhage (LH: 57, 119). Ed Dorn's, Olson-inspired, injunction in *North Atlantic Turbine* for British poets to escape inherited constructions of space by 'naming themselves and the rocks' (Dorn 1967: 41) provides an obvious background to the section on John Ford that contains the lines:

> the city is not like *The Searchers*
>
> strangers
>
> rush the frame & clutter the composition (LH: 90–1)

However, read as narrative, *Lud Heat* is less an application of Olson's projective credo than an account, in part at least, of its protagonist's failure to write such poetry. The journal entries and lyric sections describe the frustration of the poet's desire 'to construct a more generous sentence' (LH: 94), his inability to achieve that consonance with his environment which, for example, he sees and envies in the poet Chris Torrance's 'neat fast physical descriptions' and 'elasticity of vision/ deepest/ confession of ecstasy' (LH: 65). At some level, we are to understand, this failure is due to the malign influence of the Hawksmoor churches which seem to follow the poet across London as he tends the parks, cemeteries and other public places of the London Borough of Tower Hamlets in the eleven months between May 1974 and April 1975. Instead of an Olsonesque identification of poet and place, the poem thus describes the poet's growing consciousness of his antagonistic relationship with his environment expressed in his 'Theory of Hayfevers' and culminating in the sunstroke he suffers while eating his packed lunch in the churchyard of St Anne Limehouse. Instead of an identification with place, the poem charts a sense of possession by occult powers. In opening himself up to the world of mid-1970s London, the poet finds the 'Heat' commemorated in the title too much to bear. Its final lines seem to have been lifted from a Gothic novel: 'So again we service the dead, complete the stifled gesture, grasp at the arm raised in salute from the choked ground' (LH: 141).

These are lines which directly contravene Olson's demand that poetry leave the past behind in order to concentrate on the matter of living.[2] It is no coincidence that the final section of the poem should be a prose postscript dated 24 July 1975 – that is, outside of the period identified in the title, for the prose sections effectively provide the lyric and journal entries with a narrative plot centred on the Hawksmoor churches. For this reason, *Lud Heat* has a far more novelistic character than Fisher's unfinishable investigation of the same areas.

Overlying and containing the Olsonesque sections the elaborate occult schema centred on the Hawksmoor churches thus seems to problematize the poetic affiliation of the lyric sections. For this reason, *Lud Heat* effectively resembles a failed *Künstlerroman* in that it is a work which describes its own failure to come into being – a failure marked in the inter-title which identifies the work as 'Book 1' – thereby signalling its incompletion with a stifled gesture to an absent second book.

Thus, while the interplay of poetry and prose may be formally familiar from earlier encounters between the long poem and the city, in *Lud Heat* their interplay complicates the dynamics of the poem's American inheritance.

---

[2] Articulated, for example, in a 1951 letter to Robert Creeley: 'And had we not, ourselves (I mean postmodern man), better just leave such things behind us – and not so much trash of discourse & gods?' (Olson 1987: 79).

Here, the juxtaposition of poetry and prose does more than mimic the variety of the 'physical collage of urban space' (Sheppard 2005a), it also amplifies the uncertainty and indeterminacy of the poem as a whole, raising a number of questions about the relationship between the separate elements in the work. Is the prose to be read as an explication of the poetry?[3] Is 'the narrator' (LH: 96) to be identified as the author of the essays, the journal entries and the free verse? Are they to be identified with Sinclair or is *Lud Heat* better read as a form of dramatic monologue, or generic mutation, with the Olsonian project being relativized by another figuration of the city? In raising these questions the mixture of poetry and prose provides the poem with its epistemological drama and its most clearly Modernist aspect – the tension between the compulsion to resolve chaos into order, on the one hand, and, on the other, its apparent unease about the status of any order produced by that compulsion.

This tension between the search for pattern within the city's manifest contingency, and anxiety about the city as a site of signifying excess is explicitly marked even in the more expository sections such as the lengthy opening essay, 'Nicholas Hawksmoor; his churches' which provides a 'brief and nervy synopsis' (LH: 21) of the Hawksmoor material and, given its position in the text, seems to present itself as the interpretive schema through which we should read the rest of the poem. In the essay we are told that the eight churches for whose location Hawksmoor, as surveyor and architect, was directly responsible together mark out a 'major pentacle star' (LH: 15), which also incorporates other cardinal points in London's topography including the British Museum and Royal Observatory at Greenwich: 'The locked cellar of words, the labyrinth of all recorded knowledge, the repository of stolen fires and symbols, excavated god forms – and measurement, star knowledge, time calculations' (LH: 15). The constellation mapped by the churches can then be extended to take in Bunhill Fields, effectively the dissenter's Westminster Abbey, 'plague pit, burial place of William Blake, Daniel Defoe, John Bunyan' (LH: 15) and on to incorporate a variety of other 'subsystems'.

The intricacy of the web of buried spatial energy thus plotted, however, is less interesting than the pronominal dance of the paranoid subject

---

[3] According to Sinclair, the prose sections were completed after the poetry (Jackson and Sinclair 2003: 97).

registered in the essay's constant shifts between assertion and discovery, conjecture and revelation. In this, the subject exploits the ambiguity of the essay as a form which is at once authoritative and speculative, folding its mobility of viewpoint back into the public space in whose construction it was, historically, such an important agent, in order to ground in fact an assertion which can only be comfortably entertained as a conceit. Sinclair constantly exploits the impersonality of the form in order to try its own credence against its assertions – 'what we are talking about is not accident' (LH: 14) and again, 'We must examine the detail' (LH: 15) – in preparation for huge leaps of imaginative transformation: 'The power remains latent, the frustration mounts on a current of animal magnetism, and victims are still claimed' (LH: 15). These (un)easy shifts between speculation, suggestion and assertion express the dynamic of a consciousness caught up in the movement of its own conjectures, watching with a mixture of excitement and disbelief as the world arranges itself around its suppositions. The general indeterminacy of this process is registered in the auxiliary verb 'can' in the following sentences: 'We can mark out the total plan of churches on the map and sift the meanings. We can produce the symbol of Set, instrument of castration or tool for making cuneiform signs' (LH: 16) and again in the uncertain nature of the word 'possible' here and the weight of conjecture carried by the verb 'did': 'From what is known of Hawksmoor it is possible to imagine that he did work a code in the buildings, knowingly or unknowingly, templates of meaning, bands of continuing ritual' (LH: 17).

Where the moral embrace of the first person plural shapes the space of Movement verse, Sinclair's terrain is given form in the opening essay by the idea that the ley line acts as a link between the spatial and narrative sense of plot by providing a key to the coding and decoding of the topography of London as a signifying system. Once a ley line, or 'line of escape' (LH: 17), is set in motion by its passage through two significant points, it will transform everything it subsequently touches into new data, discovering hidden causalities and occluded relationships in the city's contingencies: 'The web is printed on the city and disguised with multiple superimpositions' (LH: 16–17). The lines so constructed are spatial but also temporal, for in Sinclair's scheme '[e]ach church is an enclosure of force, a trap, a sight block, a raised place, with an unacknowledged influence over events created within the shadow-lines of their towers' (LH: 20). The unacknowledged influence selects any violent crime in their shadow-line as confirmation of that influence, and the events so selected stretch from the Ratcliffe Highway 'slaughter' of 1811 to 'the battering to death of Mr Abraham Cohen, summer 1974, on Cannon Street Road' and, of course, include that staple of London noir, the 'Jack the Ripper' murders of 1888: the 'whole karmic programme of Whitechapel' which 'moves around the fixed point of Christ Church' (LH: 21–2).

The spatial and temporal in turn become textual as the essay pursues the traces of this 'unacknowledged influence' into Blake's visions in *Jerusalem* and the prose style of Thomas De Quincey's account of the Ratcliffe Highway murder in *On Murder Considered as One of the Fine Arts*: 'digressing obsessively towards overlapping versions of the truth, [he] couldn't help getting in among the authentic substrata. Unconsciously he offers hieroglyphs, disguised and smudged Egyptian ritual detail' (LH: 23). Ultimately, once it is set in motion, everything can be interpreted in light of this pattern. Confirmation of his 'hunch' that sites of the churches are related via earlier burial sites to 'the four Egyptian protector-goddesses, guardians of the canopic jars' (LH: 28) takes the form of the bout of sunstroke contracted at Limehouse church – guarded in his scheme by Selkis, the scorpion goddess 'associated with the scorching heat of the sun' (LH: 28).

However, the natural limits of this paranoid style become apparent when, after a detailed description of the layout of St Anne and its relation to Egyptian ruins, the narrator, as if chastened by the weight of evidence he has uncovered, pulls up short:

> The speed of the track increases and information fattens to excess. It is the greasy slope of madness, time-bends, over-stimulated blood hooks at the high air. Blake is too bright to be looked into – even at this distance. The whole structure becomes top-heavy and falls beyond control. Mark out a possible ground-plan for further and more calmly detailed studies. Speak of the excitement that is still there. Acknowledge energy. (LH: 36–7)

The 'excess' of meaning which opens out onto 'the greasy slope of madness' reveals the pathology inherent within the charting instinct. In this instance, it marks the recognition that the patterns of significance generated in the attempt to bring order to chaos can assume an autonomy which threatens that of the ordering consciousness, plunging it back into chaos. Clearly an interpretative system which can endow a 'goat and several collections of chickens' (LH: 29) kept in the back gardens of the houses surrounding St. Anne Limehouse with a ritual significance is too powerful as an interpretative schema: in generating meaning, it returns everything to noise.

In this dramatization of the pathological dynamic at work in the transformations of signal and noise, *Lud Heat* extends and complicates William Paulson's (1991) account of the role of difficulty in literature discussed above. The difficulty of *Lud Heat* lies not so much in the ambiguity and indeterminacy of the verse fragments – the noisiest element of traditional Modernist poetics – but in the prose, which, here, itself seems to constitute an adaptive reading strategy, a determination to impose order regardless of the psychic cost. Extended over 141 pages, the effect of this textual dynamic is queasy and vertiginous: the journal excerpts and fragmentary lyrics deny the reader the critical distance required to contextualize the narrative which appears to describe a progressive mental breakdown, while the prose sections, instead of providing context or perspective, reinforce that sense of breakdown through their relentless overdetermination. *Lud Heat*, in other words, exploits the dynamic relations between signal and noise to convey the claustrophobic sense of city life as an interpretive crisis, of city life as immersion in a semiotic economy where adjustment requires the right degree of selection and filtering: an environment whose illegibility is a function of both illiteracy and over-literacy.

The anxiety about the status of the order the poem conjures into being is amplified by uncertainties of register and genre. Tonally, *Lud Heat* veers from the authentically lyrical through mock oracular to just plain portentous: 'It was his pleasure and his duty to speak to the visitors who recrossed the seas in ancestor pilgrimage' (LH: 100–1). Its generic instability is signalled in the subtitle – *A book of dead Hamlets* – which, in addition to its topographic reference to the borough where it is set, gestures simultaneously to the Egyptian Book of the Dead and to the pin-up boy of Western melancholic introspection, (and possibly, given its concern with the cultural detritus of mid-70s London, a well-known brand of cheap cigar).

It is tempting to see Sinclair's ostentatious deployment of the ideas of occult patterning at the outset of his poem as an extension and terminus to the

Modernist experimentation with what T.S. Eliot termed 'the mythic method' (1984: 177) – the use of inherited structures and narrative paradigms as devices to give a form to the contingency of modernity. Where *Ulysses* deploys the narrative framework of the *Odyssey* to structure the random wanderings of a schoolteacher and an advertising canvasser in Dublin, Sinclair ransacks the Abacus catalogue for an esoteric equivalent to Joyce's Homeric scaffolding. However, any reading which attempts to naturalize *Lud Heat* as a late Modernist epistemological fable is problematized by its generic heterogeneity and Sinclair's own frequently affirmed commitment to the reality of his unreal city – his conviction that the bands of continuing ritual at work in contemporary London traced in his poem are more than a simple conceit.[4] As Karl Miller notes in his review quoted on the cover of the Granta edition, 'Sinclair means his dark stuff.' *Lud Heat*, in other words confronts the reader with a spatial problem and any reading must address its refusal to quarantine its sacralizing impulse within the secular enclosure of art, to reduce the occult to aesthetic strategy. The fact that Sinclair 'means his dark stuff' confronts us with the darkness of meaning within a postmodern poetics.

'These facts fade. The big traffic slams by': Art in absolute and abstract space

As an encounter between the long poem and the big city, then, *Lud Heat* is recognizably Modernist in its exploration of the tension between imposed order and revealed meaning, and typically Modernist too in its deployment of resistance to imitate the semiotic confusion of the urban environment within the text. Unusually, however, it is the promotion of occult patterning within the prose sections rather than the indeterminacy of the poetry that generates the greatest resistance insofar as it troubles the familiar partitioning

---

[4] See, for example, his 2002 interview with Mark Pilkington and Phil Baker: 'Ley lines and all of that was much more part of the project for me all the time. My book Ludd Heat was totally ley line orientated. Although I was reading John Michell, it was more to do with EO (Elizabeth) Gordon's Prehistoric London. I found that book around that time and saw that, although it was written by a nutty Christian, it gave you a series of metaphors you could use about the linking of sites in the London landscape. Once you saw it in that way, you could see how all the Hawksmoor churches linked up to give you all those paths and energies. From that everything else derived' (Pilkington and Baker 2002).

of discursive space which ordains that the occult should remain within its genre, should remain, as a conceit, framed by the secular discourse of art. The noise of *Lud Heat*, in other words, alerts us to the awkward coexistence of two kinds of space within the semiotic economies of city and text. In further demarcating these spaces and their modes of historical and discursive interrelation, it is useful to draw upon the distinction between absolute and abstract space described by Henri Lefebvre in *The Production of Space* first published in French in 1974.

In Lefebvre's terms, Sinclair's primary concern in *Lud Heat* is with mapping absolute space, that is with a space which, originally derived from features of the natural landscape, comes to be invested with symbolic meaning. Most obviously spaces such as these include churches, cemeteries and other sacred sites, but places such as crossroads, gallows or market places can also function as types of absolute space. Absolute space is distinguished by the fact that once invested with a symbolic meaning and thus separated from the spatial continuum (1991: 48), it serves to organize or structure that continuum (1991: 234). This occurs within cities, which Lefebvre suggests, tend to be generated from fragments of absolute space. However, the notion of absolute space is also crucial to the role of the city within the wider spatial economy in that, as concentrations of power and information, cities organize their surroundings both physically and symbolically:

> The city state thus establishes a fixed centre by coming to constitute a hub, a privileged focal point, surrounded by peripheral areas which bear its stamp. From this moment on, the vastness of pre-existing space appears to come under the thrall of a divine order. At the same time the town seems to gather in everything which surrounds it, including the natural and the divine, and the earth's evil and good forces. (1991: 235)

Grounded in absolute space, Lefebvre's city is both real and symbolic: it presents itself as an image of the universe, or *imago mundi* (1991: 235), which organizes a spatial economy in which everybody knows their place. It is this vision of the city that Sinclair registers in the skyline punctured by Hawksmoor churches – a city of parishes where the secular and sacred topographies appear to coincide and it is this city he attempts to map through the use of ley lines, which, as we have noted, serve as a plotting device that links topographical and textual space.

According to Lefebvre, absolute space is displaced by the emergence of an abstract or secular space in the cities of twelfth-century Europe as a result of the commercial revolution instigated by the development of primitive capitalism. Whereas in the feudal period, the 'basis of wealth was still real property, ownership of the land', the advent of primitive capitalism in Medieval Europe 'brought commerce inside the town and lodged it at the centre of a transformed urban space' (1991: 265). For Lefebvre, the emergence of this new kind of space is consequent on the relationship between accumulation and Logos:

> The space that emerged in Western Europe in the twelfth century, gradually extending its sway over France, England, Holland and Italy, was the space of accumulation – its birthplace and cradle. Why and how? Because this secularized space was the outcome of the revival of the Logos, and the Cosmos, principles which were able to subordinate the 'world' with its underground forces. Along with the Logos and logic, the Law too was re-established, and contractual (stipulated) relationships replaced customs, and customary exactions. (1991: 263)

Insofar as this abstract space, predicated on the abstraction and fungibility of value, was dependent on contractual relations, it was thus intimately bound with the authority of the written – and hence transportable – sign. As such, at a fundamental level, abstract and absolute spaces represent the opposition of the written and the spoken; the authority of speech and the power of the word.

In Lefebvre's psychoanalytically informed account, abstract space, the space of the Logos, of contract and calculation, does not replace absolute space but drives it into a feminized underground which is defined in opposition to abstract space as the space of speech: 'Religious space did not disappear with the advent of commercial space; it was still – and indeed would long remain – the space of speech and knowledge' (1991: 266). For Lefebvre, as for Sinclair, consequently, the modern European city contains two radically different kinds of space whose relationship is figured in almost identical terms. Thus, when Sinclair writes: 'These facts fade. The big traffics slam by. A work ethic buries ancient descriptions' (LH: 26), it reads like a stenographic version of Lefebvre's assertion that:

> Even today urban space appears in two lights: on the one hand it is replete with places which are holy or damned, devoted to the male principle or

the female, rich in fantasies or phantasmagorias; on the other hand it is rational, state-dominated and bureaucratic, its monumentality degraded and obscured by traffic of every kind, including the traffic of information. It must therefore be grasped in two different ways: as absolute (apparent) within the relative (real). (1991: 231)

For both writers, the burial is physical (new buildings replace old), cultural (contractual relations replace customary relations) and, particularly for Lefebvre, psychological: absolute space comes to occupy the position of the repressed, a position which he describes as heterotopical. Thus:

> With the dimming of the 'world' of shadows, the terror it exercised lessened accordingly. It did not however disappear. Rather it was transformed into 'heterotopical' places, places of sorcery and madness, places inhabited by demonic forces – places which were fascinating but tabooed. (1991: 263)

Adopting Lefebvre's terminology, the prose sections in *Lud Heat* can be characterized as explorations of the heterotopical spaces of topography and culture. In 'Rites of Autopsy', an account of Stan Brakhage's film *The Act of Seeing With One's Own Eyes* shot on location in the Allegheny Coroner's Office, the cadaver with the 'awful revelation of meat' acts as heterotopia. The conflation of body and city as forms of absolute space underwritten by the idea of the city as *imago mundi* is explicit: in this 'confrontation of the body's most deeply held fears. We move down into the very heart of the city labyrinth, breaking the first seal' (LH: 54). The most extended and explicit encounter with the dimensions of absolute space occurs in the essay 'From Camberwell to Golgotha' – an account of his visits to sculptor Brian Catling's exhibition at the Camberwell Art School in June 1974. Opposing the sculptor's understanding of absolute space to that of the 'art fanciers who stroll through' (LH: 78), the essay describes how Catling works with a vision of 'architectonic wholeness ... total invention ... not small, isolated artefacts, but a sense that the sculptor has managed to realise one detail from a whole that goes to the horizon and beyond' (LH: 81). Like absolute space itself, Catling's artefacts organize space as a totality, a space which extends from the enclosure of Camberwell Art School to Dorchester, from the city into the country and into the earth. The section is itself structured as a form of double chamber with the account of a visit to Catling's exhibition in Camberwell – predicting 'the emotion I will feel in Dorchester, the following February' (LH: 79) where, revising his notes, he receives 'from the sculptor in the city' (LH: 82) an account of his expedition to St Anne, Limehouse, dated 7 February 1975. This narrative chamber within a chamber takes us into the crypt of St Anne and also the spatial perception of the sculptor:

> This place is also like the pyramids, the isolation here is total and with candles it even looks like one of those early prints of the discovery of the king's [*sic*] gallery. Dead geometric persistence. What the masonry holds beyond decayage. Compressed, the fear of form. (LH: 86)

What Brakhage and Catling offer Sinclair are images of artists who have successfully incorporated absolute space into their media. Brakhage's art is depicted in terms of the artist's self-sacrifice: 'We are seeing something old, but corrupted. Not performed in a sacred state of grace, to high purpose – it becomes through Brakhage's sacrifice, grace-filled' (LH: 57). Eschewing the 'spurious search for "originality"' (LH: 77), the sculptor's engagement with the qualities of space itself offers the poet a vision of the pre-abstract space produced by unalienated labour: 'The eye/hand relation is brotherly. The sculptor is at ease constructing an oven or beating out a ritual weapon. The incantations he chants are the natural sounds of these hill ridges' (LH: 81).

For the protagonist of *Lud Heat*, this ability to place art in relation to absolute space remains a problem, and, read as a failed *Künstlerroman*, *Lud Heat* is partly about the desire to write such a poetry in London and the impossibility of doing so. The intimations of artistic crisis ripple through the text, and his suggestion that the narrator's non-specific sense of dread articulated through Hawksmoor's churches reflects his recognition of the historical impossibility of the projective project – of developing a verse which is true to its immediate location. The spoken space of a speech-based poetry invoked by Olson is tied to the lost heterotopic geography of London's absolute space. A geography which is overwritten by the imperatives of abstract space: 'A work ethic buries ancient descriptions.' The space of a poetry integrated into life has been usurped by Max Weber's spirit of capitalism. The space of open poetry has been taken over by the city's own communicative system, for the abstract space which defines the poet's environment is in Lefebvre's terms the space of network:

The space which established itself during the Middle Ages, by what ever means it did so, whether violent or no, was by definition a space of exchange and communications, and therefore of networks. What networks? In the first place, networks of overland routes: those of traders, and those of pilgrims and crusaders.... The communications network was simply the physical reflection – the natural mirror as it were – of the abstract and contractual network which bound together the 'exchangers' of products and money. (1991: 266)

The distinction between absolute and abstract space is thus critical to the poetics of *Lud Heat* as an attempt to find a place for poetry within the space of abstraction and informs the poem at a much more fundamental level.

'[I]n there for the duration': Poetry as workplace

This concern with the difficulty of placing poetry in a social and political context is signalled from the outset in the poem's dedication to Sinclair's fellow workers, 'Joe, Arthur, Bill and the others who are in there for the duration' (LH: 7). At once a statement of solidarity and separation, the dedication articulates the ambiguous relationship between 'the narrator' (LH: 96) and the world he describes, amplifying the profound sense of spatial unease within the poem and transferring that to the poem as an artefact. Positioned at the work's textual and ontological threshold, the dedication registers an awareness that, as artefact, the poem marks the poet's exclusion from a space of collective labour. The diegetic 'there' tropes simultaneously on the traditional idea of art's ability to confer immortality upon its subjects, and the idea that, as the objects of both textual and capitalist economies, as characters and unskilled manual labourers, 'Joe, Arthur, Bill and the others' lack the reflective consciousness to escape their objectified condition and, consequently, are condemned to endure 'the duration' of those whose time is never their own. However, the fact that the space of labour is, in this instance, both a garden and the final vestige of the public sphere further complicates the poet's exclusion from the spaces articulated through the poem.

The entanglement of those spaces is already evident in the aspirant gardener's first meeting with the foreman, 'Mr L. Wood, the red, vein-faced,

Geordie boss-man' (LH: 39) who warns of 'rough and ready language' (LH: 39) and claims a geographical solidarity with the narrator on the basis that his fellow workers are 'not friendly like us northerners' (LH: 39). This gesture of inclusion in the community of outsiders is an unwelcome reminder of the narrator's exclusion – in geographical and, more importantly, social terms – from the ground on which he wants to 'construct a more generous sentence' (LH: 94), the world in which he wants to locate his art. The 'Geordie boss-man' thus stands as the sign of a more general bad-faith that frustrates that ambition of generosity: he reminds us that, whatever the narrator's post code, *Lud Heat* belongs to the long tradition of writing which exoticizes the East End: its apocalyptic vision of rats swarming over St Anne a distant echo of Jack London's image of the peopled abyss. While the characters are 'in there for the duration', the narrator is merely down there on a visit.

The suture marked in the dedication informs the representation of space throughout the poem. Where the spires of Hawksmoor's churches articulate a lost world where spiritual and secular topographies coincide, the topography mapped out by the narrator is marked by non-identity. This is most pronounced in the poem's inversion of the spaces of work and home. Whereas the bothy, or hut, the narrator shares with his fellow gardeners is intimate and homely, even drawing Joe back from sick leave into its circle (LH: 45), the domestic world is, in contrast, shadowy and alien, a place of 'rapid sexual gratification/ in the corridor' (LH: 64). Instead of providing a shelter from the outside world, home seems to attract the forces which diminish the narrator's already precarious sense of self or 'egoic grip' (LH: 62). Thus, while he tries to write, 'in another room the electric serial/ loud & raw/ has taken something from his eye'; whereas work is described in terms of companionship, at home, company is reduced to its metonyms: 'so many call/ so many coffees wines' (LH: 42). Even parenthood as the ground of identity and provider of direction seems under threat: 'look: with/ my daughter's dungarees they give you a compass' (LH: 60).

The social/sexual disorientations evident in the inversion of the spaces of work and home are amplified by the park's uneasy place within the geography of intimacy. In the poem this is further reinforced by the dog handler from the menacingly indeterminate 'brown sex police' (LH: 43), who patrols the boundary between public space and private passion. Presenting himself as 'part of some more massive & paternal scheme' (LH: 43), the dog handler 'caresses his images'; and his lurid tales of 'Miltonic banishment' (LH: 44) are marked by their projected sexual violence: 'A swift tongue of lust flicks through his yarns' (LH: 43). The intrusion of the dog handler with his serpentine language reveals the park to be that abstract form of the absolute space of the garden:

> These urgencies. Sharpest imperatives & oldest instincts are broken into. Citizen's privileges upon their own ground are destroyed. The open lands are chained & bolted. The handler pets & fondles his wolf. (LH: 44)

The oldest instincts, the poem makes clear, include not only sex but any creative engagement with being and as such the chains and bolts include those instituted by *The Parks Department Manual* handed him by the foreman which contains such nuggets as:

> *7. Writing of Books. While occasional literary or artistic work is permissible, special consideration would have to be given for the writing of books for payment on subjects relating to an Officer's or employee's work for the Council.* (LH: 39)

The easy comedy generated by clumsy bureaucratic attempts to regulate artistic production should not disguise the seriousness of the poem's concern with the relationship between writing and labour, poetry and belonging and the different kinds of space opened up by different forms of discourse.

Finding a space for poetry involves the reconciliation of two incommensurable forms of temporality: the flash of poetic perception and the routinized response demanded by abstract labour:

- rake the sandpit of dead flies
- cut off the signalling of groundsel
- find yellow surprising (LH: 49)

The desire to write his 'more generous sentence' measures the narrator's unease in spatial terms, for his inability to accommodate reflects his inability to achieve that level of belonging and possession which is a precondition of generosity. But the spatial is also temporal insofar as the generosity of the sentence he desires to construct chimes in turn with the heresy of Origen invoked at the beginning of that section: the 'unlikely hope' (LH: 92) that the damned will burn for a fixed term, rather than eternity, and hence echoes once again the 'duration' of the dedication. The poet figures himself as providing access to the temporality of redemption, the flash of perception which will open up another temporality within the administered time of labour:

> he has a car (Ford Capri, GT)
> but asks often for the time
> & that becomes my function (LH: 50–1)

The poet can be figured as the giver of time because the flash of sudden perception which breaks through patterns of routinized response is only possible through the noise of poetic diction. But fulfilling that function, writing a poetry which can disrupt the logic of commodification and rediscover the surprise of yellow, entails finding a place for poetry within the world of abstract space. In this desire to integrate poetry into the rhythms of labour, the poet confronts the problem that 'it is what we don't notice/ that is worth remarking, & without insistence' (LH: 51) that the recorded perception is already devalued.

In this we can recognize the familiar articulation of 'the poetic' as a means of disrupting routine perception, of the poetic as noise. However, the poet's desire to achieve a more generous sentence, a sentence which can accommodate the abstract space of labour and commodification and thereby ameliorate the sentence of those who are 'in there for the duration' is subjugated or blocked by the writing of Hawksmoor: his attempt to be in the here of breath and voice is blocked by the perception that his 'here' is the city as Hawksmoor's text, a city of signs.

> The old maps present a skyline dominated by church towers; those horizons were differently punctured, so that the subservience of the grounded eye, and the division of the city by parish, was not disguised. Moving now on an eastern arc the churches of Nicholas Hawksmoor soon invade the consciousness, the charting instinct. (LH: 13)

Hawksmoor's skyline signals both the presence and inaccessibility of absolute space because it points to the city as the construction of the abstract space of the sign. If the poet cannot simply open his verse to the space in which he finds himself, it is, the poem suggests, because that space has been already textualized by the writing and rewriting of Hawksmoor: 'He had that Coleridge notebook speed, to rewrite the city: man, recognising some distillation of his most private urges in the historical present, is suddenly, and more than anybody around him *there* – had more to say than the 8 churches could use' (LH: 14). He is a writer moreover with a vision of the city as a form of order in chaos. Sinclair quotes Hawksmoor's letter to Dr George Clarke 'we have noe City, nor Streets, nor Houses, but a Chaos of Dirty Rotten Sheds, always tumbling or taking fire…' (LH: 14). But in imposing his vision of the city onto this chaos, he gives London its modern form through the use of 'risky quotations' (LH: 14) from pre-classical architecture. The quotations are risky for ecclesiastical architecture but also because they import the language of form into London. Unlike his more patrician mentor Christopher Wren, Hawksmoor never travelled to Europe to view the masterpieces of European baroque *in situ*. Instead, he ransacked the burgeoning architectural literature for examples from an eclectic range of pre-classical architecture, reflecting Europe's developing Orientalism. Hawksmoor's 'risky quotations' from Egyptian monuments are thus doubly disconcerting – they import motifs from the pre-classical world into modern London and they do so through textual transmission, through the transmission of print. Hawksmoor's skyline thus speaks of Britain's emerging imperial/Orientalist reach and its difficulty in articulating its national identity over and against the architectural language of power in Europe. But it also indicates the role of writing as a distinctly urban technology. With the transmission of images from Ancient Egypt, London inscribes itself within a system of cities – international but also inter-epochal.

In this suggestion that the city has not only been textualized by Hawksmoor but that his rewriting of London contains messages that he does not understand, that his writing, or citation, is the unwitting vector of a message from older cities, Sinclair introduces the idea of the parasite, of the writer as host, which recurs in various forms in the text, most obviously in the narrator's sense of being doubled by R.L. Stevenson who is also presented as a channel for the double aspect of London:

> We stumble into the realisation of a doppelganger principle. The feeling was already present, of a secondary personality developing, Ka assertion, inhabiting this body shell. 'Not quite myself today;' I am host to motivations

that cannot be understood ... As the ego breaks I am host to another being, who pushes through and not with the pink tenderness of new skin – but with old flesh, hard as wood. The earlier 'I do not know who I am' virus is confirmed, as this terminal caricature eases out of my face ... (LH: 109–10)

The sense of being doubled by Hawksmoor on the part of the poet leads to a 'loss of egoic grip', a sense of himself being lived by other forces:

And worse is to follow. Another of Anna's casually recounted, but vital dreams: that there are two creatures, one is her husband, the supposed protector, who is sitting upstairs in a wicker chair, while the other, also with my face, kicks down the door. Hyle is straining his collar. (LH: 110)

For Serres, the parasite is the figure of noise because it instigates a shift in the perception of information: it is a reminder that what is noise at one level is information at another. It is this shift that troubles the narrator – the sense that any sense of the here is undone by other imperatives of which he is ignorant. Sinclair's account of the city shows a similar shift in scale, from the individual to the species: 'The patients are not individual, are a strata that curves through the alternating times of the earth' (LH: 109). One of a series of images where the dissolution of the individual ego opens out onto the perspective of the species, where the ontogenetic yields to the phylogenetic, and even grander flows of energy and matter: 'We are invaded by a virus bearing the message of the stars' (LH: 110). Thus we are reminded that from the perspective of the species, the individual is only interesting by virtue of its errors, its genetic noise. Natural selection teaches that 'it is only our faults we have to offer' (LH: 103); and again, 'the pages/ of his script/ are individually handed out/ we stumble through/ "walk on by"' (LH: 93). Similarly from the phylogenetic perspective: 'Death is the fuel we are using up; its smell not unlike petroleum' (LH: 105) a perception which relates us directly to the Hawksmoor skyline which was paid for by a tax on the coal imported into the city to meet its energy needs.

More importantly, however, *Lud Heat* shifts scale in terms of its poetic practice: it effectively undergoes a form of generic mutation so that the poet becomes a character in his own poem which ends up looking more like a novel, thanks to its mythologization of London. Like the Victorian novel, *Lud Heat* provides an interface with the city but it is an interface which explores the dynamic, mutually constitutive relationship between city, consciousness and text. In confronting us with the noise of the occult and the difficulty of making sense of 'outmoded' beliefs within a modern secular environment, *Lud Heat* also confronts us with the difficulty of accommodating secular and sacred topographies within the same spatial language.

A text which registers this incommensurability or disagreement must fracture the community of which it is itself a part, the community of genre or mode, of poetry itself. Formally, this strain is registered at numerous points in the text. The shift between the meditative, confessional intimacy of the free verse section which concludes with a quote from Rimbaud: *j'ensevelis les morts dans mon ventre* (LH: 95) and the bombast and uneasy comedy of the mock-heroic prose of the following section announced with the title, 'THE VORTEX OF THE DEAD! THE GENEROUS!'[5] provides a particularly marked example. Here the open-field, ambiguous, multilayered confessional text abuts a parodically monomaniacal voice that literally screams its paranoid vision at the reader. Formally, this juxtaposition may seem fairly unremarkable: the division between, on the one side a text which seems to ask to be read as lyric and on the other a text which might be read as problematizing that request – is familiar enough. The juxtaposition of these two voices as the lyric and the satiric – works to ironize and thus destabilize any fixed perspective within the poem in a manner familiar from classic Modernist texts such as *The Waste Land, The Cantos,* and *Ulysses.* Formally, it inserts a gap between any perspective within the work and that of the work as a totality which we, as readers, have no problem in identifying as the indeterminacy that constitutes the work of art. As such, there is no difficulty in reading across that border and recuperating the formal break within a conventionally poetic economy – of treating 'The Vortex of the Dead' as a metaphor for the organizing power of myth, for example. However, as Fisher's letter attests, there are real problems with resolving these two versions of the poetic – the multilayered, ambiguous and open on the one hand and the monomaniacal and paranoid on the other – within the same frame. Alongside the familiar version of poetry as a relatively

---

[5] 'The Vortex of The Dead' seems to be a reference to the theory first expounded in 1911 by Russian 'heliobiologist' Alexander Chizhevsky that human behaviour, and hence human history, are directly influenced by solar cycles, so that solar-storms or peaks in sunspot activity coincide with upsurges in violence and an intensification of international conflict. Chizhevsky was sent to a Gulag by Stalin in 1947 for promoting this theory but it has continued to circulate, being resurrected most recently by Raymond Wheeler, at the University of Kansas, whose work informed the apocalyptic predictions that were focused on 2012.

open field of signification, we are confronted with a version of poetry as a compulsion to impart a particular vision which the sharer knows will isolate him or her from their community. It identifies the poetic with a desire to confess a vision which will lead to the speaker's rejection by the community that validates his or her language. It is a formal division that in effect presents an alternative version of the poetic as a language that simultaneously reveals the interdependence of individual and community, ego and collective and puts that relationship at risk.

The juxtapositions of these voices within *Lud Heat* present us with two versions of the poetic whose relationship is dissensual, which will not add up or be contained in a single frame: on the one side, a poetic which is plural and multivalent and on the other, a poetic which is mantic or 'vaticinal' – which points to an aporetic dimension within the poetic as a form of communication which dissolves community, a sharing which produces separation. It is this dissensual aspect of Sinclair's un/poetic that is registered in Fisher's concern about the extent to which Sinclair 'means' his metaphors. Fisher is troubled by Sinclair's literalism, his insistence on the matter of his mythology and suggestion that buildings actually generate energy, and his letter registers the ways in which *Lud Heat's* literalism disturbs the proper relationship between the poetic and the mythic described by Eliot's insistence that the 'mythic method' is 'a way of making the modern world possible *for* art'. For Eliot, in other words, myth is an operative principle, a mechanism for rendering coherent that which would otherwise be incoherent. In this, it implicitly identifies the proper relationship of poetry to myth as one of subordination. Poetry contains myth as a gesture towards a lost coherence. It points to a lost moment of plenitude, a fiction of origin. And as such, myth functions as the sign of signs, of an absent that engenders the present of modernity.

Consequently, in disturbing that proper relationship between poetry and myth, by presenting versions of the poetic which refuse to occupy the same frame, Sinclair is also, implicitly challenging that Modernist narrative about the relationship of (fragmented) present to (organic) past and (alienated) society to (immanent) community. In effect, by refusing to treat myth as the sign of absence, of a lost immanence, he is pointing to the ways it continues to operate in producing immanence in the form of essentialized communities.

This concern with the operation of community is evident in the content of Sinclair's mythic method. Informing *Lud Heat's* occult topography is the fact that 'The Romans regarded East London not as a place for the living but as a necropolis for the dead' (LH: 27). This fact serves as a reminder of the important relation of funerary rites to the construction of community. Funerary rituals, Jean Luc Nancy (1991) suggests, are how communities essentialize themselves and take control of the perception of finitude by which they are constantly threatened. Rituals are, in Nancy's terms, a machinery for the playing back of immanence, an idea echoed in Sinclair's description of Hawksmoor's churches: 'We are pushed towards the notion of these churches as Temples; and as cult centres. Courts and gardens where the living communicate with the dead and receive wisdom from them' (LH: 28).

In this sense, *Lud Heat* becomes an excavation or recovery of the connection between community and the production of death, a connection which, although forgotten beneath the abstract space and time of capital, remains, as we have seen, inscribed in London's topography: 'These facts fade. The big traffics slam by. A work ethic buries ancient descriptions' (LH: 26). The boundaries marked out by the pattern of Hawksmoor churches are in this sense then typical of boundaries in general. They are the lines through which community reproduces itself as the same through the production of an Other, an Other whose repeated murder is performed in ritual. And, as the point of entry for successive populations of immigrants, East London is the area where the management of the border is most acute and where the dangers from essentialized notions of community as 'blood-land' (LH: 47) are consequently always nearest the surface.

Lud Heat registers the actuality of this concern in its depictions of the crumbling welfare state – 'who will pay the surgeon', 'rats scale the rubbish on the South Downs' (LH: 90, 94) – and by carefully recording the electoral triumph of the recently founded, whites-only political party, the National Front in the neighbouring borough of 'Hackney South & Shoreditch' (LH: 130).

In other words, myth as an essentializing force for group cohesion is still very much operative in East London in 1974. And Sinclair's mythic topography effectively transforms myth from a signifier of rupture and absence into the marker of the intimate connections between immanence and violence which persists in the contemporary political landscape.

Where Victorian novelists sought to provide an overview of the new social reality of the industrial city and Modernist writers sought to involve the reader in the active production of meaning, Sinclair in *Lud Heat* performs a generic mutation, invoking a space which is fundamentally topological – where the active consciousness of the poet producer/reader becomes a character in the city which he produces. He thereby reveals the mutual implication of the city in the sign and the sign in the city. Sinclair's subject has abandoned the exclusive communalism of the British Poetry Revival where poet and reader are united in the activity of producing meaning, for a more compromised and complicit existence in the chaotic edges of cultural production, a region where the gated communities of high Modernist difficulty are forced to re-engage with the semiotic hoi-polloi of Hawksmoor's 'chaos of dirty rotten sheds'. The Hawksmoor skyline – part Modernist difficulty, part Gothic schlock and part demotic chaos thus becomes the signature of a new city where the compromise of commodification attendant on any truck with the sign is explored as a constitutive element of the urban rather than denied in the name of community.

3

The Vessels of Wrath: Noise and Form in *Downriver*

The empty vessel

Uniquely among Sinclair's published works, the novel *Downriver* (1991) concludes with a statement of the time and place of its completion: 'November 1989, London' (D: 407). In tethering the text so insistently to the diegetic, this piece of paratext seems to set up a deliberate tension with the title. It constitutes itself as an act of defiance to the process that will drag it inexorably downstream – published 1991, first paperback edition 1992, first Vintage edition 1995, first Penguin edition 2004 – the process, that is, that will carry it away from its source in that particular time and place, a time not so much of revolutions but of radical dissolutions, of walls that are suddenly no longer there. But, in commemorating its origins in that faultline, the dateline also ties the text to the momentous and as such represents a stake too in the sense of a wager – a wager about the unknowability of what those signs will come to mean. It signals not only ignorance of what significance will attach itself to that date and its relationship to the 'HAPPY ENDING' (D: 407) whose possibility is both ventured and queried in the final words of the text but also a question mark about where London will end up in the world they presage.

The sinister historical resonance of the title suggests one possible answer to the question of London's eventual destination. Given that the phrase 'selling down the river' originates in antebellum America and refers to the practice of disciplining slaves with the threat that they will be sold 'downriver' to endure the supposedly harsher conditions on the Southern plantations, Sinclair's title intimates its understanding of the nature of labour conditions in a globalized

economy in which the cultural and economic relation of 'global cities' to national
territories has become increasingly tenuous. As such, *Downriver* harbours
within its title an allusion to the wider reconfiguration of space predicted in
another text with which it shares its particular moment. In his essay 'The End
of History?', Francis Fukuyama gives his now notorious interpretation to the
events of 1989 with his vaticinal announcement that they signalled

> not just the end of the Cold War, or the passing of a particular period of
> postwar history, but the end of history as such ... That is, the end point of
> mankind's ideological evolution and the universalization of Western liberal
> democracy as the final form of human government. (Fukuyama: 1989)

Given that the History behind which Fukuyama seeks to place a period is
precisely that which the grand theorists of the novel, from Georg Lukács to
Mikhail Bakhtin to Ian Watt invoke in their accounts of the development of
the form, it is evident that one of the things '1989' could come to mean is the
end of the novel itself; that the triumph of 'Western liberal democracy' with
whose structure of experience extended prose fiction is historically associated
entails that the novel may turn out to be one of the cultural artefacts whose
destination lies 'downriver'. Sinclair's narrator contemplates precisely this fate
when he confronts a wall of concert posters consisting of a 'hyperactive collage
of quotations; many from William Burroughs, some from Joyce, some even
from Jean Rhys. Authors whose works would finally exist only as names on
hoardings: *memento mori* to bands who went out of business before the paste
was dry' (D: 237).

When reading Sinclair's dateline in conjunction with Fukuyama's essay then,
this insistence on the significance and particularity of the time of *Downriver*'s
composition becomes a sign of history and the end of History and as such a
sign both of witness and of the problems of witnessing. Its diegesis signifies
a concern with simultaneously bearing witness and bearing witness to the
inadequacy of such witness that distinguishes *Downriver* from texts which are
conventionally described as postmodern. Rather than the ludic exploration
of the ontologies of the fictional in a world devoid of metanarrative ascribed
to the postmodern text by its major theorists (Hutcheon 1988; McHale 1989;
Jameson 1993), *Downriver*'s engagement with the relationship of narrative and
witness is better suggested by describing it instead as a *post-historical novel* – a

novel that is intent on exploring its own place as a novel in a world devoid of the History upon which it was thought to depend.

This post-historicism is most clearly manifest in the novel's ambivalence to its own form. As Robert Sheppard notes, insofar as it resembles a 'formulation [that] deliberately avoids the word "novel"' (2007: 54), that ambivalence is even encoded in the over-elaboration of Sinclair's title: *Downriver (Or, the Vessels of Wrath) A Narrative in Twelve Tales.* Instead of identifying itself with a genre, *Downriver* prefers the genre-less 'narrative' and 'tales'. These more elusive terms are themselves complicated by the ambiguous notion of the vessel, which insofar as it signifies something which both contains (holds within bounds) and transports or communicates, serves as a topological figure for the ambivalence of Sinclair's attitude to form as that which communicates its own containment.

The title's allusion to Romans 9:22 – '[What] if God, willing to shew [his] wrath, and to make his power known, endured with much longsuffering the vessels of wrath fitted to destruction' – points to the role played by the vessel as a figure in the theological dispute about omniscience and free will, mercy and vengeance, which will return as narratological questions in *Downriver.*

Most obviously, the text functions as a vessel of wrath in its mordant satire of Thatcherism and Margaret Thatcher as 'The Widow', while the separate vessels – the 'twelve tales' – correspond to twelve sections (not chapters) of interwoven stories which are loosely organized around a series of mysteries involving the exploration of areas of London with connections to the river, most of which easily resolve themselves into metaphoric vessels. Thus, in the quest to discover the identity of Edith Cadiz, it is clear that Cadiz herself is a vessel insofar as she is a figure who, like Thomas Pynchon's V, seems to have several historical avatars. The function of rooms as vessels that contain and communicate is explored in the tales describing the disappearance of David Rodinsky from the Princelet Street Synagogue in the 1960s and the locked-room murder of Mary Kelly by Jack the Ripper in the Prima Donna's tale. In the tale dealing with the investigation of 'the railway murders' and their relation to the demonic Spring-Heeled Jack, the train functions as a vessel for the transportation of, among other things, industrialized time, an image literalized in the account of the 'woman whose job it was to entrain daily for Greenwich to capture and fetch back the "right time", so that the watchmakers of Clerkenwell could make a show of precision, repair their damaged stock with transfusions of the real' (D: 170). The vessel of wrath, however, has its most literal incarnation in the account of the narrator's attempt to determine the precise location of the sinking of the SS *Princess Alice*, a Thames pleasure steamer whose wreck in 1878 with the loss of some 650 lives prefigures that of the *Marchioness* in 1989 in which fifty-one guests at the birthday party of merchant banker Antonio de Vasconcellos were drowned.

The ambivalent attitude to the topology of form indicated in the notion of the vessel further reflects Sinclair's acute sensitivity to the parallels between the role of 'enchantment' in the production of cultural and commercial value; his sense that his own activity as a writer is inseparable from the wider economies of the city; and his understanding that the viability of his project is determined by its ability to discover areas whose aesthetic interest has yet to be realized: 'Obviously, Spitalfields was burnt out (caned by the supplements) – but Bow was effervescently marginal, a desert crying aloud for re-enchantment' (D: 235). Spitalfields, the area between the City and East London had, in other words, already been reimagined and prepared for development, Bow, further East was the next likely territory to undergo this process. In *Downriver*, this sensitivity to the implication of cultural and commercial economies is focused through the satiric account of the narrator's attempts to make a documentary about the London that is vanishing in the wave of post-1986 development, the landscape of an industrial and commercial city rendered obsolete by the financial revolution instigated by the deregulation of the stock market previously based in the City of London. The novel thus presents its own concerns remediated through the language of the TV-pitch perfected by the producer, Sonny Jacques:

> 'I like it!' he shouted, ... 'A re-enchantment of that which was never previously enchanted. Yes! And we set that against the state art of the Silvertown Memorial, those bragging *vertical* energies, laying claim to emotions they have not earned. The public river and the unregarded wasteland. God, it's almost a title! We've got it. We've got our pitch'. (D: 236)

The idea of the novel as simultaneously a property to be pitched and a place of labour whose value is tied to the fluctuations of value elsewhere in the economy is reflected in the ambivalent place of the novel within Sinclair's oeuvre. Thus, while *Downriver* invites formal and thematic comparison with contemporary London novels such as *The Satanic Verses* (1988) and *London Fields* (1989), it is also clear that the term novelist fits Sinclair far less comfortably than, for example, Salman Rushdie, Martin Amis or A.S. Byatt. In part this uneasiness is because Sinclair's novels – five to date[1] – form only part of a more wide-ranging and experimental oeuvre in which poetry, documentary, travel writing, film and collaborative projects serve to challenge the cultural centrality traditionally ascribed to the novel. Rather than jewels in the crown, Sinclair's novels jostle for position within a wider conception of the writer's work which is constantly foregrounded in his text. In *Downriver*, the narrator's self-conscious self-presentation as 'a jaunty witness, a paddler in the narrative shallows' (D: 249) whose materials are 'recycled more often than a Brick Lane pint' (D: 350) encourages us to see the novel as just one possible arrangement of materials which will be recombined until they have lost their market value.

> Fredrik had done a number in the *London Review of Books* on a novel I had recently published; which would otherwise, despite the gallantly double-glazed 'doorstopping' of my publisher, have sunk into necessary and well-deserved obscurity. Fredrik suggested that Spitalfields was, currently, a battleground of some interest; a zone of 'disappearances', mysteries, conflicts, and 'baroque realism'. Nominated champions of good and evil were locking horns in a picaresque contest to nail the ultimate definition of 'the deal'. We had to get it on. There were not going to be any winners. If we didn't move fast, any halfway-sharp surrealist could blunder in and pick up the whole pot. (D: 93)

Finally, however, it is the novel as a vessel of narrative that is the most important locus of the ambivalence. In the relationship between novel and narrative, the vessel becomes a figure for the dual status of narrative as both a way of knowing – Louis Mink's 'primary cognitive instrument' (1987: 185);[2] – and a form of making. Where the accent has been placed on the loss of the real attendant on the linguistic turn, and the demonstration by, for example,

---

[1] *White Chappell, Scarlet Tracings*, Downriver (1991), Radon's Daughters (1994), Landor's Tower (2001) and Dining on Stones (2004).

[2] Louis Mink: 'Narrative is a primary cognitive instrument, an instrument rivaled, in fact, only by theory and by metaphor as irreducible ways of making the flux of experience comprehensible' (1987: 185).

Hayden White, that history is inseparable from rhetoric and narrative causality (White 1975), this ignores the emotional source of narrative in the desire to testify, to tell the story as a form of witness, and hence the loss of witness. *Downriver* as such becomes a vessel which communicates the wrath born out of its inability to speak the truth from which its narrative springs.

In *Downriver* consequently, noise tends to take the form of the return of the unselected: the unselected by virtue of which narrative is constructed and the unselected in the name of which narrative wishes to speak. To examine the productive function of that return of the unselected, this chapter will examine *Downriver*'s mapping of this world firstly in narratological terms through Sinclair's use of the 'locked-room' mystery genre as a means for exploring the underlying noise of narrative as Mink's 'primary cognitive instrument'. It then considers Sinclair's exploration of the novel as the marker of the shifting relationship between secular and sacred space in the wake of Ayatollah Khomeini's fatwa on Salman Rushdie issued on 14 February 1989. Finally, it explores *Downriver*'s presentation of the possibilities of critique in the context of the cultural cynicism which it identifies as marking its cultural and philosophical moment in a world without sides.

'[N]o female sound': Noise and narrativity in *Downriver*

Downriver, Sinclair has said, was conceived as an act of atonement. It 'started out as a series of tales that would give some kind of meaning to the pain of the victims of Jack the Ripper, whose voices had, I felt, been left out of *White Chappell*. There was no female sound in there' (Potter 1994: 46). His concern with restoring a 'female sound' is literalized in the opening sentence: ' "And what," Sabella insisted, "is the *opposite* of a dog?" ' (D: 3) Sabella Milditch's expression of Alice-like exasperation is directed at a cultural logic exemplified by her husband, Henry Milditch, and the narrator's dismissal of every book they mention as ' "a dog", "a howling dog", "an absolute dog" '. It is an exasperation at what Patrick Wright (to whom the novel is dedicated and who finds a fictional analogue in the character Fredrik Hanbury) has termed 'the entropic view of history' (Evans 1997: 135) current amongst the English Left after a decade of Thatcherism and which Sabella glosses as the sense that '[e]verything is finished, burnt out. Nothing is what it used to be' (D: 3). Her complaint, in other words, identifies a view of history rooted not in post-colonial melancholia so much as despair at the dissolution of the post-War consensus underpinning the ideals of the welfare state – a despair which extended from the consequences of monetarist policy for the fabric of social life to a more general loss of conviction in the possibility of belief itself.

For Sabella, however, this general condition of cultural despair has immediate and practical implications. The direct cause of her exasperation lies in her husband's plans to move the family out of inner-city Hackney to 'some Suffolk fish dock'. Rejecting Henry's 'decent-minded' talk of the problems of 'inner-city schools and the rising tide of litter and urban violence' (D: 4), she points out that, for her, this will mean an unwelcome return to the values of an all-too-familiar Victorian geography of gender. While her husband will be free to enjoy all the amenities of a re-masculinized metropolis such as the Groucho club, she will be left imprisoned in the provinces, wading through 'reprints of Wilkie Collins': '"*Bollocks* to urban violence," Sabella screamed. "You'll dump me out in the sticks with your rotten kids, while you slide down the motorway. You'll only crawl back when you need a few quiet days to sleep off the excitement."' (D: 4) Henry Milditch's response to his wife's objections to her proposed rustication, forcibly evicting her from his 'book-room', provides a symbolic enactment of the themes of displacement explored further in the novel, while her prognosis of a re-Victorianized metropolis which has become the haunt of predatory males fairly describes the position of most of the other female characters in *Downriver*.

In his gesture of atonement, of attempting to make up for something previously 'left out', Sinclair links the origins of *Downriver* with that desire to create a whole by making good a lack that Georg Lukács identifies as distinguishing the novel from the epic. It is this tension between the need to constitute itself as a totality – to make a world – in the face of a commitment to a freedom which is in principle limitless that leads Lukács to produce his classic definition of the novel as 'the epic of an age in which the extensive totality of life is no longer directly given, in which the immanence of meaning in life has become a problem, yet which still thinks in terms of totality' (1971: 56). Lukács means by this that insofar as the novel strives to give an aesthetic form or sense of completeness to a depiction of a society which valorizes the individual and the principle of individual freedom, the possibility of totality and necessity are confronted as problems, or in his memorable phrase, the novel is constantly confronted by a 'bad infinity'. For Lukács, the novel as the vessel of a liberal commitment to freedom, is in other words, haunted by the possibility that things could be otherwise, by a lack of necessity and a lack of completeness. Beyond the ambition of restoring a sense of gender imbalance within his fiction then, Sinclair's identification of the absence of a 'female sound' in his earlier work, *White Chappell, Scarlet Tracings* can be read as indicative of a more structural concern with the logic of narrative as a form of knowing which is starred by the sin of omission. It indicates a concern, that is, with the ways in which narrative as a means of making sense of the world involves a process of selection which bears with it the negative trace of its exclusions, the exclusions which we have identified with the concept of noise.

Downriver has its source in a concern with the ways in which the desire to tell a story requires another's silence. Specifically, it registers the ways in which a fascination with determining the identity of a Victorian serial killer works to occlude the identity of his victims, how the mystery of one person's identity leaves us incurious about that which we think we already know, the identity of his victims. Mary Ann Nichols, Annie Chapman, Elizabeth Stride, Catherine Eddowes and Mary Jane Kelly are the names of the women supposed to have been killed by Jack the Ripper, which is to say, that, no matter how intensely the details of their lives are scrutinized, their bearers do not exist in their own right. Rather, they exist by virtue of a narrative in which their allotted function is that of the victim. Recovering the 'female sound' that is absent from *White Chappell*, in other words, is not simply a question of telling the story of Jack the Ripper's victims,[3] for the Ripper would remain their creator; it is rather a question of exploring the possibility of attributing agency and motive to the role that narrative logic demands be devoid of agency or motive, that of the victim.

---

[3]   This is the strategy of Alan Moore and Eddie Campbell in the graphic novel, *From Hell* and the 'Connoisseurs of Crime' in *Downriver* who speculate that the third of the Ripper's five 'canonical' victims, Elizabeth Stride may have turned to prostitution after losing two children in the SS *Princess Alice* disaster.

The impulse to atonement, to 'give some kind of meaning to the pain of the victims of Jack the Ripper' that provides the initial impetus for *Downriver* finds its clearest expression in 'Prima Donna', the tale that deals with the death of Mary Kelly, thought to have been the Ripper's 'final' victim. The tale's subtitle '(The Cleansing of Angels)' aligns Sinclair's concerns with providing a voice for the silenced with Walter Benjamin's invocation of the Angelus Novus to formulate a 'tradition of the oppressed' in his 'Theses on the Philosophy of History' (Benjamin 1969). In his ninth thesis, Benjamin invokes the Angelus Novus as the sign of a perspective from which causality appears as chaos: 'where we perceive a chain of events', the angel sees instead 'one single catastrophe which keeps piling wreckage upon wreckage and hurls it in front of his feet' (1969: 257). As such, the Angelus Novus stands as a more general sign for narrative's exclusions – for that which is unselected in the process of making sense of history in terms of progress or development.

In 'Prima Donna', Sinclair explores the opportunities afforded by the conventions of Gothic fiction including the found manuscript and the locked-room murder to invest the role of victim with agency. Presented as a manuscript dictated by Mary Kelly from beyond the grave to obsessive Ripperologist John Millom, it begins: 'I had not, I think, been dead beyond two or three months when I dreamed of the perfect murder' (D: 202) and describes how Kelly re-imagines, or remembers, her death so that '[s]he is no longer trapped in his story, like a fly in amber' (D: 208–9). The Prima Donna's tale explores the ways in which the representation simultaneously erases and preserves the represented, in the same way that the Ripper creates his victims – as 'the canonical five' for example – by murdering them.

From her allusive account of the events within the locked room, it is evident that Kelly achieves her release from the amber of narrative by detaching the narrative focalization of her tale from her person: 'I saw the outline of a girl's body, frosted with unstable light. I saw my own double, kneeling sadly over the body, then moving into the shadow' (D: 203). The mechanics of the reversal by which she transforms herself from victim into her murderer's murderer are confused but turn upon the parallels between sex and murder as ritual. The Prima Donna describes how her eventual murderer/victim, a blind surgeon – we assume Sir William Gull – would visit her regularly in her room for an hour on terms set by him, each time locking the door behind him as he entered. During these visits where she performed the rituals he demanded of her, they were 'shadows miming desire in a house of the dead, a museum of trapped reflexes' (D: 205). Eventually, she introduces rituals of her own which, awakening his desire, transform him into her victim, signalled by the fact that he is no longer able to leave when his servant calls for him after an hour and that she, rather than he, locks the door on his arrival. She achieves her triumph when he finally kills her and in so doing disappears. However, this account is subverted by the tale's final paragraph: 'Footsteps on the cobblestones, and a single knock at her door. The dream of perfect murder fades' (D: 209). The violence here is to narrative: finally the tale is that of a dead narrator and reveals itself to be (just) a dream.

No sooner is the tale over than we are plunged into competing interpretations. For 'Sinclair', the Prima Donna's rituals seem to describe the little death of the lovers' out of body experience: 'the madness of love-death ... the metaphysical poets mingling of souls' (D: 210). Millom however insists on a more radical interpretation. He suggests that Kelly recognizes that mastery can only be exercised over subjects who resist and thus that apathy and indifference are the ultimate forms of resistance: 'The woman *allowed* the surgeon to enact the deed that was his inescapable destiny. She could not change the events of history, but only the meaning' (D: 210). In her 'indifference', which mirrors our indifference to the identity of the Ripper's victims, she forces him to assume her identity:

> The blind surgeon wanted something that excited him more than honour, more than sanity, more even than life. He wanted the one crystal absolute she denied him – yes, apathy; he wanted it so much he was prepared to pass over the borderline of identity, become her, and suffer her vengeance *within her flesh*. (D: 210)

Apathy is the most prized quality in narrative as an economy of affect organized around desire. Consequently, apathy is the only affect that can disrupt the economy of desire that drives the narrative and can thus release its victim.

'Sinclair's' resistance to this interpretation reminds us of what is at stake in this attempt at atonement. The attempt to give a voice to the excluded leads us back only to an encounter with the narrator's obsessions and the Prima Donna's tale presents us with an allegory of narrative as a site of exchange, where identities shift and the boundary between narrator and narrated, presenter and represented dissolves. 'Sinclair' as the author of *White Chappell* may believe himself to be immune to the obsession with 'atrocity' exhibited by Millom, to operate at a critical and cultural distance from the popular interest in Ripper narratives, but in this surgical detachment he, like Gull, simply denies his parasitic dependence on the obsessions which motivate his 'characters'.

Narrative thus emerges from the Prima Donna's tale as a site of furtive exchange and contagion: 'White hands break free of his cuffs, to flap around the lamp, as he signals his triumph. "Gotcha!" He has implicated me in horror, infected me with a small corruption from which there is no immunity' (D: 210). Although he resents Millom's explication of the Prima Donna's tale, preferring his more innocent vision of the 'the madness of love-death' (D: 210), it is clear that his desire for innocence reflects his inability to cope with the more disturbing version of their relationship:

> Through the focus of repeated ritual acts the woman infiltrates the surgeon father's consciousness – so that when the inevitable moment comes, she takes responsibility for her own death; leaving him with nothing, an achieved emptiness. (D: 210)

The 'achieved emptiness' echoes Lukács' 'bad' infinity. Sinclair attempts to figure his resistance and antipathy to Millom through appeal to the Freudian plot when, in a trope repeated across his oeuvre, he suddenly recognizes the manuscript as his own: 'The manuscript was in my own hand....But I have no memory of its composition. The risks were too great. I had sworn to finish with all this compulsive night stuff' (D: 211). The locked room is given its conventionally Freudian furnishing as the site of the unconscious: it is a symptom of the writer's ignorance of his own writing and as such locates the Other within the same.

In attempting to give voice to that which has been left out, narrative confronts its inability to escape its own will to knowledge. No matter how elaborate the narrative construction intended to provide a space for that which has been left out, – the tale within a tale, the unreliable narrator in an unreliable narrative – the narrator is condemned to discover that the supposedly excluded is its own production. As Peter Brooker puts it, '[w]omen figure in this story... less as actors than the creations of man's fevered sexual imagination' (2002: 102). As such the content of the Prima Donna's tale is less interesting than its form, the ways in which Sinclair attempts to create a space for the excluded and specifically his use of the idea of the locked room. Thus, if the 'female sound' is not to simply collapse into the unknown known of the unconscious and become thereby an object of symptomatic analysis, it is instructive to consider the ways in which the structure of the Prima Donna's tale works to revise the Ripper narrative or undo the work of narrative-as-Ripper. Specifically, it is worthwhile considering some of the ways in which the idea of the locked room works as a figure for narrative's exclusions, to consider the way the idea of the locked room serves as a figure for the productive tension between omniscience and ignorance.

The locked room

In presenting the Prima Donna's tale as a locked-room murder, Sinclair draws on the fact that Kelly, having lost the key to her room at 13 Miller's Court, would bolt and unbolt the door by reaching in through a crack in the window next to the door (Connell 1995). Thus, while it is technically true that Mary Kelly's mutilated body was found in a locked room, this detail says more about the social and economic circumstances of her life than the mystery of her death. The process that transforms the elements of the banal – a lost key, a broken window – into elements of mystery is, however, significant. For the Prima Donna's tale in gesturing towards the locked-room mystery as genre invokes another local text which turns on a similar tension between the messiness of everyday life in the East End and the exactitude of form.

Israel Zangwill's novella, *The Big Bow Mystery* (1892) which recounts the murder of a middle-class philanthropist and trades union activist in a lodging house in Bow near Whitechapel is frequently cited as a paradigmatic instance of the locked-room mystery genre. The interactive dimension of the genre – the rule that the reader be provided with all the clues necessary for a solution – is a critical aspect of the locked room story and suggests its function as a compensatory fantasy. Within the confines of the locked-room mystery, readers are granted an agency – the materials necessary to solve the mystery – which they signally lack in real life, where, as in the case of Mary Kelly, violence is always experienced as, in some way, inexplicable. Zangwill's flawless logical puzzle, however, bears the imprint of the true story of the murder of Miriam Angel by Israel Lipski in nearby Batty Street in Poplar in 1887, a murder in which the messiness of true crime is compounded by allegations of institutionalized racism (Friedland 1984).[4] This uneasy congress between true crime and the locked-room mystery provides another variation on the theme of narrative as Ripper. In Zangwill's case, the satisfaction of the tale is also explicitly and satirically contrasted with the political impotence of the working class whose representatives furnish the victims – murdered and falsely accused – of the tale.

By the time of its publication in 1892, Zangwill was writing within a recognized genre whose origins are usually traced to the publication of Edgar Alan Poe's *Murders in the Rue Morgue* in 1841. The literary critical significance of the *Murders in the Rue Morgue* as the 'first detective story' has been much discussed for, in addition to establishing a template for later detective fiction, it is also possible to see within Poe's 'tale of ratiocination' the lineaments of proto-modernism (Merivale 2010). With its creation of the detective hero, the mystery, of which the locked room can claim to be the paradigmatic example, represents a shift away from the conventions of narrative omniscience towards the problematization of the epistemological that Brian McHale identifies as the 'dominant' of Modernist fiction (1989: 9). According to McHale's 'general thesis',

the dominant of modernist fiction is epistemological. That is, modernist fiction deploys strategies which engage and foreground questions such

---

[4] 'Zangwell [sic] based his novel on an actual case of great public interest in 1887. A woman named Miriam Angel was heard moaning in her locked room in a boarding house on Batty Street in the East End of London. Other roomers broke down the door of her room, and found her dying in bed. A doctor was brought in quickly and discovered she had been poisoned with prussic [sic] acid. Then more moaning was heard. Under the dying woman's bed was a man named Israel Lipski, who had apparently taken some poison too. Lipski recovered, and was charged with Angel's murder. He would claim he was forced to go into the bedroom by two men, who then poisoned Angel and framed him. He was found guilty of the murder, and was eventually hanged. But first there was a great movement led by the editor William Stead, who felt the trial was unfair. Stead's attempt almost freed Lipski (Home Secretary Matthews and the trial Justice, Sir James Fitzjames Stephen reviewed the evidence, only to reaffirm the verdict after Lipski apparently confessed). It [sic] one wants the full story, read Martin Friedland's THE TRIALS OF ISRAEL LIPSKI'. http://en.wikipedia.org/wiki/Israel_Lipski [accessed 1 July 2011].

as …: 'How can I interpret this world of which I am a part? And what am I in it?' Other typical modernist questions might be added: What is there to be known?; Who knows it?; How do they know it, and with what degree of certainty?; How is knowledge transmitted from one knower to another, and with what degree of reliability?; How does the object of knowledge change as it passes from knower to knower? What are the limits of the knowable? And so on. (1989: 9)

However, where Modernist fiction in McHale's taxonomy works to problematize questions of what constitutes knowledge, of what and how we know, the locked-room murder effectively works to reinforce the claims of omniscience.

It does this in two ways. Firstly, insofar as it opposes rational explanation with supernatural appearance, the room becomes the arena for an emblematic struggle between reason and its Other. As this confrontation inevitably results in the triumph of reason over the supernatural, the locked-room mystery presents itself as a fable about Enlightenment and omniscience. It presents knowledge as a condition which is achieved through struggle, or the exercise of reason, rather than that into which we are born (omniscience). Read as a fable about Enlightenment, the locked-room mystery constitutes a statement about the place of omniscience within a realist narrative economy. With its roots in a theological world view all too plain, the problematic nature of omniscience in a realist representational economy has long been evident. As Nicholas Royle points out '[o]mniscience is not simply a hyperbole, it is an incoherent and flawed plot device in a story that critics and theorists have been telling for a hundred years and more' (2003: 260). Omniscience denies a space to the unknown; it denies the agency of the unknown both as a motor of scientific inquiry and as the basis of a Freudian model of the psyche. In the Enlightenment plot, the unknown as ignorance is that which has to be overcome in order to produce enlightenment; in the Freudian plot, omniscience denies the structural importance of the unknown as the basis of knowledge.

Focusing on the importance of the unknown, the development of detective fiction in general (and the locked-room mystery in particular) in foregrounding epistemological problems represents an important episode in the management of omniscience. In the locked-room mystery and detective fiction generally, omniscience is displaced from narrative to genre. It moves away from the focalizer's relationship with the focalized to the reader's recognition of the kind of world represented by the text. In both its classic and metaphysical traditions, detective fiction as an epistemological puzzle is defined by a number of assumptions about what constitutes an acceptable solution to the mystery and resolution to the story, not least, that the solution should not involve a supernatural agency. It instigates a division between the narrator-detective as the heroic epistemologist and the author-creator who must ensure that the murder be solved in an acceptable fashion. Thus, the locked-room murder represents simultaneously a move away from the category of the omniscient and an affirmation of the possibility of omniscience, of knowledge as the only condition of narrative closure. The locked room is, in other words, a means of dealing with our discomfort about the idea of omniscience, of staging the disappearance of the author-god while guaranteeing that he remains in the background to ensure the recognizibility of the fictional world; to police the distribution of the sensible as it is articulated in the understanding of what constitutes a 'good' story or what linguists would term a 'well-formed formula'.

In narratological terms then, the locked room is always a product of focalization: it is the figure of an epistemological limit, a place where we cannot go. However, given that the resources of narrative include omniscience and omnipresence, the locked room invites us to read it as a fiction about fiction; as a figure for what is concealed within narrative itself – the space where, despite its omniscience and omnipotence, narrative cannot enter. It is this space, the space occupied by the 'victim', which I have suggested is created through the imperative of selection and which consequently is the realm of noise.

In this respect, the locked room functions much like Ross Chambers' revision of Eve Kosofsky-Sedgwick's notion of the closet (Chambers 2002). For Sedgwick, the closet is the figure for containing the incoherence in ideas about (homo)sexuality – namely, that sexual identity is both biologically determined and culturally constructed. According to Chambers, Sedgwick's closet is 'a device to deny [that] incoherence by policing the separateness of the "really gay" from the general instability of identities, and which thus, when read symptomatologically, reveals that general instability' (2002: 167).

In Chambers' development of the concept, the closet becomes a figure for the containment of the aporia generated by 'paradigmatic' thinking in general: it is the space of aporia where we discover the illusory nature of the claim that a binary opposition saturates the field. Thus, where paradigmatic thought encourages us to concentrate on the differences that divide the members of two sets or paradigms, it masks the differences that separate the members of the same paradigm which could themselves be the basis for another articulation of the field.

A good example of this process is found in Zangwill's *Great Bow Mystery* whose solution requires the reader to recognize that the persona of detective and murderer are not mutually exclusive, and in general, the locked-room mystery relies upon presenting alternatives which, at first sight, seem to exhaust the logical possibilities of the situation. In other words, as a strategy for dealing with the problem of omniscience, the locked-room mystery, even as it constitutes itself around a space denied to omniscience, deploys another paradox elaborated by Edgar Allen Poe: the art of misdirection or paradox of hiding in plain sight.

As such, the locked room functions as a closet for dealing with the problem of the unknown. The locked room reclaims the unknown as an operational category, it creates a place for the unknown within the world of scientific omniscience, as that which will be discovered, and hence as the necessary supplement of omniscience. However, as a scene for staging the operational unknown, the ignorance which sustains the ideal of Enlightenment, it also points to the absence of a more radical unknown, the unknown which is unknowable and to which Emanuel Levinas gives the term the Other, the unknown, that is, which haunts narrative as noise.

The violence that is always the implied content of the locked room aligns the violence implicit in representation with that implicit in the claim that two possibilities exhaust the field. Within *Downriver*, this tension is rehearsed in the supposition that the first and third person exhaust the field of narrative focalization. In *Downriver*, the act of narration is foregrounded as an integral part of the drama. Like Marlow in Conrad's *Heart of Darkness*, (which, as Brian Baker observes, is a 'major intertextual presence' (2007: 92) within *Downriver*), 'Sinclair' makes narration part of the drama of narration. 'Sinclair' records his own birth as narrator at the outset of the narrative: 'I knew then that my days as a dealer were almost over. I didn't want to touch whatever lay on the floor of the Tilbury shop. But I had the queasy sensation there ought to be a story in it' (D: 5). Similarly at the narrative's conclusion, he reviews a number of possible exit strategies, including his eventual choice, the 'dreary postmodern fraud' of handing the job over to a guest narrator.

While 'Sinclair' functions as the primary narrator within *Downriver*, his first person narration is interspersed with a number of third person or omniscient narrators whose relation to the 'Sinclair' narrative is complex. Sometimes they appear to be narratives authored by figures within the first person narrative – Millom and the Prima Donna's tale, Bobby Younger and the story of Arthur Singleton – at other times they appear to be experiments by 'Sinclair' himself. All of the third person narratives, however, concern victims. These include the stories of Victorian cricketer, Arthur Singleton; Dr Adam Tenbrucke, 'the owner of a shelf of Conrads', Cec Whitenettle, a train driver and the mysterious Edith Cadiz. The subjects of the third person narrative are all, in one way or another marked out as sacrificial victims. The division between first and third person narrative thus articulates within the structure of the text a thesis about narrative and power which is made explicit when, 'Sinclair' surrenders the task of narration to Joblard in the final section: 'There is, I assure you, a measure of safety in being the one who holds the pen' (D: 378). The third person is vulnerable, dispensable: ' "I" is the man in possession, but *he* is also possessed, untouchable. "I" is immortal. The title of the survivor. There has always to be one witness to legitimize a massacre. Anerian at Catraeth' (D: 378).

The distinction between narrator and narrated is, in other words, one of power and his most explicit demonstration of this power dynamic occurs in the account of Edith Cadiz. That story is introduced in a manner that emphasizes the operation of narrative desire, the way in which narrating a story constitutes a form of imaginative possession (Cadiz begins life as a photo of an unknown woman who catches 'Sinclair's' eye) about whom a group of men begin to speculate moving between the identity of the woman depicted and the commodified form of the representation – the photo. After this careful framing of Cadiz as a figure for narrative desire the lurch into the third person in the subsequent section is almost as dramatic as when the diary narrative of, Esther, the heroine of Wilkie Collins' *The Woman in White* is taken over by her nemesis, Count Fosco. The lurid account of Cadiz's double life as a nurse and as a prostitute who is eventually murdered by Labour MP, Meic Triscombe, identifies the third person as a thin disguise for fantasy. The assumptions implicit in the third person narrative are then identified in the disavowal of the following section which begins '[i]t is not known, and I do not know what happened to Edith Cadiz' (D: 79). This denial of omniscience constitutes a refusal of responsibility and an opening to the possibility of responsibility, to invent a character and to surrender any claim to 'know what happened' to her is the only possible counter to the obsessive quest for the identity of the Ripper, a radical openness which exposes the fiction of fiction's relation to its totality.

If the locked room serves as a general narrative figure for fiction's implication within the problematic relationship of omniscience and ignorance, Sinclair's attention to the relations of narrative and fiction to the claims of totality and the productive function of the unknown acquires an immediate political urgency in the wake of the publication on 14 February 1989 of a fatwah against the novelist Salman Rushdie by the Iranian cleric Ayatollah Moosavi Khomeini.

'[No] sides to take': The fiction of disorientation

Downriver directly references the consequences of Khomeini's fatwa on Rushdie and the burning of copies of the *Satanic Verses* in Bradford on January 14, 1989, on three occasions. Describing the wind tunnel effect associated with skyscrapers on the empty streets of Canary Wharf, the new financial capital down river from the City on the Isle of Dogs, he suggests the ubiquity of the Rushdie affair when he writes: 'A bruised wind, frustrated, bounced from the tall buildings, sibilating like a host of linkpersons struggling with the revised pronunciation of "Rushdie."' (D: 284) Rushdie's name, the image suggests, is everywhere – in the wind, but also, running through the interstices of the mediascape occupied by the linkpersons or continuity announcers between programmes. Carefully, however, the image of the wind tunnel effect also ties the 'revised pronunciation' to the archetypal structures of capital, suggesting that the revision of Rushdie's name is related to the revisions of the city-scape, which can itself be read as the emblem of the wider reconfiguration of global space attendant on 'the end of history' and the dissolution of the of the geopolitical landscape of the Cold War.

The novel's second reference to Rushdie reflects on the implications of this geopolitical reconfiguration for the immediate practice of the novelist in relation to the notion of public space: its implications, that is, for the novelist's imaginative freedom to explore every aspect of life. Contemplating the fact that the novelist as novelist is now excluded from his *habitus*, public space, with an inversion of the familiar racist expression 'they all look the same to me', Sinclair notes his ambivalent feelings to his familiar territories:

> [Sinclair] daren't set foot in Whitechapel. With his bald dome and spectacles, his notebook, he might be mistaken for Salman Rushdie. They'd hack him to pieces on the cobbles of the brewery ... We all feel guilty, guilt as a constant, a hangover of guilt: even if we haven't read a word of it. There are no sides to take. (D: 371)

The novelist's edgily hyperbolic contemplation of his imagined exclusion from the street encodes his perception of the novelist's and the novel's new roles at the frontline of an emerging arena of negotiations about global space. Those new roles are discursive, insofar as fiction becomes identified as the shibboleth separating the space of Enlightenment from the literalism of a 'mediaeval' religion, separating an enlightened 'us' – good readers – from a barbaric and literalist 'them' – bad readers, but it is also material insofar as the spatiality of a new form of conflict becomes map-able with the cultural space of literary production. It is a conflict in which targets are authors, publishers, translators, the staff of hotels occupied by translators and publishers, readers, bookshops and clerics who refused to condemn the book and Muslims caught up in the reaction to the controversy. As Paul Weller notes, in the course of 1989 the novelist appeared to be one of the main protagonists in a '20th century Holy War, [which] with its terrifying righteousness on both sides, may be on the point of breaking out sporadically but repeatedly in airports, shopping streets, suburbia, city centres, wherever the unprotected live' (2009: 117).

Despite 'Sinclair's' claim that '[t]here are no sides to take', for Peter Brooker at least, the third reference to the Rushdie affair suggests that Sinclair inclines towards a liberal fundamentalist view, while Baker detects a latent racism in his depiction of the Bengali community on and around Brick Lane:

Banglatown, as it was vulgarly called, replaced the perished dream of
Spitalfields. The 'born-again' Huguenots dumped their Adam fireplaces,
and ran. The stern fathers of the One True Faith sent columns of black
smoke twisting skywards as they redressed the violations of the culture of
drunkards and apostates that surrounded them. Vulture priests, percolating
hatred beneath their turbans, bearded in a nest of absolutes, spittled their
chanting congregation with infallible accusations. (D: 265)

Brooker is attentive to what he terms Sinclair's limitations, noting that while
'earlier immigrants are an acknowledged, sometimes considered presence, the
newer ethnic community of Bangladeshis, whose great Mosque now occupies
the site of a former synagogue in Whitechapel's Fournier Street, are as if
invisible' (2002: 103). This invisibility, Brooker suggests constitutes a notable
omission in the work of an 'artist who would notice everything in his chosen
territory' (2002: 103). His blindness to the presence of the majority population
in his chosen territory, Brooker believes, is indicative of the extent to which
Sinclair 'falls prey to the power of "whiteness" whose apparent transparency is
the very sign of its undeclared but hegemonic ethnicity' (2002: 103). It is also
indicative, he suggests, of 'the continuing unresolved relations of Islam and the
West' (2002: 103).

Rather than reading this invisibility as an absence, however, if we view
Downriver as an exploration of the possibilities of the novel form in a post-
historical context, the supposed failure to include a substantial Bengali
presence within the novel, and thus, implicitly, to address the issues of a multi-
faith, multicultural community also constitutes a comment on the orthodoxy
of the novel as a form whose historical function is to provide some form
of formal resolution to social conflicts. This commitment to the novel as a
dialogic form attains the status of a postmodern orthodoxy which is summed
up by Carlos Fuentes when, in 1989, he writes in *The Guardian* that '[i]n the
novel, realities that are normally separated can meet, establishing a dialogic
encounter, a meeting with the other', presenting the novel, in other words, as a
'privileged arena' which facilitates 'bringing together in tension and dialogue,
not only opposing characters, but also different historical ages, social levels,
civilisation and other, dawning realities of human life' (Fuentes 1989). Rushdie
indicates his own commitment to this view of the novel and its failures in
conversation with James Fenton:

what I tried to do was to bring two worlds which happened to be present inside me – more than two worlds actually – India, Islam, the West – these three worlds all of which are present inside me in a very vivid way – I tried to bring them together. I tried to describe each in terms of the other. Well it didn't work. Whatever one may feel about *The Satanic Verses* as a novel, if you look at the *event* of the *The Satanic Verses* it pushed those worlds further apart. (Fenton 1991: 31)

Given that the view of the novel as a dialogic form for the encounter of that which society holds apart achieves the status of a postmodern orthodoxy, whose liberal assumptions are made ever more visible by the Rushdie crisis, Sinclair's 'failure' to embrace a dialogic model of the novel indicates a sensitivity to the ideological imperatives that inform the postmodern orthodoxy of the novel as a form which can contain conflicting voices while remaining blind to its own liberal assumptions of the notion of a privileged arena. Rather than a privileged arena for the exploration – and resolution – of social conflict – *Downriver* can be seen to explore the conditions of the novel in a space where, with its ideological investment in liberalism, it must consider its adequacy to map a new spatial configuration in which as just one 'voice' its claim to totality is self-evidently problematic.

John Berger suggests one strategy for mapping the terrain inhabited by Sinclair's book when he writes on the relationship of *The Satanic Verses* to the *Koran*:

The two books at this moment represent two notions of the sacred. The Koran is a sacred book in the most traditional and profound sense of the term ... Rushdie's book has become a sacred cause to the European world because it represents the artist's right to freedom of expression. In Europe, as has been pointed out before, art has replaced religion. (Berger 1989)

However, while Berger's characterization refuses to oppose 'sacred' and 'secular', as faith and reason, it presents the new spatial dispensation in terms of the clash of civilizations promulgated by Samuel Huntington rather than any more nuanced appreciation of the multiple tactical and hybrid articulations of that spatiality. This more nuanced version of the realities of the post-colonial and post-Cold War dispensation is reflected in, for example, Mica Nava's vision of a city characterized by 'increasingly undifferentiated, hybrid, post-multicultural, lived transformations which are the outcome of diasporic cultural mixing and indeterminacy' (2007: 13).[5] Sinclair's narrativization of London as 'grimoire' (D: 407), in other words, runs counter to the cosmopolitan narrative of London as a vibrant city of creative energy arising from an unproblematic ethnic diversity and counter to the 'indiscriminate celebration of mixing or hybridity' that Rebecca Walkowitz associates with Rushdie (2006: 132).[6]

The cultural and aesthetic space explored in *Downriver* is characterized neither by the clash of civilizations – 'there are no sides to take' – nor by the hybridized forms associated with multiculturalism and the new cosmopolitanism explored in the novels of Rushdie, among others. Sinclair's gothic vision of the metropolis precludes any celebration of the cultural opportunities of the metropolis insofar as it marks his fixation with the revenance of evils attendant on the return to those Victorian values vaunted by Margaret Thatcher but whose true content is articulated by Sabella in the novel's opening pages. Rather than conflict or clash, or celebration of hybridity, Sinclair maps a space of dissensus where sacred and secular constitute constantly shifting boundaries within a malleable landscape. In such a landscape, Sabella's demand to know 'the opposite of a dog' becomes meaningless.

Opposition in a world without sides

In her demand to know 'the opposite of a dog', however, Sabella expresses the fundamental problem of negotiating a landscape where there are no sides, while the cynicism etymologically encoded in that question is simultaneously

---

[5]   Writing on the protests against the filming of Monica Ali's *Brick Lane*, Dominic Head notes: 'The sorry episode was a kind of pantomime of cultural misunderstanding, with the various players fulfilling their allotted roles. The self-appointed leader of the protest, for example, dutifully displayed ignorance of the point of novel writing (if one can trust the quotation ascribed to him): "it's not a fiction book ... this is all lies". Yet we might wonder if there were really other motivations, apart from the convenient "refusal" to accept fiction as fiction. The reporter for *The Hindu* found that locals were apt to repeat the allegation that the protest was a "publicity stunt" by a group of traders. As with the protest on the book's publication, there is a prospect that the fresh protest was mobilized by a traditional contingent in Brick Lane, chary of the theme of female emancipation in Ali's novel. That only two women attended the "damp squib" of a protest tends to reinforce this suspicion. In this interpretation of the affair, the traditionalists' repudiation of the novel as "lies" rather than "fiction" has more purpose: it implies a partial understanding of how novels work to promulgates ideas, and to play their part in the cultural mediation of behavior' (2008: 77–8).

[6]   Rebecca Walkowitz writes that 'Rushdie is widely associated with the indiscriminate celebration of mixing or hybridity, in part because his novels seem to perform this celebration, in their exuberant combination of genres and cultural references, and in part because his essays call for "*mélange*" as a practice both of cultures and of writing' (2006: 132).

the novel's target and the condition it must overcome in its quest to discover the possibility of testimony in the post-historical condition. Within Sinclair's satire of Thatcherism, cynicism is presented not merely as the cultural dominant of neoliberal Britain, it approaches the condition of a philosophical absolute which threatens to negate any possible notion of an opposite or of an oppositional text such as Sinclair's. It is this despair which gives a peculiarly philosophical resonance to Sabella's demand to know 'what *else* there is' (D: 3).

For *Downriver*'s narrator, Sabella's question marks, as the narrative's incipit, the precise moment of his transformation from a dealer in books to their producer: 'I knew then that my days as a dealer were almost over. I didn't want to touch whatever lay on the floor of the Tilbury shop. But I had the queasy sensation there ought to be a story in it' (D: 5). However, if he is to succeed in turning from a dealer in books to their producer, and thus reversing the prevalent cultural logic, it is implied, that the 'narrator' must find an answer to Sabella's question – to discover, that is, the possibility in a world gone to the dogs, of any meaningful form of opposition.

A fuller indication of the nature of that problem is set out in the third of the book's twelve sections when a voice that hovers somewhere between the narrative and the authorial declares that '[t]he great shame and dishonour, of the present regime is its failure to procure a decent opposition' (D: 72). The disorientating effect of this statement lies in its rejection of the traditional *dispositif* of British parliamentary politics and assertion that the apparent division between government and opposition masks their underlying identity as two sides of a single 'regime'. Effectively, the verb 'procure' transforms the constitutional principle, enshrined in the term 'loyal opposition', that both governing party and opposition form part of a larger whole which derives its power from the throne into a restatement of a Foucauldian vision of the complicity of power. This is then given a satiric performance in the portrait of the 'opposition' Labour MP, Meic Triscombe, 'the standing member' for Hackney. In his account of how Triscombe deploys Bevanite rhetoric as an aid to sexual arousal and conquest, Sinclair suggests the more general cultural exhaustion of socialism as a rhetorical resource. The history of working-class struggle has become a source of faux sentimentality cynically deployed by career politicians. Triscombe effectively foreshadows the capitulation of New Labour and the rise of the belief that the electoral defeat of the Conservative party could only be achieved by an opposition which adopted many of the core assumptions of monetarism and the importance of a 'business ontology' (Fisher 2009: 11) in spheres of society previously regarded as the proper concern of the state. As such, the pain of the historical victims of class conflict should be added to the sum of what has been 'left out'.

However, in addition to signifying the failure of political opposition, Triscombe also serves as a metonym for a wider cultural complicity that includes all oppositional forms including, it is implied, satires of Thatcherism such as *Downriver*:

> Never have there been so many complacent dinner parties, from Highbury to Wandsworth Common, rehearsing their despair: a wilderness of quotations and anecdotes....Writers were glutted on hard-edged images of blight....The worse things got, the more we rubbed our hands. We were safely removed from any possibility of power: blind rhetoric without responsibility. (D: 72–3)

Here, Sinclair registers the paradox remarked by Dominic Head, that Thatcherism 'generated an apparent renaissance in English fiction...even though writers were largely hostile to the political ethos associated with Thatcherism' (2008: 59–60). He presents us with a vision of satire as a fundamentally parasitic mode which draws on the energy of that which it denounces and hence of 'wrath' as a source of pleasure.

As such Sabella's question points beyond the problem of opposition as a cultural form – real existing opposition as it were – to a problem with the notion of opposition as a logical category. In this, Sinclair's satire of Thatcherism can be usefully aligned with the characterization of the postmodern developed in Fredric Jameson's influential essay, 'Postmodernism, Or, The Cultural Logic of Late Capitalism' first published in *The New Left Review* in 1984. In its concern with the (im)possibility of opposition, *Downriver* explores the condition indicated by Jameson when he writes that:

> some of our most cherished and time-honoured radical conceptions about the nature of cultural politics may...find themselves outmoded. However distinct those conceptions – which range from slogans of negativity, opposition, and subversion to critique and reflexivity – may have been, they all shared a single, fundamentally spatial presupposition, which may be resumed in the equally time-honoured formula of 'critical distance'...we

all, in one way or another, dimly feel that not only punctual and countercultural forms of cultural resistance and guerrilla warfare but also even overtly political interventions like those of *The Clash* are all somehow secretly disarmed and reabsorbed by a system of which they themselves might well be considered a part, since they can achieve no distance from it. (1993: 48–9)

Echoes of Jameson's account of the postmodern aesthetic as dominated by 'parody and pastiche' are clearly audible in Sinclair's description of the architecture of the Canary Wharf development on the Isle of Dogs, the setting for the 'Isle of Doges (PLC) Vat City' section which describes the experience of postmodern pastiche as an alteration in the fabric of space and time. As the narrator's companion, Davy, says:

> You realize we may actually have been flung back into an ahistorical anomaly: a confirmation of [Stephen] Hawking's absence of boundaries, a liquid matrix, a schizophrenic actuality that contains the fascinating possibility of finding ourselves placed in postmodern docklands and *quattrocento* Florence, *at the same time*. So that all those greedy pastiches have become the only available reality, 'real fakes', if you like. (D: 297)

Davy's musings on the 'real fake' register the experiential dimension of what Jameson terms the 'crisis of historicity': he registers the pastiche of postmodern docklands as simultaneously a particular style with its own specific temporal and spatial location, the equivalent of '*quattrocento* Florence' and as an assertion, '*at the same time*', of the impossibility of construing any totality (historical or spatial) within which styles or periods can be causally related. It is the greed of pastiche that locates this versioning of the postmodern, echoing Jameson's description of architectural pastiche as 'the random cannibalization of all the styles of the past ...' (1993: 18). The postmodern is morally located as the architecture of greed, a greed which has consumed time and location itself. As Jameson writes: 'Faceless masters continue to inflect the economic strategies which constrain our existences, but they no longer need to impose their speech (or are henceforth unable to) ...' (1993: 17). Sinclair here, in other words, extends Jameson's idea of the loss of critical distance with the conceit that the end of History has made all historical periods contemporaneous, and that this is registered in the fabric of the city – not simply as an architectural palimpsest but as the aesthetic of a new present. Without the causality of history and of any accepted narrative which will establish a causal relationship between past, present and future, we find ourselves in a space where all 'periods' are contemporaneous, not simply as architectural styles but, critically for Sinclair, as forms of imagination.

> We arrived here by an act of will: *was it our own?* What if the inevitable return of our natural cynicism and disbelief has let slip Conrad's *Heart of Darkness*, renegades from Dickens's prison hulks or any other composite monsters – including those from this fiction you are supposed to be writing? If the imagination is primary, then anything we can imagine must lie in wait to ambush us. (D: 297)

This meditation on the temporal impact of the postmodern, however, occurs in the most elaborately satirical section of *Downriver*: an account of how the Vatican has leased the Isle of Dogs which is intended to suggest the sacred role of high finance within a supposedly secular world. As such, Sinclair retains a formal and principled commitment to satire within a postmodern enclave and the discovery that satire is, against the prevailing cultural logic, thriving in new locations, downriver, suggests that we need to press Jameson's argument that satire cannot survive the loss of critical distance a little harder.

In Jameson's terms, *Downriver* explores the problems of (self)representation in a cultural landscape which has lost any sense of 'critical distance'. For Jameson, however, this loss of critical distance is to be understood as an effect of the shifting organization of the modes of production as capitalism enters its 'late' phase. And as such the apparent loss of critical distance is only apparent: a Marxist theory of cultural production can still serve as an interpretative horizon. In understanding the relation of the loss of critical distance to the cynicism invoked by Sabella, Peter Sloterdijk is a more useful guide. Where Jameson relates the celebrations of postmodern irony to the mutation of capital, Sloterdijk identifies a cynical postmodernism – a loss of belief in the possibility of belief – as integral to the concept of enlightenment itself. For, insofar as the notion of enlightenment is predicated on the assumption that appearance is never identical with truth, that truth can only be revealed through the process, or labour, of unmasking, cynicism describes the fundamental motion of enlightened reason which inevitably culminates in the assumption that all forms of belief are deceptive. Hence,

> In the shattered world of multiple perspectives, the grand views of the whole, in fact, belong more to simple souls than to those who are enlightened and educated by the given order of things. No enlightenment can occur without destroying the effect, thinking from a point of view, without dissolving conventional morals. Psychologically this goes hand in hand with a scattering of the ego, literarily and philosophically, with the demise of critique. (2010: xxxiii)

For Julian Wolfreys, Sinclair's text performs this crisis of critique in its refusal to conform to the demands of a critical object: 'Iain Sinclair's texts cannot be read', he argues, 'they are unreadable in a very real way, which has nothing to do with the language, the syntax, the grammar or any other formal element. They are unreadable inasmuch as everything that is to be said already finds itself on the surface of the text' (2004: 162). The text, in other words, actively disrupts the space claimed by the critic, the space of unveiling, where truth will be displayed beneath the surface.

The ontological implications of the loss of critical distance identified by Wolfreys are comprehensively demonstrated in Sinclair's reading of John Tenniel's 'Alice in the Train' illustration for Lewis Carroll's *Alice Through the Looking-Glass* (see Figure 3.1). 'Sinclair's' reading of the illustration which he purchases as a postcard instigates a number of spatial disruptions which should be separately noted. Firstly in its virtuoso display of the language and techniques of cultural and textual analysis, it disrupts the spatiality which distinguishes the object from analysis or the space of the critic from the producer or author. Sinclair's fluency in the language of critical discourse is evident in sentences where the self-reflexive and parodic are held in a state of productive imbalance: 'With the advent of the Guard at the window – asserting his status, inside and outside at the same time – the illustration lays claim to a moral complexity that is the cartoon surrogate for "Las Meninas"' (D: 179). In directing us to one of the seminal scenes of post-structural reading, Foucault's account of Velasquez's painting 'Las Meninas', Sinclair's text not only makes plain its refusal to assume the passive role of object for analysis, it also asserts a claim to contain post-structuralism within its

Figure 3.1 From Lewis Carroll's *Alice Through the Looking Glass*

discursive universe – not just as an object of pastiche and as a problematic which is both represented and exemplified.[7]

Further, the well-known ambiguities of Carroll's text allow Sinclair to explore the implications and consequences of that collapse of critical distance for the practice of close reading. Sinclair's account reveals how Tenniel's illustration discloses a paedophilic subtext within Carroll's scene. He notes how the 'Gentleman's crossed leg, with bulky folds of material at the knee,

---

[7] Foucault reads 'Las Meninas' as the marker of a new episteme in Western art and the conception of space. It marks the break between the classical and the modern: 'Perhaps there exists in this painting by Velasquez, the representation as it were, of Classical representation, and the definition of the space it opens up to us. And, indeed, representation undertakes to represent itself here in all its elements, with its images, the eyes to which it is offered, the faces it makes visible, the gestures that call it into being. But there, in the midst of this dispersion which it is simultaneously grouping together and spreading out before us, indicated compellingly from every side, is an essential void: the necessary disappearance of that which it resembles and the person in whose eyes it is only a resemblance. This very subject – which is the same – has been elided. And representation, freed finally from the relation that was impeding it, can offer itself as representation in its pure form' (1991: 16).

supplies the Goat with a mythically engorged member' (D: 179) and goes on to indicate the implication of the sexual within the imperial when he notes the 'area of furious cross-hatching [that] spreads like a stain from the knees of the Gentleman in White to Alice's hooped stockings, tracing the undisguised coastline of Africa' (D: 179–80).

However the post-Freudian, post-colonial eye which (once it has been pointed out) cannot not see the sexual symbolism in Carroll's proto-surrealism, or register the proximity of the feet of Alice and the Gentleman in White, has to exist alongside an innocent eye. It is not that we see innocence corrupted by experience, Sinclair suggests, but rather that the two perspectives are mutually productive: it is only once we have recognized the real identity of her fellow travellers, that we can see the true strength of Alice who remains the most potent figure within the composition:

> But all of us, puppets and audience, are dominated – transfixed – by the mongoose-will of the blonde girl. Self-contained, she sits as if she were attending a lecture, with slides, on Faraday's electro-magnetic current, or the Discovery of the Source of the Nile ... Alice can cancel them all, reassert the sanctity of the carriage, travel alone. They are shadows. (D: 180)

Disenchanted and innocent perspectives are held in a mutually productive relationship: we are not viewing a lost innocence but an innocence which becomes visible only by virtue of experience. However this Blakean marriage of contraries does not exhaust Sinclair's reading of reading. In a parody of the popular hermeneutics practiced by Jean Overton Fuller who claimed to have proven that Jack the Ripper was the painter Walter Sickert (and subsequently by Patricia Cornwell[8] and Dan Browne), Sinclair suggests that if we pay attention to the discrepancies between Tenniel's and Carroll's account of the scene we can see that Tenniel is 'playing detective ... he codes his etching with the solution to the railway murders that had not, *as yet*, been committed; but which we can now unravel on his behalf' (D: 181). The quest soon spirals out of control with the depiction of Alice supposedly revealing details of the Railway Murders known only to the police but which

---

[8]   For more on Jean Overton Fuller and Patricia Cornwell, see Fiachra Gibbons' 'Does this painting by Walter Sickert reveal the identity of Jack the Ripper?' (Gibbons 2001).

implicates Sinclair's companion, Joblard and then 'Sinclair' himself before dissolving into a banality about the act of writing: 'In the end every writer confesses. It proves nothing; a kind of boast' (D: 183).

At one level then, Sinclair's text problematizes the space of critique by refusing its position as an object for analysis: it has already registered and incorporated the theory that will be utilized to make it produce academically sanctioned meanings and interrogated the motivation of such production. However, where in the postmodern aesthetic elaborated by Jameson this produces an empty world of pastiche and irony, in Downriver the erasure of the space between subject and object demanded of critique generates something like the dynamics of the future anterior, the 'preposterous' tense (Bal 1999: 6) that allows us to say what we will do as if it was over and done with. The supposed object – the text, or the victim – becomes that which will have been, which will come to be seen as.

The dissolution of the space of critique, in other words, does not necessarily involve a collapse into postmodern relativism and cynicism. Rather, in demonstrating the productive and dynamic relationship between subject and object it indicates the possibility for an ethics of narrative which can arise only once the notion of an original or lost innocence has been undermined. It is this ethics which informs Sinclair's satire.

The 'vessels of wrath': Satire and cynicism

Insofar as it invokes a lost ideal against which to measure the deviance of the present, satire would seem to be an intrinsically normative, communitarian and conservative mode. As John Clement Ball observes, it would be '[a] remarkably enduring commonplace of satire theories is the notion that satire, even at its most revolutionary, gazes nostalgically and conservatively back upon a privileged golden age' (2003: 9). It is a commonplace that requires some reworking in the case of Sinclair insofar as one of the principal targets of his satire in *Downriver* is the notion of a return to Victorian values that played such an important part in the rhetoric of the Conservative governments lead by Margaret Thatcher (Samuels 1992). This intent to reveal the 'true' meaning of this Thatcherite appeal to Victorian values is marked in the opening vignette, which, as we have seen makes explicit just what that return would mean for middle-class women such as Sabella: banishment from the liberties of the city and sequestration in the country.

In this instance, it is still possible to align Sinclair's satiric attack on Thatcherism with the conservativism of the mode. *Downriver* could be read as a denunciation of Thatcherism as an ideology which disguises its radical content (neoliberalism and the dissolution of society) through an appeal to a fake conservativism (Victorian values) which is exposed in the name of a true conservativism whose lost object is the post-war consensus of the welfare state, the organic community sacrificed to the market mechanisms commemorated in 'The Isle of Doges' section. The lost community, in other words, might be construed as the progressive vision of history. In the absence of any positive statement of the lost community, however, this gloss seems unsatisfactory, and the real character of Sinclair's satire is suggested when, in the same mode, the narrator dwells on the decision to resolve the crisis in the prison service as it struggles to cope with growing numbers of 'technical offenders' and 'evicted mad' by reintroducing Victorian prison ships, or hulks:

> Market forces suggested privatization on the American model. But we had our own well-tried methods. We had thousands of years of dark history to draw on. The hulks had been pressed back into service. I could not believe what I told myself I was seeing. (D: 335)

Here, it seems that the true target of Sinclair's satire is less the notion of a return to faux Victorian values which mask the horrors of the Victorian city than the notion of return itself: the compulsion, that is to invoke a vanished community, which will serve as a basis for the critique of the present. Sinclair is more concerned with history as revenant – as the source of monsters which are released by the compulsion to return to a lost golden age than with the accuracy or inaccuracy of the version of history presented by the politics of the day.

That it is the use of the past in general, rather than any specific version of history that Sinclair targets, is suggested in his depiction of Meic Triscombe's opportunistic exploitation of working-class struggle, another return and another appeal to a lost golden age which becomes the measure of pure cynicism. It is, in other words, the appeal to the past in order to denounce the present that provides the most sustained target of Sinclair's satire.

As such, Sinclair's satire raises questions about the relationship between satire and community traditionally presupposed in accounts of satire as a mode. The question is thus: 'is a non-normative satire possible or does Sinclair's satire involve rethinking the notion of satire's ties with the community and consequently rethinking the notions of community?' The problematic of community as the basis of satire is illustrated in one of the novel's most elaborate satirical set pieces centred on the Canary Wharf development on the Isle of Dogs in the 'Isle of Doges (Vat City PLC)' section. Developing the common satirical image of neoliberal Britain as a PLC, Sinclair examines the impact of globalization on ideas of the sovereign state and the national imaginary. The conceit that the Isle of Dogs has been leased to the Vatican works at a number of levels. Firstly it comments on the religiosity of adherence to the 'voodoo economics' of neoliberal policy and the role of finance in general – referring, in other words, to the actual occupants of Canary Wharf. At the same time, it points to the irony that this papal religiosity should be the ultimate product of the spirit of Protestantism and that the Anglo-American economic model should have such a corrosive effect on the integrity of one of the nations whose self-image was forged in opposition to Roman Catholicism. As such, the Isle of Doges satire returns us to and inverts the popular anti-papal tradition of satire of the protestant revolution in the sixteenth and seventeenth centuries. This Hegelian irony where the spirit of Protestantism produces papery is summed up in the observation that 'an involuntary return to the point of departure is, without doubt the most disturbing' (D: 53). At the same time it returns us to the tension between the production of sacred and secular space discussed above.

But if Sinclair's satire returns us to earlier registers of the mode, it does so in full consciousness of the ambiguities of its practice. If, as Sloterdijk suggests, 'ideology critique is satire which has forgotten to laugh', Sinclair's satire is imbued with the savage melancholy of an ideology critique which can no longer believe in the possibility of critique. Sinclair's satire is practiced, in other words, in the belief that it is complicit with that which it denounces. This complicity is dual. It lies in the knowledge that no form of cultural resistance can resist the logic of commodification and thus the denunciations of capitalism simply serve to strengthen it. It also takes the form of a recognition that, as a mode, satire draws its material from the disorder it depicts – that as a 'mediator between the real and ideal' (Guilhamet 1987: 16) it partakes, parasitically, of both, or, to paraphrase Sinclair 'the worse it got the better we liked it'. Following Gramsci's thesis that hegemony requires counter-hegemony, that resistance legitimizes oppression, Thatcher is the true 'female sound' in *Downriver* in that the text takes its energy from her.

In his conflation of Thatcher and Victoria in the figure of 'the Widow', Sinclair returns us to the iconography of Britannia familiar from the political satire of Gillray and Cruikshank in the eighteenth and nineteenth centuries. The elaborate satire around the commissioning of the monument to the consort is traditional in form, exposing the total cynicism of power and the venality of place-holders. Sloterdijk suggests something of the ambiguities involved in satire's medial position, its parasitic character, when he notes that:

> Every struggle leads necessarily to a reciprocal reification of subjects. Because enlightenment cannot give up its claim of imposing better insights against a self-obstructing consciousness. Thus ideology critique acquires a cruel aspect that if it ever really admits to being cruel, claims to be nothing more than a reaction to the cruelties of 'ideology'. (1987: 15–16)

In other words satire must first posit what it denounces, it must imagine the world it wishes to destroy, produce the real as well as the ideal. On the grounds that 'it is impossible to outrage the baroque realism of the dying century', the satirist always has license to '[i]magine the worst and then double it' (D: 357). The satirist can always produce cruelty and depravity in the name of the satirized other.

It is in this context that Sinclair's insistence on the productive power of the imagination assumes its importance and his suggestion that, as 'conspirators looking for a conspiracy', the Widow is 'a blue rinse succubus, draining the good will of the people' (D: 267). Just as 'the gods are our needs made manifest, the Widow is the focus of our own lack of imagination; the robot of our greed and ignorance. Therefore she is indestructible' (D: 267). Ultimately, it seems, Thatcher is the product of a collective failure of imagination, of the inability to imagine anything better.

As satire then, *Downriver* most fully reveals the topological conditions of its status as a vessel of wrath. In its satire of Thatcherism, it acts as a vehicle for the cultural anger at the values of Thatcherism that demand expression, that demand a vessel; but at the same time it confronts its readers with the possibility that Thatcherism may itself be produced by the same mechanism that produces satire – the desire to return to some original, normative vision of community. Satire as much as Thatcherism, it implies, is the product of a failure of imagination – a failure to recognize the mutually productive relationship of present and past and insofar as the past stands for the radically Other, a failure to recognize the mutually productive relationship of self and Other.

4

Between Archive and Ash: *Rodinsky's Room*

The solemn mystery of the reappearing room

If in the 'Prima Donna' section of *Downriver*, the locked room acts as a space for managing the tension between formal closure and the messiness of history on the one hand, and the problem of omniscience, on the other, it returns to other ends in the section titled 'The Solemn Mystery of the Disappearing Room'. Here, Sinclair provides one of a number of accounts of the story of David Rodinsky:[1]

> Rodinsky, a Polish Jew from Plotsk or Lubin or wherever, was the caretaker and resident poltergeist of the Princelet Street synagogue: an undistinguished *chevra* without the funds to support a scholar in residence. He perched under the eaves, a night-crow, unremarked and unremarkable – until that day in the early 1960s when he achieved the Great Work, and became invisible. (D: 134)

Apparently another 'locked room mystery', in its various versions the story of Rodinsky's room provides one of the most important examinations of the theme of noisy or dissensual space in Sinclair's oeuvre and is the subject of the book length collaborative work with writer and visual artist Rachel Lichtenstein, *Rodinsky's Room* (1999). Collaborative works tend to be placed at the margins of an oeuvre, but in Sinclair's case, the idea of collaboration seems structural and central: as a collaborative work, *Rodinsky's Room* thus in itself constitutes a form of dissensual space. In *Rodinsky's Room*, Sinclair's

---

[1] His first account of Rodinsky's room is in a 1988 *Guardian* article titled 'The Man Who Became a Room'. He returns to it again in *Rodinsky's Room*, *Dark Lanthorns*, and *London Orbital* (both the film and the book).

text distributed over five separate sections is inseparable from Lichtenstein's also spread over five sections and an Afterword. Thematizing the problem of the archive, or the storage of cultural knowledge, the book presents us with an example of that problematic in its own form and as such Sinclair's treatment of the topic of Rodinsky's room is most usefully discussed in relation to his and Lichtenstein's textual cohabitation.

Rodinsky's room is located in the garret at No.19 Princelet Street in Spitalfields, London. From 1932 to sometime in the late 1960s, the room, once a Huguenot weaver's workshop, was home to a family of Jewish immigrants from Kushovata, a shtetl, or small town, in the Pale of Settlement on the periphery of the Czarist empire near Kiev. Rodinsky's mother and father, Haicka and Barnett Rodinsky, had fled persecution in Russia to join the well-established Jewish ghetto in Whitechapel sometime in the 1920s. His father, a tailor, survives only as signature on a birth certificate and a sepia photo. Contemporaries only remember Haicka bringing up two children on her own in the Princelet Street garret: a daughter known variously as Bessie, Bertha or Brendall and a son David, born in 1925. Following the death of Haicka and incarceration of Bessie in the Claybury Mental Hospital, Woodford, North London, David Rodinsky lived on in the room alone until he 'disappeared' sometime in the late 1960s. With the dispersal of the East End Jewish community to the suburbs, the synagogue was decommissioned and abandoned and the room was left untouched for fifteen years until it was 'rediscovered' in 1981. When it was opened, along with Rodinsky's personal effects, his clothes, his wallet, his spectacles case, and 'stiffened pyjamas and fossilized blankets', the room was also found to contain hundreds of heavily annotated books in numerous languages and a vast collection of personal writings scrawled in exercise books, on chocolate wrappers and on scraps of paper of every conceivable provenance, again in a variety of living and dead languages (RR: 27). Inevitably this *mise en scéne* was interpreted as an originary absence that demanded a narrative recuperation. Within the symbolism of urban space, this garret that textualizes itself becomes the stuff of local legend, the stuff, that is, of the legend that produces a locality. For as Michel de Certeau observes '[i]t is through the opportunity they offer to store up rich silences and wordless stories, or rather through their capacity to create cellars and garrets everywhere, that local legends (*legend*: what is to be *read*, but also what *can be read*) permit exits, ways of going out and coming back in, and thus habitable spaces' (1988: 106). No longer a synagogue, No.19 Princelet Street becomes the perfect place for staging a synagogue and it is this space that determines what can be read. As a lighting technician working on a production of *The Golem* in the 'deactivated' temple tells Lichtenstein on her first visit:

> 'I heard that when they first opened the room, a mummified cat was found sleeping in his bed. There were hundreds of books up there, containing mystical formulas, and it is believed [Rodinsky] managed to transport himself out of the room without ever leaving.' The lighting man leaned closer. 'His boots were still there, standing in the corner, filled to the brim with dust' (RR: 22).

Sinclair and Lichtenstein are drawn to the room for very different reasons and thus encounter two very different *legenda*. For Lichtenstein, the granddaughter of Polish immigrants, Rodinsky's room is a last remnant of the all-but-vanished Jewish community of the East End into which her grandparents, Gedaliah and Malka Lichtenstein, had settled in the 1930s. For Lichtenstein, the room thus represents a connection with her own past, with the 'colourful characters' who had both 'fascinated and terrified' her as a child, and, through them, with the lost traditions of the Ashkenazy. As such, the room is a further means of realigning her own diasporic identity with the collective narrative of twentieth-century history, 'the black spider of the holocaust' (RR: 86). This process of realignment began, she writes, on the death of her grandfather when she was seventeen: 'When he died I panicked, realizing that with him was buried the key to my heritage. I became determined not to let it die with him. A week after his death I took the first step towards a reconnection between my past and my present and reclaimed by deed poll the surname Lichtenstein' (RR: 19).

Noise as *lieu de mémoire*

Lichtenstein presents us here with an exemplary illustration of what Pierre Nora terms a *lieu de mémoire*, or 'memory site', whose existence he suggests is indicative of the destruction of lived tradition by modernity, those sites both physical and symbolic which 'exist because there are no longer any *milieux de mémoire*, settings in which memory is a real part of everyday experience' (1996: 1). For Lichtenstein, both the room and her name express a sense of the past which is symptomatic of the loss of lived tradition. They are the products of a world where, as Nora writes:

> The equilibrium between the present and past is disrupted. What was left of experience, still lived in the warmth of tradition, in the silences of custom, in the repetition of the ancestral, has been swept away by a surge of a deeply historical sensibility.... Memory is constantly on our lips because it no longer exists. (1996: 1)

Substantially the same perception of the way in which space is produced as the consequence of a temporal crisis, of spatiality as an expression of a structural disruption of the relation of past to present, is also evident in Sinclair's first description of Rodinsky's room in a piece he wrote for the *Guardian* in 1988 titled 'The Man Who Became a Room' and which is taken up almost verbatim in the passage from *Downriver* quoted above:

> Patrick Wright has alerted me to a fable that is acquiring great potency in the amoebic principality of Spitalfields – the myth of the disappearance of David Rodinsky. Rodinsky, a Polish Jew from Plotsk or Lublin or wherever, was the caretaker and resident poltergeist of the Princelet Street synagogue ... He perched under the eaves, a crow, unremarked and unremarkable – until that day in the early Sixties when he achieved the great work and became invisible. It is uncertain how many years passed before anyone noticed his absence. He had evaporated, and would remain as dust, his name unspoken, to be resurrected only as a feature, a necessary selling point, to put alongside Nicholas Hawksmoor in the occult fabulation of the zone that the Eighties demanded to justify a vertiginous inflation in property values. (Qtd. RR: 32)

As this suggests, however, while both share an interest in the room as a site which dramatizes the relationship between time and space, Sinclair's interest, unlike Lichtenstein's, lies in the room's function as a nexus of narrative and capital and consequently, its place in the constant reconfiguration of London as a field of energy at once imaginary and real. Despite the dismissive tone, the potency of the fable within Sinclair's text is attested by the regularity of its recurrence being visited on separate occasions in *Downriver* (1991), *Lights Out For the Territory* (1997), *Dark Lanthorns* (1999) and *Dining on Stones* (2004).

Room as archive

As is clear from Lichtenstein and Sinclair's distinctive lines of approach, Rodinsky's room marks a complex site within the figuration of place and temporality in a postmodern urban topography. In one direction, it points us towards the Holocaust and the question of representation of a time which is irredeemably post-Auschwitz – which, as Andreas Huyssen notes, 'has become a cipher for the twentieth century as a whole and for the failure of the project of enlightenment' (2003: 13). In another direction, it points to the assault on community and tradition launched by free market economics under the banner of Thatcherism in 1980s Britain. To reflect the complexity of its position at the nexus of these diverging urban narratives, it is useful to invoke the concept of the archive, for the prominence of the archive in recent theory is due in large part to a perception of the inability of any grand narrative to represent the multiple dimensions of the spaces contained within *Rodinsky's Room*. Thus, if the loss of nostalgia for the lost grand narrative defines the postmodern condition for Jean-François Lyotard (1984: 41), 'the obsession with the archive' is its corollary for Nora:

> The less memory is experienced from within, the greater its need for external props and tangible reminders of that which no longer exists except *qua* memory – hence the obsession with the archive that marks our age and in which we attempt to preserve not only all of the past but all of the present as well. The fear that everything is on the verge of disappearing, coupled with anxiety about the precise significance of the present and uncertainty about the future, invests even the humblest of testimony, the most modest vestige, with the dignity of being potentially memorable. (1996: 8)

Like Rodinsky's room, the archive is another space whose dimensions measure a crisis of temporality. As Derrida points out in his essay commemorating the opening of the Freud museum in London, the archive as *arkheion* is from the outset aporetic. The word *arkhé* 'names at once the *commencement* and the *commandment*', names both the command to remember, to archive, to keep and the commencement of an institution of archivization (1996: 1). Or, in Dragan Kujundzic's paraphrase: 'Remember: no memory or testimony is possible without the archive! Remember: memory and testimony are possible only without the archive!' (2003: 166)

The beginning of the archive signals the end of memory, the externalization on a material substrate of what was internal and living for the purpose of preservation. The command to remember is thus the command to let go, to forget. As such, the archive is always the graphic materialization of an absence, a trace whose subject is temporality.

The rise of the archive signals not only the absence of 'living' tradition but, in historiographical terms, the absence of any narrative grand enough to stitch together past, present and future. It comprehends too a shift in the material substrate of temporality. The narrative in its linear progress seems inadequate to contemporary perceptions of spatiality, whereas the archive opens out directly onto cyberspace (Mackenzie 1997; Liu 2002). In this situation, the plurality and democracy of the archive seems to offer an alternative means of storage and of transmission – preserving the past and the present for an eventual retrieval. However, the very openness of the archive is its limitation. As Nora notes:

> Now that historians have abandoned the cult of the document, society as a whole has acquired the religion of preservation and archivalization. What we call memory is in fact a gigantic and breathtaking effort to store the material vestiges of what we cannot possibly remember, thereby amassing an unfathomable collection of things that we might someday need to recall. (1996: 8)

As the site of memory postponed, the archive, even as it promises to preserve the past denies the possibility of transmission, for if, as Derrida suggests, the 'archive has always been a pledge, and like every pledge, a token of the future', it is a pledge which can never be honoured (1996: 18). Whereas the logic of narrative through the prospect of closure holds forth the promise of an ending that will retrospectively determine the significance of every incident, the plurality of the archive which is in its very nature unbounded always admits the possibility of further additions. The archive archives 'the material vestiges' of a departed intention. It archives the material inscription of that intention and the faith in the possibility of transmission. The transmission, however, depends on the technologies of classification and retrieval and these are precisely the technologies thrown into question by the drive to archive. As Derrida points out, the idea that the archive preserves the past is illusory, for the archive is constituted through the technologies of classification and retrieval: 'the technical structure of the archiving archive also determines the structure of the archivable content even in its very coming into existence and in its relationship to the future. The archivization produces as much as it records the event' (1996: 17). As such, the materialization of Rodinsky's room as an empty chamber, a room which is not merely empty but which points, Marie Celeste-like, to its own emptiness, becomes the emblem of the emptiness of the 'material vestige' and of the archive itself. It is full of its own emptiness.

The imperative of an age which is compelled 'not only to keep everything, to preserve every sign (even when we are not quite sure what it is that we are remembering) but also to fill archives' (Nora, 1996: 9) is already at work in Rodinsky's room when Lichtenstein arrives upon the scene. The logic of archive has already erased any trace of origin: 'The room no longer existed in its original state, as an abandoned tomb. The room had been dismantled, the contents boxed up by the Museum of London, then taken to storage rooms to dry out in stable conditions before being returned to the synagogue' (RR: 27). Lichtenstein, however, invests that logic with a religious force. Confronted by a text without any natural boundary – which literally runs up the walls in faded inscriptions on the wallpaper behind the door and is even inscribed on the piano – 'faint traces of pencil on the ivory keys: strange indecipherable symbols, written in his own hand' (RR: 27) – Lichtenstein becomes obsessed with the preservation and cataloguing of every slightest trace of Rodinsky's presence in the chamber. In the process, her fervour works a strange transformation upon the objects she collects (archivization produces as much as records the event) such that marks which should naturally be understood in terms of simple use value once touched by emptiness take on a fetish quality: 'In the centre of the wooden ceiling was a rusty gas lamp, surrounded by a charcoal halo from constant use… The floorboards were bent and cracked next to the enamel sink where I presumed he had washed every day' (RR: 27).[2]

---

[2] One of these traces will eventually be recuperated in the narrative economy. In the final paragraph of Lichtenstein's 'Afterword' to the 2000 edition, she writes: 'Just before we left the grounds Monty invited us all to wash our hands. He explained the significance of this for those who did not know: "The ritual act of cleansing our hands symbolizes our resolve to improve ourselves and our lives, and to put thoughts of death and decay behind us." Then he said to me: "You have set him free, now it is time to move on."' (RR: 339)

Lichtenstein and noise as redemption

In Lichtenstein's fetishization of the trace, we see how the severance of any organic link between present and past, the loss of those 'ideologies that once smoothed the transition from past to future' (Nora 1996: 2), effectively sets in train a binary logic for the arbitration of worth. Either everything is worth saving or nothing is worth saving. In the absence of any ritual or narratological means of determining what from the past should be preserved, we enter a world structured by the polarities of archive and ash, total recall or total annihilation.

In Lichtenstein's text, those polarities are literalized in the comedy of the rubbish bags: 'A large amount of Rodinsky's clothes, saucepans, shoes and other personal items were thrown away. I arrived one day to find them bagged up on the street, and sneaked them back upstairs' (RR: 28). The shuffling to and fro of garbage bags measures the ontological gulf between the sacred and the profane that must be subsumed within the archive. In a world without saints, everything has the potential to be a contact relic: even a bus ticket can be sacred. Indeed, *Rodinsky's Room* archives this principle in the form of the legend of the *lamed vavnik* which Lichtenstein learns is,

> a pre-Hasidic myth about the thirty-six righteous men who always live in this world. Their good deeds stop the world from being destroyed. Their power rests on the fact that no one knows who they are or where they live. They do their work in secret and are not rewarded. When they die another is born. (RR: 242)

Or, in Sinclair's take on the same myth: 'any spittle-flecked ranter might be a millennial messenger' (RR: 196).

The comedy of the garbage bags reveals too the intimate association of theology and epistemology, for if we do not know which questions to put to the archive because we do not understand the nature of the mysteries it contains, anything and everything could turn out to be the 'vital' clue (with the implication too that the archive always harbours evidence of crimes yet undiscovered). In both its theological and forensic aspects in principle, the archive insists that nothing is immaterial.

As such the archive confronts us with the problem of interpretation, of how to make sense of this compendium born out of the fear of forgetting.

Lichtenstein's response to this problem of reading is essentially Modernist in its combination of the theological and epistemological. In the fragmented text of Rodinsky's room, she sees the absence of a human figure and consequently she attempts to make sense of that absence by restoring the missing figure in the form of an authorial intention. After immersing herself in Rodinsky's poly-lingual text which seems Joycean in its range, stretching from Irish drinking songs to transcribed jingles, she concludes: 'It was my belief that he was trying to write a book on the structure of language itself' (RR: 98). In so doing, perhaps inevitably, Lichtenstein invokes the trope of prosopopoiea: 'Gradually, over time, through careful examination of his vast collection, a faint image of a man began to emerge: a scholar harbouring secrets, a meticulous annotator of texts, a comedian, an enigma' (RR: 28). And once invoked, the logic of prosopopoiea is invincible: no sooner has she endowed the absent with a face then she feels its gaze upon her neck: 'More often than not the cold, or the overwhelming sensation of being watched, would drive me out of the room, with the hairs on the back of my neck prickling. But every day I would be back at the table, fascination overcoming fear' (RR: 28). The trope closes the circuit between the obsession with possessions and the sensation of possession.

Insofar as the archive lays upon the present, the obligation to preserve the past for the future, prosopopoiea is the trope of archival retrieval as J. Hillis-Miller suggests when he notes that '[r]eading is one major form of the responsibility the living have to the dead'. The archive confers upon the act of reading if not the giving of life, a strange kind of efficacy – the ability to animate the dead:

> For Plato, as for Yeats, such shades are able to keep in existence only because, so to speak, they have drunk the blood of language spoken by the living. They exist only so long as we go on giving them our blood in individual acts of reading and in individual acts of prosopopoeia, ascribing a face, a voice, and a personality to those inanimate black marks on the page. The moment no one, anywhere, is reading Plato, all the figures in his dialogues will die again. (1995: 74–5)

However, while the archive is predicated on this obligation of the living to the dead, the localization of that unified voice, the voice of the father, of the patri-archive, once it is inscribed in physical media and has surrendered itself to interpretation cannot survive its dispersal, no matter how often the garbage bags are taken back upstairs. As Kujundzic notes:

> Every archive has something of the jealous God. It imposes the keeping of the idiom, the name of the singular event, close to itself and one with itself. But, at the same time, the archival impulse requires inscriptions, writing, graphic traces and translation, in order to launch itself into historical and material existence. (2003: 174)

No unitary meaning can ever be recovered from the archive, and that is, in Derrida's psychoanalytic reading of the archive as the vehicle of monotheism, the crime, the repressed fact adduced by every bus ticket and annotated chocolate wrapper it contains.

In Lichtenstein's case however, the prosopopoiea uncovers not a face within the archive so much as a face upon the archive. She figures Rodinsky's features not from his writing but from his reading, suggesting that he has drawn his self-portrait in the passages he chooses to translate from an English-Hebrew dictionary (RR: 301). Rodinsky reveals himself through his transcriptions, his annotations, his movement across the texts of others. Rodinsky is less a voice than a diasporic trace across numerous dead and living languages. To embody that text, Lichtenstein believes it is necessary to trace it back to an origin, to go back to the place from where it came. Inevitably, it is in the journey back along the bloodline to Poland and the borders of the Ukraine that Lichtenstein confronts the logic of the archive in its full complexity.

For Lichtenstein, Poland is the product of the archive. As her plane descends she is physically assaulted by the memory of '[p]hotographs retrieved from cardboard boxes in Warsaw, Jerusalem, London and New York. Images that burn into the skull and cannot be erased' (RR: 204). Despite her resolve to 'experience Poland in the Nineties' (RR: 206), it is these images which define her vision of the country. As she joins two-dozen American Jewish academics for a conference and tour of Poland's Jewish sites, they travel the country looking out on a world seen entirely in terms of its missing Jews. So too, the Poles with whom she feels most comfortable are those that share that perception: 'Poles who feel the loss, who see the footsteps of the former Jews embedded into their streets, hear the whispers in their music, taste the remnants in their food' (RR: 211). Without that perception of absence, she reflects, 'we become invisible time travellers, our activities totally alien from the lives of the Poles we see through the rain-smeared windows of our bus'.

But in Poland too she confronts the ambivalence of the archive in the form of an unease at the relationship between industrialized murder and industrialized remembrance: 'For the first time I recognized that I was not alone in my obsessive pursuits but part of a worldwide phenomenon in my generation' (RR: 212). And although she welcomes that sense of community, there remains a constant sense of the incongruity of this 'horror tour' (RR: 227). She records her vision of the '[g]risly tourists, speeding through the sodden countryside, stopping to pay homage to the deserted sites of where our ancestors once lived'. The archival instinct becomes the focus of that unease: 'As we arrived at each site, most of the Americans would jump in front of the monuments, swapping cameras with each other, to catch on celluloid the moment of "being there". Warped tourism, horror snapshots' (RR: 233). The same bureaucratization of experience that structures the memory industry is also that which made the Holocaust possible. As Kujundzic notes, 'the first computer, the IBM-owned Holledrith machine, was first put to use on a grand scale for the systematic archivization of the European Jewry in rounding it up for the concentration camps' (2003: 178). So too the efficiency of Dutch bureaucracy is frequently cited as an explanation of the deportation of 107,000 of the 140,000 Dutch Jews. 'There is no archive fever without the threat of this death drive, this aggression and destruction drive,' suggests Derrida. As such 'archive fever verges on radical evil' (1996: 19–20).

Inevitably in a landscape understood primarily in terms of the mass graves lying just below its surface, the return to Poland is figured as a return of the repressed. But the return is double. As a return to the scenes of horror encoded in her own and Rodinsky's family histories, it is motivated by the need to remember and give names to the nameless victims of history – to lay ghosts to rest. But in returning to a Poland which seems to have been untouched by modernity, the affluent descendants of Poland's persecuted migrants sporting Nike trainers and free to travel where they please confront both the remoteness of the past and the possibility of its revenance. Looking out on the medieval landscape familiar to their ancestors 'the wooden houses, their yards teeming with chickens, and the peasant women at work in the fields' (RR: 229) – the Western tourists are also haunted by the spirit of anti-Semitism that this archivized landscape has seemingly preserved intact. A workman intrudes his presence between the travellers and the synagogue they want to explore: 'He was grinning inanely, pointing at us and asking, "Juden?"' (RR: 223) Because the archive does not allow the possibility of decay, because it preserves intact, it is the source of what Derrida terms the spectral (1994): in abolishing the division between past and future, it constantly confronts us with the possibility of the return of that which we had thought we had left behind.

Apart from the grinning spectre of a revenant anti-Semitism, Poland also serves as a reminder of the economy of memory. 'Yiddishkite is in vogue in Poland at present' (RR: 223), notes Lichtenstein while one woman from San Francisco aims to retrieve as much Judaica as possible from Eastern Europe to give as wedding presents: 'They should be in Jewish homes' (RR: 210). The irony of this aspect of Lichtenstein's encounter with the *lieux de mémoire* is suggested in Adorno and Max Horkheimer's poignant observation that '[t]he respect for something that has no market value and runs contrary to all feelings is experienced most sharply by the person in mourning, in whose case not even the psychological restoration of labor power is possible' (1972: 216). According to Adorno and Horkheimer, the functionalism of an exchange economy where worth is always measured in terms of value-for-another denies anything more than 'sentimental' value to those objects whose worth is known only to the mourner, for mourning 'becomes a wound in civilisation, asocial sentimentality, showing that it has still not been possible to compel men to indulge solely in purposeful behaviour' (1972: 216). Yet, as Lichtenstein discovers in Poland, the industrialization of mourning means that even the mourner must haggle in the market place. 'I had never been brave enough ... to walk away crossly from the rudeness of some of the Poles I met, who would treble the price of Jewish artefacts on a market stall or try and gain a fee for showing you around an old building that could have been your grandfather's home' (RR: 224).

Sinclair and the production of absence

In Poland Lichtenstein discovers that the *lieu de mémoire* is always already inscribed within the rationalized space of a functionalist economy – indeed it is a product of that economy. As his *Guardian* piece suggests, it is the relationship between the realms of memory and the realms of capital and their territorialization through narrative that interests Sinclair. He is less concerned with the absence of Rodinsky than with the creation of absence itself. Thus, he focuses on the strange alchemical process through which the impotency of a casual disappearance, 'unremarked and unremarkable', assumes the potency and (economic) power of the Invisible: an absence which can provide a motor for a particular kind of fiction – 'the occult fabulation of the zone that the Eighties demanded to justify a vertiginous inflation in property prices'. For Sinclair, Rodinsky's 'disappearance' thus signals more than the simple loss of the 'warmth of tradition, the silence of custom', it marks a further reconfiguration of a city which is constantly being remade through telling and selling, tale and retail.

In Sinclair's reading, Rodinsky's story marks a very particular instance in that general structural dislocation of temporality within a very specific locale – the zone that separates the financial centre of the City from the proletarian quarters in the East End – Whitechapel, the ghetto home to successive waves of Huguenot, Irish, Jewish and Bangladeshi immigrants. The emergence of Rodinsky's room is to be understood within the context of the shifting narrative topography of London which is itself to be understood within the framework of the more general economic context created by Thatcherism. As it plays out within the sphere of memory, the Thatcherite assault on notions of community – 'there is no such thing as society' – corresponds to the systematic destruction of *milieux de mémoire* in favour of *lieux de mémoire*. The reconfiguration of society in terms of consumption rather than production, the transformation of workers into consumers, paves the way for the commodification of memory, the creation of the past 'as the final colony in the American World Empire', as it is caricatured in *Dining on Stones* (DOS: 100).

Accordingly, Sinclair approaches Rodinsky's room in Princelet Street via his memories of working in the ullage cellar of Truman's Brewery on nearby Brick Lane in the 1970s. For a writer 'thirsty for stories', the ullage cellar 'was the ultimate resource, a living metaphor' (RR: 61). Sinclair's ullage cellar is in effect a proletarian Eden where the warmth of tradition takes the form of hammocks slung between the hot water pipes and the silence of custom is marked by the 'brewery bells' that let the plumbers know when to 'pop down the betting shop to catch the last race, before signing on for overtime'. It is here amidst the inefficiencies of a yet-to-be-rationalized, pre-Thatcherite, industry structured by collective labour agreements that the stories that constitute communal memory thrive. The brewery is in Nora's terms, a *milieu de mémoire*, a repository of the male lore of the East End. Within the interstices of its soon-to-be-archaic collective labour agreements are woven the collective memories of violence that mark a working-class community's relationship to the territory, turf and earth it occupies but does not own:

> They remembered nights of fire-watching, the bomb that landed in the Jewish burial ground, depositing shattered corpses on the roof of the gravedigger's shelter. They remembered everything about the war. There was a Ripper specialist who photographed with a plate camera, all the relevant sites. There were Cable Street marchers, pro and anti-Mosley. There were geezers who had made up the numbers with veteran gang boss Jack Spot, and honoured him for his raids on the blackshirts ... (RR: 63)

In this memory economy, the story of Rodinsky's room is conspicuous by its absence: in all the 'formless afternoons in the complementary bar', there was no mention of the vanishing caretaker of Princelet Street. It is not simply that the room had not been discovered, the room could not be discovered:

> This was an unrequired story.... Rodinsky was an empty space, a lacuna; that which was not to be uncovered, something sealed and forgotten.... He wasn't visible or invisible. He had neither presence nor absence. His story hadn't been formulated. It was too early to fit into the Spitalfields canon. It belonged to an era that had not yet been rediscovered, or reinterpreted. Like the ghetto itself, the floating zone between the City and the covert world of the East End, the myth was on ice. In limbo. Unactivated. With the reimagining of the area that the developers, the energy pirates, of the Eighties would enforce – the need to ground their presumptuous brochures in a neverworld of Huguenots, dancing Hasids, and blandly sinister Masonic serial killers – Rodinsky, his curious history and his spontaneous combustion, would be dragged into the light. (RR: 63–4)

Rodinsky's is an Eighties story; it forms part of the process through which Spitalfields is territorialized as a potential area of investment, the conversion of a zone of transit into an area with its own marketable identity. It is part of the process through which a number of synecdoches are unified in a proper name:

> I'd heard no mention of the tale in the Seventies – because it hadn't been formulated. Spitalfields was still an antiquarian conceit. The area, when I spoke of it was Whitechapel. Friends referred to 'Brick Lane' or 'Cheshire Street'. 'The market'. 'The bagel shop'. 'The back room of the Seven Stars'. (RR: 67)

No longer a place *of* immigration, Whitechapel reincarnated as Spitalfields becomes *about* immigration – literalized in the vague plans to turn No.19 Princelet Street into a 'museum of immigration and false memory' (RR: 8) but more spectacularly in the recreation of a 'Huguenot experience' in the Severs house in nearby Folgate Street. In place of rituals that assert the continuity of past and present, the Severs House sacralizes faux rituals which pointedly assert the lack of connection: ' "Leave ash be", says a warning note pinned to the side of the fireplace. "It's about what you have just missed." ' (RR: 10); where the paying guests 'don't know how they are expected to behave. They want to signal their appreciation that *they* understand, but they've been forbidden speech' (RR: 9). Rodinsky's disappearance thus becomes the means of transforming a zone of transit into a neighbourhood but a neighbourhood without community and a neighbourhood whose past has been manufactured, artificially arrested by blue plaques at a particular moment. As such, it is symptomatic of the wider vision of the city elaborated in Sinclair's work as simultaneously centripetal in its concentration of capital and centrifugal in its tendency to disperse and alienate communities. As Robert Bond notes, in this reading Rodinsky's story takes its place in the process analysed by Henri Lefebvre in which 'the urban core becomes a high quality consumption product for foreigners, tourists, people from the outskirts and suburbanites' (2005: 175).

> Composed. Contrived. Authenticated. Grant us a ghost in the attic, a broken weaver's loom, and we will do you a dozen kosher Georgian units, at 200k a throw, for the Far Eastern catalogue. Hong Kong bankers were buying up Heneage Street apartments, site unseen, before Chris Patten had got his dogs out of quarantine. (RR: 64)

At the same time, the original proletarian inhabitants of the urban core are displaced to the amnesia of the suburbs, the *banlieues de mémoire* – as part of the creation of a memory owning democracy whose relationship with the past is manufactured by the heritage industry.

As a re-immigrant, returning from the amnesia of the suburbs, Lichtenstein rescues Rodinsky's story from the heritage fables of property developers and reterritorializes it in the darkness of twentieth-century history. Critically, her possession of, and by, Rodinsky exposes the 'inappropriate and inconsequential rituals' (RR: 79) of complicit art, literally when she disrupts a performance in the synagogue which involves ripping up sacred texts left abandoned in the building: 'She snatched back the relics, thereby becoming part of the show' (RR: 79). Sinclair's own method however can best be described as an interrogation of the visual images and surfaces thrown up by the mimetic technology of the nineteenth century – Adorno and Horkheimer's 'sequence of instantaneous experiences which leave no trace' in order to uncover the traces which will allow for a different configuration of the archive.

Sinclair attempts to reveal the palimpsestic presence of Rodinsky in his room-as-archive by placing his story in relation to other ghostly presences in the narrative ecology of East London. He advertises his method in the opening paragraph of 'Witnessing Rodinsky': 'I pillaged legends, stole names (Swedenborg Gardens) back from their well-earned obscurity. Understood how men became places. How they could be recalled from the great dream, where proper human beings with birth certificates mingle with immortal fictions, with Sherlock Holmes, Fu Manchu, Dr Jekyll, Dr Mabuse and with the Golem of Prague' (RR: 61). This easy congress between fictional and historical ontologies is accomplished through the deconstruction of the paradigmatic – syntagmatic opposition in a technique which is both associative and metonymic.

One such trajectory begins with the wardrobe in a Danny Gralton photograph of Rodinsky's room which is perceived in its metaphorical aspect as the emblematic space of the refugee and an avatar of Rodinsky: 'part barrier, part entrance to a parallel dimension (the mirrored panels access the worlds-within-worlds aspect). Takes its place in the mythology of the Holocaust. The secret space that becomes a room for refugees' (RR: 69). From this room in which fugitives 'vanish into their clothes, as in a Magritte painting', he moves to David Hartnett's depiction of a fictional Jewish Ghetto in the novel *Black Milk*. He notes the thematic correspondence of a young woman who moves from being a detached observer into a participant and eventually a prisoner of the tale, before finally disappearing into a wardrobe and notes too the coincidence of the heroine's name: Rachel. But it is the cover picture which provides the link. The photo depicts a 'performance of a Rachel' standing against a brick wall located in the flat of the photographer, Marc Atkins. Atkins lives in the apartment of a former rabbi in another deactivated synagogue in nearby Heneage Street. A letter from the son-in-law of the rabbi arriving out of the blue informs him that he had met Rodinsky in that room in 1948 – the wall in the picture belongs to the room in which Rodinsky 'was seen for the last time' (RR: 73). Atkins, he notes, 'by whatever accident, had found the perfect location in which to photograph an absence' (RR: 74).

In this way, by concentrating on the analogous and the coincidental, Sinclair creates a web of stories and associations to reveal the presence of Rodinsky as absence in settings as unlikely as the stage set of Harold Pinter's *Caretaker* and Nicholas Roeg and Donald Cammell's *Performance*. David Rodinsky becomes Davies, Pinter's tramp – '[h]is consciousness stretches as far as the limits of the metropolitan imagination, to the outer edge of Rodinsky's *London A–Z*' (RR: 77) – modelled on the disappearance of Pinter's Ashkenazy uncle Judah. He becomes the legendary 'chat artist' David Litvinoff – whose silent presence connects the popular and gangland cultures of late-1960s London emblematized in Mick Jagger and James Fox's role reversal in Roeg's *Performance*. In David Livitnoff, the type of what John Sears terms the 'central modern myth, that of the unrecognised and now only posthumously acknowledged creative genius' (2005) Sinclair most clearly suggests the possibility with which *Rodinsky's Room* constantly flirts: that the text itself is haunted by the presence of an invisible third author for whom the other two simply act as scribe (Sears: 2005). It is a conceit which returns us to the problem of where to put *Rodinsky's Room* forcing us to recognize that the dramatic interest of the project lies in the structural tension between a narrative about the archive (Lichtenstein's text) and an archive of narrative, a compilation of anecdotes, a constellation of London's collective memory.

In the interleaving of these two texts, narrative and archive struggle continually to contain one another in a contest which breaks the bounds of the original text in which they are forced to cohabit. Within *Rodinsky's Room* itself, space is carefully apportioned: Sinclair gets the first word in the section significantly titled 'Rachel Lichtenstein in Place', and Lichtenstein concludes the first edition with 'David in Focus'. Sinclair, however, circumvents that perspective in *Dark Lanthorns* (1999) – the record of his walks along routes marked in Rodinsky's *London A-Z*. Lichtenstein then incorporates that text within the 'Afterword' to the second edition of *Rodinsky's Room*. Sinclair revisits the topic in the 2004 novel *Dining on Stones* and cameos Lichtenstein in the 2002 film *London Orbital*. As a tour guide to the Jewish East End, Lichtenstein effectively takes possession of the Rodinsky material. This compulsive return to Rodinsky's empty chamber, Sears suggests, 'acts as a metaphor for the apotropaic function of all symbolic repetitions, the warding off of death, its totemisation and reduction to something repeatable, therefore momentarily conquerable' (2005).

Ghost storage

In a note titled 'On the Theory of Ghosts' collected in the back pages of their *Dialectic of Enlightenment*, Adorno and Horkheimer identify a 'disturbed relationship with the dead – forgotten and embalmed – [as] one of the symptoms of the sickness of experience today' (1972: 215). This 'sickness' they attribute to the fact that '[i]ndividuals are reduced to a mere sequence of instantaneous experiences which leave no trace, or rather whose trace is hated as irrational, superfluous, and "overtaken" in the literal sense of the word'. They continue:

> What a man was and experienced in the past is as nothing when set against what he now is and has and what he can be used for. The well-meaning if threatening advice frequently given to emigrants to forget all their past because it cannot be transferred, and to begin a completely new life, simply represents a forcible reminder to the newcomer of something which he has long since learned for himself. (1972: 216)

Apart from the suggestion that modernity makes migrants of us all, the peculiarity and beauty of Adorno and Horkheimer's theoretical oddment is that it reverses the normal ontogeny of the haunted house. Whereas we might think that hauntedness marks the refusal of place to submit to the exigencies of function or the persistence of a certain spirit against the claims of the present,

Adorno and Horkheimer suggest rather that we are haunted because we live in a space that makes no provision for the dead. In what is in effect a materialist theory of the immaterial, they suggest that it is the unacknowledgeable despair at the rationalization of a space which subordinates everything to its own functionality that leads the living to summon up the dead. For the ghost is, in Adorno and Horkheimer's view, simply the manifestation of an anger at the reduction of experience to functionality which can never be articulated because it evades the categories of rationalized expression. As such, the problem of ghosts comes down to a problem of storage. A ghost story is a story not of possession but of possessions, of holding on and letting go.

In different ways, both Lichtenstein and Sinclair's accounts of Rodinsky's room represent elaborations on this problematic. Lichtenstein summons the dead out of a despair at a loss of 'tradition'. She wishes to preserve the room as an archive of that which it is impossible to remember historically. For her, as we have seen, the room becomes an emblem of Benjamin's 'tradition of the oppressed' (1969: 256): the tradition of those whose lives are excluded from the narrative of History; those whose lives, as such, constitute the noise of History as narrative. On one reading at least, this represents an ethics of the forgotten, an ethics which effectively installs the noise of History as an ultimate ethical horizon whose material form is the archive, an archive which is simultaneously coterminous with Benjamin's 'debris' (1955: 258) of History.

For Sinclair, however, the logic of redemption that informs this ethics culminates in the blue plaque memorials of the 'heritage industry' and 'blue plaques induce guilt, forcing us to remember those who might prefer to be forgotten. But we can't allow it. We want to hold them there, in place to give meaning to our own temporary existence' (RR: 6). Blue plaques exist, in other words, not to commemorate the dead but to shore up our own sense of identity, to mark out the narrative through which we give meaning to our lives. Blue plaques, as the sign of a cultural craving for origin and identity mark the refusal of *Nachträglichkeit*, the perception of the dynamic relation between present and past: that the 'dead moment only exists as we live it now' (WST: 112).

And, perhaps inevitably, given Adorno and Horkheimer's theory that the origin of ghosts lies in the instrumentalization and bureaucratization of space, it turns out that the explanation of Rodinsky's disappearance lies in a simple administrative error. The elevation of this tale of dereliction and urban alienation into a London legend it transpires rests on confusion about the status of Rodinsky's tenancy within the synagogue. His legend is the product of a misplaced social services file. Rodinsky, like his sister, Lichtenstein discovers, was eventually committed to a mental institution where he died after the community in which he 'made sense' had abandoned the East End for the suburbs, leaving his room as a small and incomprehensible piece of the Ukraine transplanted intact into London. 'The Rodinsky family did not successfully make the transition to the new world', she writes, '[t]heir attic room became a microcosm of the mystical world they had left behind, but in Whitechapel their sentiments were deeply misunderstood' (RR: 232). Rodinsky's secret thus proves to be that of Adorno and Horkheimer's modern migrant – he was simply unable to leave the past behind. As Sinclair writes:

> And then, very gradually it breaks on us: the room *is* the drama. Rodinsky will never appear. There is nothing he could say. He is an absence. He doesn't belong in his own story. The incontinent clutter of things, uncollectable sub-antiques, displaces his consciousness. He is represented by whatever has survived his disappearance. The room is the map of a mind that anyone capable of climbing the stairs can sample. Rodinsky's life has been sacrificed to construct a myth, mortality, ensuring immortality. (RR: 174)

5

Roadworks: Orbiting the Orison

The symbolic function of the road in Sinclair's work is indicated in a memorably condensed fashion in the opening pages of *White Chappell, Scarlet Tracings* when the narrator's fellow second-hand book dealer and travelling companion, Dryfeld, begins a discourse on toads and motorways:

> 'If the A1 had anticipated itself, Darwin would never have had to leave these shores. It's all here, Monsieur. Only the fittest and most insanely determined life forms can battle across the river of death to reach the central reservation – but then, ha! They are free from predators. They live and breathe under the level of the fumes. They stay on the grass spine, leave the city, or the sea-coast, escape, feral cats and their like, and travel the country, untroubled, north to south. The lesser brethren die at the verges. And are spun from our wheels, flung to the carrion. Grantham's daughter, this is your vision'. (WST: 12)

While it is unlikely that Margaret Thatcher would have recognized her 'vision' in Dryfeld's riff, Friedrich Hayek, one of the principal sources of her economic theory, would almost certainly have agreed with this identification of the relationship between (social) Darwinism and the operation of the free-market mechanism which achieves efficiency through its disposal of the weak and superfluous. For Hayek, free-market capitalism, insofar as it constituted a self-organizing system, was at the most basic level a 'natural' mode of economic organization whose operational logic was replicated throughout the natural world and could even embrace the relationship of toads and motorways (Hayek 1978; Hunt and McNamara 2007). Alan Marshall commenting on the development of the 'Economy-Ecology' analogy in postmodern science notes that this thesis has received even more extreme statements by Robert Ayres and Michael Rothschild who, taking this argument to its logical conclusion, '[regard] capitalism as an inevitable, natural state of human economic affairs.

Being for or against a natural phenomenon is a waste of time and mental energy' (2001: 142).

As such, Sinclair presents us here with an image of a contradiction which runs throughout liberal thought as it is manifest in the concept of noise. Where liberalism conventionally looks to the road as a symbol of the free circulation of goods and information, Dryfeld's commentary indicates that it is as a barrier, or a 'river of death', that its true function within (neo)liberal thought is revealed. It is only through the discipline of the market, through a submission to its ruthless efficiencies, that we will reach the promised land. The promised land, however, Dryfeld's analogy suggests, will resemble not so much a garden as the everywhere and nowhere, the no-place, of the central reservation. The road leads only to its own unresolved spaces.

The passage occupies a totemic position in Sinclair's oeuvre. As the opening scene of *White Chappell, Scarlet Tracings*, it marks Sinclair's shift from poetry to fiction and his narrator's transition from assistant gardener to second-hand book dealer, a change in career which reflects Sinclair's own move from his position as small-press owner and temporary labourer to book dealer specializing in the works of the American 'beat' writers. In this move from the production to distribution of literature, Sinclair's career change mirrors the wider structural and ideological changes in the British economy. As he remarked in a lecture at Birkbeck in 2011, the world of the council gardeners commemorated in *Lud Heat* had vanished when he returned the following year. The Park Department had been outsourced; the permanent staff disbanded; and all their knowledge and experience had been lost.[1] In swapping his socialized lifestyle of communitarian production for that of a traveller and trader in used goods, Sinclair is in step with the tenor of the times: the suggestion attributed to Employment Secretary Norman Tebbit, that in Thatcher's Britain the unemployed should 'get on their bikes' to search for work identifies mobility as a key element in the economic formula of neoliberalism, and with it, the road.

---

[1] 'The sad thing was that we returned a year after we left and we went back to the hut but there was nobody there, there was one person who said well it's all been rationalized and we've all been let go and there's going to be gardeners coming in from the outside. And at that moment you recognize this sense of place and sense of, however grudging and bitter it was about what they were doing, the sense of responsibility for keeping a landscape beautiful and alive, was gone for good, and the people that came in just blasted away like industrial cleaners and then were off in the van and away' (Sinclair and Boal 2011).

The dynamics of the new economic reality is captured in the company of book dealers described in *White Chappell* who join forces to raid provincial bookshops but keep their information and discoveries secret from each other. As dealers or brokers, they are emblematic of the parasitic economy of the middlemen who make their living through establishing connections between the consumer and the consumed: they produce goods not through labour but out of the back of a car, and as such, are the central figures in an information economy where money is made literally on the road. The road as that which separates and connects becomes the locus of value production in a post-industrial economy, and, as Brian Baker notes, roads are central to most of Sinclair's work from this period, providing the narrative continuity in his novels in the absence of plot (2007: 162–3), and in his non-fiction projects, it is the road that provides the immediate focus of the *London Orbital* project and his account of following the journey up the Great North Road out of Essex taken by peasant poet John Clare in 1841. Consequently, it is the road as the locus of noise that will be explored in this chapter.

The politics of bus stops

The *London Orbital* project, which, in addition to the film and book of that name, can also be extended to include the novel *Dining on Stones* (2004), is intimately linked with Sinclair's hostility to the Millennium Dome (now the O2 Arena). The inspiration for the walk around the M25, Sinclair explains, 'started with the Dome' and '[a]n urge to walk away from the Teflon meteorite on Bugsby's marshes' (LO: 4). An account of his motorway walk consequently must begin with an examination of his critiques of the 'Teflon hedgehog' which, having begun in an article commissioned by the *London Review of Books*, were then bundled in the pamphlet *Sorry Meniscus* (1999) and were later reprised in the opening section of *London Orbital*.

His critique of the Dome is important too because it is one of the points in his text where his voice seems indistinguishable from the more general chorus of disapproval directed at the government's determination to waste money on 'the most expensive tent in the universe' (SM: 23) and as such a point where his text seems closest to the reactionary grumblings more 'usually associated with the *Daily Telegraph*' noted by MacFarlane (2005: 4) and the generalized abhorrence of modernity that Heartfield decries as 'Londonostalgia'. Inevitably Sinclair's rhetoric in these pieces chimes with the general chorus of disapproval within the press and national media. However, despite the fact that the financial mismanagement, organizational chaos and lack of coherent vision surrounding the Dome and the 'Millennium Experience' provided an obvious target for general criticism and satire, Sinclair's writing on the subject encodes important elements of his broader critique of neoliberal urbanism.

For Sinclair the significance of the Dome lies less in its exemplary function as a waste of public resources than its function as a symbol of the essential continuity between Tory and New Labour visions of the city. As a Tory project the Dome could be derided as 'a pointless but vaguely patriotic symbol sprayed over with cheer-leader slogans' another exercise in the 'happy-clappy imperialism' familiar from earlier Tory injunctions to 'rejoice' and celebrate Britishness (SM: 19). The fact that Tony Blair's New Labour government took over the already derided project when it took power in 1997 effectively transformed the Dome into an emblem of the underlying continuity of the ideological assumptions of Tory and New Labour. As an expression of New Labour values the Dome is far more sinister than in its original incarnation as 'a classic Tory scam' (SM: 16) for it comes to symbolize Labour's endorsement of the neoliberal premise that the market represents the ultimate horizon of politics. It becomes, in effect, a symbol of the post-political condition: an emblem of a general loss of faith in politics and democracy.

In its staging of the city, the Dome represents a repartitioning of the sensible that erases the noise of politics. Under New Labour management, the Dome typifies a neoliberal concern with what David Harvey terms the 'entrepreneurial city' (1989a), in that it promotes the city as a place to do business within the global network of investors rather than concentrating on the immediate needs of its inhabitants. As such it is a 'folly that would soak up funds that would otherwise be wasted on keeping electoral promises, restoring schools and hospitals' (SM: 37). Further, it marks the imposition of a virtual city upon the concerns of the actual: 'What we could all use is another bridge, another tunnel, but that's not on the New Labour agenda. Too expensive, too much hassle. Too heavy, too Soviet. Too ... pedestrian' [ellipsis in original] (SM: 21).

Consequently Sinclair's immediate strategy in *Sorry Meniscus* is to juxtapose the vision of the Dome with the practical realities of moving through the physical space of the city. 'It was the vision in the brochures that counted, virtual reality. The world as it should be, if only we could believe' (SM: 34). Deciding to see whether it is possible to reach the Dome by public transport from within London, he leaves Hackney for Greenwich: 'The Millennium urban Experience copywriters spoke with breath-taking self-confidence of a "twelve-minute" ride from the centre of town' (SM: 53). However, the Docklands Light Railway (another public-private partnership) leaves him stranded at a bus stop in Cross Harbour on the Isle of Dogs where,

> A couple of old ladies, huddled against the cruel zephyrs and down draughts that swept through this Blade Runner architecture, remarked 'You see plenty of those bleeders', as yet another empty link-bus met the train. Meanwhile they were left waiting, half an hour or more, for the standard Island-inhabitants' cattle-carrier. (SM: 58)

The snatch of conversation records in cameo form the spatial division produced by neoliberal urbanism. As city administrations devote their energies to improving the city's competitiveness in the global market where Sassen's 'global cities' compete for investment capital, large sections of the population are confronted not only with their political disenfranchisement but with the fragmentation of urban space. The redirection of funds away from service provision to entrepreneurial initiatives effectively leaves Londoners who are reliant on the public sphere stranded at bus stops.

The result is a city structured around two types of space. There is the city addressed to the space of international capital, where link buses shuttle between sites valorized by the language of public-private investment, while the local population inhabit a series of unprofitable spaces which are increasingly discrete and unconnected. It is a spatialization of the city which, in Sinclair's hyperbolic account transforms the former Imperial metropolis into a version of its colonial Other: 'The question becomes: is it possible to reach the Dome by public transport without help from Thomas Cook, a limitless budget and a posse of native guides' (SM: 67).

The strategy of investment in prestigious projects that will increase the city's international competitiveness, creates a space which is fractured not only in terms of its interconnections with other areas within the city, but which also confronts the population with its disenfranchisement from the space of the neoliberal city which is traversed by systems to which they have no access:

> The others on the platform live there. A gang of youths, confident in the non-appearance of anything resembling a train, take off down the tracks. And they are right. Masked carriages stacked with nuclear waste or whatever, rattle through at high speed, but passenger trains are a rumour. There is only speaking in tongues feedback from the public address system. The occasional word could be picked out of the acoustic froth....At the end of the last century it was possible to get into the City in about ten or twelve minutes by train or tram. Now there are only mobs waiting for phantom buses. There's a culture of waiting. Coming down from Lewisham to Greenwich, I discovered people whose lives were based around the time spent at bus stops. They reminisced, they kvetched. They discussed various ailments and fantasised on their chances of ever reaching a doctor's surgery or out-patient's clinic. And then they went home. (SM: 68–9)

This culture of waiting, of waiting for buses and waiting for the temporary disruption of public space to be restored is, Sinclair implies, permanent for it is precisely the space of discrepancy engendered by neoliberal visions of urban regeneration: the space which fails to live up to the reality presented in the 'lap top fantasy' and the promotional brochure.

> We are being asked to endure the noise, dust, pollution of a 24-hour building site, as vindication for the heavenly pleasure park that is, just, around the corner. It's a long just: long enough to give the advertisers and image-enhancers time to whet our appetites, convince us that this Disneyland trade show is something we can't do without. Meanwhile, we must tolerate railways that don't work, public roads with private security barriers, river paths that run up against plywood fences, naked dirt from horizon to horizon, and a quadraphonic Serbian soundtrack. (SM: 52–3)

As Guy Baeten (2007) has noted, the identification of civic failure with the moral failure of the underclass is central to neoliberal strategies of urban regeneration. Merijn Oudenampsen (2007) addressing what he terms the 'city renovation yo-yo' notes that areas designated for regeneration are first identified in terms of urban blight as symptomatic of urban dysfunction, as empty of viable economic activity and or social coherence and then, '[o]nce the necessary mental space for radical intervention has been created, the new plans are presented in which special emphasis is placed on the area's wonderful economic opportunities'. As a result '[a]n almost obligatory element in plans for urban renewal has become the SWOT [Strength, Weakness, Opportunity, Threat] analysis, in which the location is unquestioningly seen as strength and the population as weakness' (2007: 121).

A consequence of this dystopian/utopian yo-yo is that the reality of under-investment in infrastructure, the failure of the post-regeneration city can also be identified with the moral failure/weakness of the population. The city's failure is imputed to the individual's unwillingness to embrace risk, to live for the future, to realize their true potential as human beings. As Sinclair notes '[i]t was the vision in the brochures that counted, virtual reality. The world as it should be, if only we could believe' (SM: 34). If reality seemed to suggest otherwise, this was because of a failure to believe, a failure of vision, a failure to see: 'The blue river. The orchards. The gardens' (SM: 34):

> Reality, out there, was always in need of a little cosmetic enhancement. Design buffs on the Millennium Experience payroll see the sorry isthmus with its muddy horizons, its earth-movers and excavators, its razor-wire fences and surveillance cameras, as an Arcadian grotto. They have no problem with deferred pleasure, they read the future like a transcendent comic strip. Old Thames is rejuvenated in a Mediterranean blue. There are avenues of potential trees, future forests. Docklands is a garden city, clean, broad-avenued, free of traffic, and peopled entirely by vibrant ink spots. (SM: 47–8)

However, in the Dome, Sinclair recognizes something more than just another exercise in the neoliberal strategy of urban regeneration. In Sinclair's reading, it exemplifies the tension between market and creativity that lies at the heart of the reconfiguration of civic government in the global context. It symbolizes the hubris of a system which believes that it can eliminate the excluded, that fails to recognize the necessity of the hidden. The significance of the Dome is connected to its site. Where the 'Millennium Experience' brochurists impose their laptop fantasies on Greenwich, he claims that earlier generations recognized the necessity of such waste land. Thus nineteenth-century colourists baulked at Bugsby's Marshes. The swamp defied their imagination. Its karma was too terrible. They knew the story and knew that any proper human settlement needed its back country, its unmapped deadlands. The Peninsula was where the nightstuff was handled: foul-smelling industries, the manufacture of ordnance, brewing, confectionery, black smoke palls and sickly sweet perfumes. (SM: 48)

As such, Bugsby's marshes give topographical expression to the wrong which Rancière places at the heart of the polis. It is the spatial equivalent of the necessary miscount.

> The Peninsula thrives on secrecy. For as long as anyone can remember much of this land has been hidden behind tall fences. Walkers held their breath and made a wide circuit. Terrible ghosts were trapped in the ground. A site on the west of the Peninsula, now captured by the Teflon-coated fabric of the Dome, had once featured a gibbet where the corpse of some pirate, removed from Execution Dock in Wapping, would be left to decay. (SM: 49)

The choice of this site for a faux celebration of all that is best about Britain symbolizes the hubris of Blair's vision of Britain where image is all that matters and the reality of the site and its cultural memory can be discounted without a second thought. In this the Dome symbolizes the wider logic of capital: the transformation of places with their own specific associations and memories into what Marc Augé (1995) termed 'non-places', the anonymous functional spaces of hypermodernity. The Dome performs this logic in that it is, in Sinclair's account literally all surface: the notorious struggles to find a content for the 'Millennium Experience' exemplify the tendency to reconfigure place as a content-less space. Having created an artificial structure in the middle of a wilderness, any content will itself be pure surface, inescapably simulacral.

The Dome's displacement of content to surface also mirrors the more general process of displacement attendant on the spatial logic of neoliberalism in which Londoners are pushed out of the increasingly spatially fragmented city and into the homogeneity and anonymity of the suburbs and dormitory towns that surround the metropolis, losing in the process access to the multiple narratives and associations of the city and the possibility of the chance encounter which constitute the positive noise of the metropolitan life.

The London Orbital or M25 motorway epitomizes this process. It is emblematic of Augé's no-place and is intended to facilitate the depopulation of the metropolis by making the city more accessible to the towns beyond its perimeter. In walking the M25, then, Sinclair is in his own terms carrying out a form of exorcism. By recovering a sense of place for this non-place, he intends to counter the 'vampiric' logic of neoliberalism which transforms place into space by erasing, denying and repressing cultural memory.

The road as parasite

If the M25 typifies the non-place of Augé's supermodernity, the place which is *in* but not *of* its place, it also forms a perfect *habitus* for Michel Serres' parasite whose position is 'to be between', which, having its being in relation, is most at home in those spaces which seek to efface their intermediality. For Serres, as we have seen, whether in information theory, biology or social relations, the parasite interferes with and upsets an existing set of relations and thereby provokes some form of reaction or response which ultimately stimulates the further transformation of the organism or system. In their study of new media development, Jay Bolter and Robert Grusin (2000) extend this insight into a principle of technological causality. It is entirely possible, they demonstrate, to write the history of new media in terms of successive attempts to overcome the noise of mediation – every new form of media attempts to deliver greater immediacy by eliminating the noise, or mediality, of that which it replaces. The same logic applies even more directly to road-building, for insofar as new roads are built when old roads no longer serve their purpose, the driving force of the parasite as noise is seldom more evident than in road-building programmes.

Like all motorways then, the M25 is conceived as an empty channel of communication, its function as medium is to facilitate the movement of travellers and goods with optimum efficiency from point *a* to point *b*. As Sinclair notes in his attention to the road's 'acoustic footstep' (LOf),[2] it is also a perfect expression of pure mediality: a channel of communication designed,

---

[2] '[A]coustic footsteps are what the road planners call the distance from which you can hear the motorway … and the motorway planners have the right to plant as far back as the acoustic footsteps stretch' (LOf).

to erase all traces of its own presence. Sinclair's 'project of restitution', in walking the M25 involves restoring a sense of place to this non-place by paying attention to its noise. By walking the '[d]ull fields that travellers never notice' (LO: 16) he aims to reinscribe this archetypal interstitial highway within a detailed cultural and topographical locale and thereby to discover within the M25 as non-place a place which is neither local nor global. Given that all roads are, to a greater or lesser degree, noisy, and that the characteristic of non-place is its aspiration to global uniformity, the difficulty of Sinclair's project lies in hearing the noise of this particular road.

That particularity, his walk reveals, is to be found in the road's symbolic resonance, its ideological content as a speech act. As Sinclair's detailed cultural history makes clear, the M25 was a project conceived as an affirmation of the Modernist faith in the future but which carried an entirely different ideological message on its completion in 1986. For a government intent on restricting the role of government to the removal of obstacles to social and commercial mobility, the road, and road-building embodied the neoliberal political project.[3] It is no coincidence that whereas Harold Wilson's 'white heat' of technology delivered Concorde, Margaret Thatcher's vision of a car-owning democracy ensured that the M25 and the Channel Tunnel would be foremost in her governments' civil engineering legacy. As a means of releasing the creative potential of a society held in stasis by outmoded political and social identities, the M25 perfectly mirrors the neoliberal conception of government, existing for the sole purpose of facilitating free movement.[4]

Indeed, insofar as it is intended to stimulate the circulation of goods and people necessary for the efficient operation of a free market, the road can even be said to replace the political machinery of democratic representation with the far more immediate mode of self-representation that, in neoliberal thought, is played by the free market. The M25 is, in effect, the public space of neoliberalism. As the host of one of the phone-ins featured so prominently in the film's sound track points out 'every one of you, every last one of you, will at

---

[3] As Joe Moran notes, Thatcher's 'consistent support for what she called "the great car economy" was based on a strong association between road-building and entrepreneurialism' (2005: 96).

[4] 'Neoliberalism is in the first instance a theory of political economic practices that proposes that human well-being can best be advanced by liberating entrepreneurial freedoms and skills within an institutional framework characterized by strong private property rights, free markets, and free trade. The role of the state is to create and preserve an institutional framework appropriate to such practices' (Harvey 2005: 2).

some time have been on the M25' (LOf) and, as an irate lorry-driver reiterates, 'everything you touch in your house has been transported by truck at some stage of the game, if there was no lorry drivers out there this country would come to a [fade]' (LOf). The idea of the traveller as a postmodern everyman provides the perfect expression of the neoliberal assault on occupation- or location-based identities. It encapsulates a world where workers have become consumers, and rail-passengers are interpellated by station tannoys as 'customers'. The psephological consequences of this shift in representation are revealed in New Labour's identification of 'Mondeo man' as the key to electoral success after 'old' Labour's defeat in the 1992 general election.[5] In consciously shifting its notional demographic away from the inner cities of the urban poor to the newly affluent constituencies surrounding the M25, Labour recognized that electoral success meant it could no longer be seen as the party of the poor. It abandoned a politics of location for one of aspiration based, as Joe Moran points out, on a car whose name is a 'made-up word meant to sound like "world" in several languages', and which was, in fact, 'one of the first cars to be conceived as a truly global product' (2005: 103).

However, as those radio phone-ins make clear, by 2001, the M25 has come to signify not greater mobility but the constant frustration of traffic jams and congestion. It has delivered not increased personal freedom but a new kind of boredom: 'More than other motorways the M25 is designed to test thresholds of boredom. It eliminates any romantic notion of boredom, but for the addicted it has its attractions, it is mainline boredom, it is true boredom, a quest for transcendental boredom' (LOf). What should have been an empty channel for better communication has become pure noise. Indeed, the phone-ins (themselves, another legacy of the Thatcherite liberalization of the airwaves, and hence the public sphere) point the same lesson: instead of liberating creative potential by increasing the opportunities for communication they have become a forum for reflecting on the failure of the road as a medium of better communication. Their constant message is 'it's not working' (LOf).

---

[5] The phrase has its origins in a speech given by Tony Blair at the 1996 Labour Party conference: 'I met a man polishing his Ford Sierra. He was a self-employed electrician. His dad always voted Labour, he said. He used to vote Labour, too. But he'd bought his own house now. He'd set up his own business. He was doing quite nicely. "So I've become a Tory", he said .... In that moment, he crystallised for me the basis of our failure, the reason why a whole generation has grown up under the Tories. People judge us on their instincts about what they believe our instincts to be. His instincts were to get on in life. And he thought our instincts were to stop him' (qtd. Moran 2005: 102–3).

What the M25 teaches, consequently, is not simply that it is impossible to build an empty road, but that Serres' maxim that 'where there are channels, there must be noise' (LOf) has profound ideological implications. Sinclair's *London Orbital* project is in effect an attempt to fathom the political implications of that lesson, for insofar as the pure mediality of the M25 reflects the neoliberal emphasis on government's own function as a form of pure mediality, its intent to simply remove the obstacles preventing individuals from fulfilling their economic and social potential, the failure of the M25 will tell us something about the failures, or parasitic dynamic – the cracks in the mirror – within the neoliberal project.

The parasitic dynamic of the M25 is starkly revealed in the apocalyptic backdrop to Sinclair's project in the form of the 2001 foot and mouth crisis. Built to facilitate the unrestricted circulation of goods and people, the motorway network has enabled the centralization of livestock slaughter. However, through the centralization of livestock slaughter, the motorway network is also instrumental in transforming an outbreak of foot and mouth disease in Northumberland into a national epidemic which results in the slaughter of seven million sheep and cattle and the effective closure of the countryside to tourism, thereby removing the countryside as a commodity from the circulation of goods. Liberalization, in other words, requires unprecedented levels of state intervention and the effective closure of the national transport system. As such these apocalyptic images identify the motorway as the site of a fundamental ambiguity within the ideology of the free market: the knowledge that the free circulation of goods and people also facilitates the free circulation of disease – that the road is both the bringer of life and of death. Encoded within the mythology of the road is the idea that the principle of the free market disrupts the conceptual landscape of internal and external, inner and outer, us and them: the road as the place of the parasite opens the way to alien invasion, but it reveals that the alien is already within the system. As an emblem of all the ambivalences aroused by the idea of the free market itself, the M25 becomes in effect a site of the mediality repressed by the neoliberal abolition of the political: it marks the recognition that a free market does not decrease the power of the state but paradoxically necessitates an even stronger state to police the freedoms it institutes.

Again Serres' account of the parasite is instructive in elucidating the chiasmic logic at work in the ambivalences generated by the road and how they relate to the apparent paradox through which the desire for the unmediated representation of the free market should result in increased, rather than diminished, levels of security and control. For Serres, we have seen, any dialogue is predicated on an agreement to exclude the noise of the media that makes the dialogue possible: 'To hold a dialogue is to suppose a third man and to seek to exclude him; a successful communication is the exclusion of the third man' (1982: 67). Rather than a supplement or obstacle to communication, the parasite as noise is the enabling condition of communication. But it is also clear that in the agreement to exclude, this model of communication is the obverse of that invoked by Jürgen Habermas as the basis of communication within the public sphere which is predicated on the notion of universal inclusion (1989). Following Serres' logic, we can say that in Habermas's model of the public sphere it is the idea of exclusion itself which is excluded. One is constituted as a member of the public by entering a space which is defined by the principle that no one can be excluded and as such it is the knowledge of exclusion which is repressed, which if acknowledged would dissolve the public sphere. In this respect, the M25 in problematizing the notion that a free society should be open to all is very noisy. It becomes in effect a figure for the problematic relationship of inclusion and exclusion within the politics of neoliberalism. Within the film, this is signalled through the mixture of roadside footage from Afghanistan with that of the M25, to indicate the road's inscription within a global economy of oil. Given that this is an exercise in psychogeography, however, the logic of the repressed should be sought not at the level of manifest content but in the project's formal meditation on the principles of exclusion and noise. The *London Orbital* project explores the M25's noise through its own noise, its own mediality.

To theorize the noise of the road, in other words, is not to represent it. If Sinclair's project as an exercise in cultural history provides a general map of the ideological contours of the M25, as a textual event, it registers the road's noise through attention to its own mediality – by foregrounding the noise of his own project in order to reveal how his own strategies of representation are implicated within those transforming the wider political culture. Typically, the mediality of the *London Orbital* project, like most of Sinclair's other projects is foregrounded by its exploration of the nature of textual boundaries. It challenges any naive notion of representation through an insistence on its own mediality through its constant invocation to a missing object: the walk.

Sinclair highlights the *nachträglich* function of the walk as the absent origin within his poeisis in his observation that '*[w]here* a road goes informs every inch of it' (LO: 46), for '*Where*' Sinclair's road goes is, of course, into his notebooks: the final destination of his walk is always the text. But, in accordance with the logic of *Nachträglichkeit*, and despite his admonitions against 'wankers spouting Baudrillard, Derrida, flannel about flâneurs' (DOS: 87), its end is also (always-already) its occasion, for the text is both the walk's destination and its point of departure – its motivation. In the case of the *London Orbital* walk, however, the road has at least two destinations, two texts: the book published in 2002 and the film, made jointly with Chris Petit, also released in 2002, both titled, *London Orbital*. This doubled destination effectively doubles the road. What Petit terms the 'split nature of the project' is reflected in the split screen format of the movie, a doubling which, apart from demonstrating a seemingly natural affinity between the pairings film/driving and writing/walking, doubly emphasizes the irretrievable nature of the event that serves as a putative original: 'the more polished the paragraph the less I trusted the memory' (LOf). *London Orbital*'s status as a film haunted by a book or a book haunted by a film of a road haunted by its destination establishes the buzz of mediality as a constant background noise within the texts.

To take one small example, the barking dog woven into the film's opening soundscape finds a referent in the book where we read, 'I heard a sound, a howling, that was to be one of the defining characteristics of my motorway walk: the chorus of the boarding kennels. Domestic animals are dumped out on the fringes where their din will cause least offence' (LO: 15). The interplay between film and book enacts, in this case, the drama of the M25 as an acoustic event – it registers the place of the motorway in the social economy of noise. We need the book to hear the dog's bark as message rather than noise, but it is the film that actually allows us to hear the howling.

Serres effectively describes the topology of this intertextual zone in detail in his example of somebody leaving a conversation at the dinner table to answer the telephone. Telephone and table constitute two distinct noise/message systems, he points out. It is Serres' stochastic region 'on the edges of messages, at the birth of noises' (2007: 67) in which we are located by the intertextuality and intermediality invoked by Sinclair. Adopting the language generated by the road itself, we might say that each text, book and film takes place within the other's 'acoustic footprint', each version constantly sounds the exclusion of its Other. The film quotes the book as the book annotates the film, and together they invoke the road as itself the primary figure of selection – this path of all possible paths – whose silenced Other is to be found in those '[d]ull fields that travellers never notice' (LO: 16).

As the interview with Sinclair and Petit included among the DVD extras makes clear, these versions of the walk as an absent event inhabit very different niches within the cultural ecosystem. Whereas the book, 'which comes out quite attractively from Penguin is able to sell quite large numbers of copies' (Sinclair and Petit 2002a), the film, 'as far as television is concerned … may as well not exist' (2002a). It survives in the interstices of the TV schedules, airing only in the small hours of the morning with the result that 'nobody knows whether they've watched it: it comes along at a point where you are either asleep or drunk, or you have maybe stayed up and seen a bit of it and then fallen asleep … it ceases to be discrete imagery and becomes part of this mindstream of nocturnal television' (2002a). Sinclair attributes the different fortunes of the film and the book to an effect of cultural *Nachträglichkeit*: 'I think this film was a very accurate reflection of what the M25 itself is, which is wholly posthumous, because when that road was opened in 1986 it was too late and people imagined it being opened in 1956 which is really where it belonged and the film is rather the same: it is something that exists in another era, doesn't belong now and people don't really know what it is, and it has no place' (2002a). The road can no longer be seen, he suggests, because it exists as spectacle within another era, it belongs to the Modernist city, the city of boulevards. As a medium, or emblem of pure mediality, the road is invisible: it exists as a site of the repressed, flowing seamlessly into the 'mindstream of nocturnal television'.

Given that there is, then, a very real problem in representing the M25 – in making the viewer see the M25 rather than *just* a motorway, it is not surprising that it is the film rather than the book that offers the greatest scope for reflection on its own mediality, and Chris Petit's self-reflexive discussion of his problems in determining the nature of his subject provides an extended meditation on the nature of the mediation represented by the motorway. In his narrative, Petit effectively articulates the problem confronting every reader of Sinclair: the sense of their own belatedness, the uncertainty regarding their own position in relation to the text, whether they are there as interpreter or witness: 'Where Iain had already walked the motorway and amassed a huge archive of material, I was left with little to do except to find the split nature of our project by electing to drive in pursuit of nothing around the world's biggest bypass' (LOf). In his quest to discover the nature of his quest in, and on, the road, to discover the rationale of his film, Petit must also contend with Sinclair's proprietorial promptings. Sinclair 'warned that by driving it, I risked becoming one of Bram Stoker's undead' and recommends that, to help him define his quest, Petit read 'the literature of the future written over a century past' (LOf). Sinclair's helpful hints tie the meaning of the M25 to time travel. The H.G. Wells quote, delivered by postcard, describing the unpleasant sensations of travelling in time anticipates his own subsequent quotation from Wells' 'speculative fiction', 'The Time Machine': 'There is no difference between time and any of the three dimensions of space except that our consciousness moves it along' (LOf). Significantly, however, Sinclair misquotes Wells, transforming the original 'moves along it' (which assigns time an external objective reality) into the more subjectivist 'moves it along' – which seems to make time an effect of consciousness. The parapraxis is important insofar as Petit's eventual solution to the problem of filming the M25 involves a refinement of Sinclair's misquotation: it is not consciousness that moves on time but consciousness as embodied in technology.

Initially, Petit ascribes his inability to film the M25 to the nature of the motorway. 'After several weeks of attempted cutting, the M25 firmly resists editing, resists linear interpretation once anecdote is refused entry into the equation' (LOf). As a circular motorway, the London Orbital refuses narrative: it is neither a road to the future nor away from the past. Rather, as the world's biggest bypass, it is about avoidance: 'it was always seen as the solution to a problem, a bureaucratic dream that took decades to realise' (LOf). As such, the M25 is about boredom and repetition. Petit's moment of epiphany finally comes when he realizes that the problem lies not in the subject but in the medium, film:

> The real problem with the M25 is that it resists filming as much as it resists editing. This seems partly to do with the new digital technology which lacks the emulsion shadows and chemical quality of film. Tape is ubiquitous. Too flexible and too accommodating. It can shoot anything. Tape is flat, tape is

over-bright and electronic, tape is logging, a hand-held diary. Film comes in ten-minute rolls, tape in 60-minute cassettes. The M25 is anti-cinema and tape is anti-image. What other than a surveillance camera would want to record its ceaseless undramatic motion? The lesson was hard to learn. Several thousands of shots and miles of footage but there was no reason to cut. Editing made no sense in relation to the subject and in the end after many wasted hours it was those camera sentinels that guarded the road which pointed the way. That tape was after all the answer. The M25 only begins to make sense if you don't switch the camera off. (LOf)

In this perception that the M25 as a subject marks the shift from one technological grouping (film/analogue/chemical) to another (tape/digital/electronic), Petit effectively locates the road, and with it, Sinclair's project, at the juncture of two paradigms of representation. Film as the medium of cinema is associated with a moving camera whose perspective, particularly in the road movie, represents the protagonist's onward movement through time and space. The M25 is 'anti-cinema' because it is predicated on repetition: the *London Orbital* becomes a tape loop. In effect Petit maps a paradigm shift in subjectification onto the technological transition from film to tape, analogue to digital. Film is active, it organizes time and space around the perspective of the camera which, in its dynamism, acts as a representative of the imperial *cogito*, moving forward, composing, and, in both senses, relating. Tape, Petit suggests, is about recording, about keeping track. Whereas the movement of the camera mimics that of the individual, the static surveillance 'sentinels' are emblems of the carceral gaze of the Foucauldian state. The individual is transformed into an object that moves across a static frame. That appears, disappears and reappears.

Along with its disruption of the narrative organization of space and time invoked by film, the surveillance tape invokes a wholly new sense of space and temporality:

We move through a flat, brightly lit and brand new electronic world where everything is surveyed, where everything is shot to death. Cemeteries full of dead TV, beyond the reach of archive and collective recall, which no one can be bothered to remember. Like the road itself, film perhaps represents the end of something rather than the beginning. Film is past, tape is future. Digital technology is the start of a new kind of time: instant, disposable, re-recordable. The freedom of the handy-cam revolution to make a personal cinema but at the same time something more controlling security, surveillance, private porno movies, speed traps, the literalness off reality TV, loss of privacy and individuality as previously understood. Whatever is happening with this new technology, it marks a fundamental revolution in the level and type of voyeurism and a different way of looking at things, less nostalgic, new, unsuspected, kinds of boredom. (LOf)

In flooding the world with 'dead TV', tape institutes a new temporality of the sign, and it is within this temporality that Sinclair locates his text. In erasing the affective power that structures the economy of memory, tape's ubiquity creates the cultural condition which Huyssen terms the 'hypertrophy of memory' (2003: 3) but which could equally be described as the hyper-inflation of memory insofar as it involves the devaluation of the image as memory's currency. The effect of this hyperinflation is spectral. As we have seen in the discussion of *Rodinsky's Room*, insofar as the command to remember etymologically present in 'archive' is also the command to forget, there is, as Derrida observes, always a spectrality inherent within the archive. However, in creating a realm 'beyond the reach of archive and collective recall' tape institutes a wider spectrality in dividing the world between the recorded and the unrecorded. The injunction to record, to archive – 'you forgot the camera!' – even as it cancels the memorability of the record erodes the value of the unrecorded. Only the recorded is real but the recorded is also the forgettable. Memory takes on the flat literalness of reality TV.

Sinclair elaborates on the political and social implications of this division in his 2005 interview with Colette Meacher. The emergence of CCTV technology, he claims, has radically 'transformed the gaze' with which both city and citizen are seen.[6] For example, the most iconic imagery of the July 2007 London bombings, he suggests, did not come from the 'inert and

---

[6] 'I think the city has been completely altered by this form of gazing and that indeed consciousness is shifting into a battle between the virtual and the actual and the whole machinery of government and politics is involved in this virtual presentation, which is their trashed version of the sublime. In which they conjure up the Millennium Dome as an island of the sublime, an Arcadian wonder – a shimmering thing of blue waters and orchards, which doesn't exist. Underneath it is a disregarded reality, which is a kind of grim poetic, dystopian imagery, smell and filth and dirt. These two sides co-exist. The sublime has been corrupted, moved on by the persuaders and corrupters and the tricksters who are endlessly hosing it over you. I think the overwhelming experiences that you describe – a sense of your identity dissolving into this massive, shifting world – is not available to us any more' (Meacher 2005).

old-fashioned' TV cameras, but was 'captured on phones in the tunnels'. As a result of the ubiquity of recording technology, the present has never seemed more present: 'This new thing has evolved, an eye in the palm of your hand, a device for seeing and communicating in present time'. The fusion of the digital and the human seems to have eliminated the gap between representation and represented, to have made the present immediate. But as a result of this new immediacy, 'what you see is totally different'. Acting as host for its content, the new technology/media has fundamentally altered the 'psychic climate' of the city: 'The technical possibilities create an expectation of disaster. The budget is so big, there has to be a bombing or an assassination to justify it. Surveillance technology incubates future shock'. Resisting this extreme statement of the parasitic relationship of media and content, Meacher counters with the common-sense view that most people find the presence of CCTV cameras 'reassuring' and argues that 'it's not as if installing cameras will criminalize the criminals; the criminals are criminals anyway! The cameras simply catch them in the act' (Meacher 2005).

In response, Sinclair notes how the technology has brought about a fundamental realignment between the image and the idea of the criminal. In the society of the spectacle the image has assumed a totemic function. The affluent believe they can protect their property by installing CCTV, he claims, 'as if the image will somehow magically protect them without affecting their own lives or behaviour'. What happens in effect is criminality ceases to be a matter of legal procedure – '[y]ou're only a criminal if you're caught. That's the definition of a criminal. Until you've been accused and proven guilty you are of no interest to the system' – and becomes an aspect of visibility with the ubiquity of surveillance technology effectively making criminality a matter of retrieval and processing: 'Most of Hackney is on a provisional caution. They're waiting for the bureaucrats to find time to process them'. As such, the technology institutes a faultline within the idea of representation between the surveyors and surveyed which becomes evident in the act of looking back: 'taking pictures of IKEA is actually a crime even though all their cameras are taking pictures of you. You're not allowed to be self-conscious. You have to pretend that you're in a movie and that you've agreed to it'. In the world of constant surveillance innocence and guilt become effects of mediality and of a relationship to mediality, such that even self-consciousness attracts suspicion.

The mantra that the innocent have nothing to hide transforms the act of hiding into a proclamation of guilt and makes self-evidence the distinctive attribute of innocence. The open society has become addicted to the gaze that transforms citizens into the performers of their own innocence. In such a society only the naive can continue to believe that innocence and guilt are qualities which exist independently of their representation:

> CM: Ultimately, the cameras won't do anything other than portray events as they're occurring.
>
> IS: There are no events as they're occurring. (Both laugh) (Meacher 2005)

Within the film, what Petit's mini-essay reveals then is that in *London Orbital*, tape is both the medium and the message. In the interview that accompanies the DVD, Petit explicitly identifies tape and the new digital cameras as the media that made it possible for him to make the film. In the film, as we have seen, tape enables the surveillance technology and security culture whose emergence the film maps onto the construction of the M25. The chiasmic logic which transforms a technology of liberation into a technology of control which is omnipresent in both the film and book, is written into the logic of the M25 itself as the emblem of a neoliberal promise of greater individual freedom which has delivered instead an ever-stronger, and more intrusive, state, and a culture ever more obsessed with security.

An unpeopled country: Misrecognition and reforgetting on the Great North Road

Sinclair's second road follows a route which is in marked contrast with his first. Where the London Orbital in endlessly circling the metropolis signals the termination of an idea of mobility in a condition of stasis, the Great North Road, or A1, explored in *Edge of the Orison* (2005) is first and foremost the road to and from the capital. As such it serves as a metonym for the road taken by the billions who have made the emblematic journey from the country to the city, and particularly, the dispossessed and landless workers whose surplus labour has historically fed the city's growth. The Great North Road is, in this respect the road that connects the urban and the rural, but also the road that links the city with its topographical and conceptual outsides: the country and by association, that most contested of categories, Nature. More immediately it is the road taken in 1841 by the 'peasant poet' John Clare (1793–1864) in his flight from an Epping Forest mental asylum back to his native Northamptonshire. It is Clare's account of how, as a child, he set out to walk to the edge of the horizon, or 'orison' in his dialect-influenced spelling, and found himself 'out of his knowledge' (EO: 30) that supplies Sinclair's title and establishes a further contrast with the horizonless circuits of the M25 where disorientation occurs not through an experience of the unfamiliar, but through the endless repetition of the same.

As the title suggests, the tone and tempo of this road trip are also markedly different from *London Orbital*. Rather than the promotion of a 'thesis' (EO: 6), this walk finds its pretext in a story of a family connection between Clare and the forebears of Sinclair's wife, Anna, who also came from Northamptonshire. This genealogical quest, the pronounced emphasis on family – Anna accompanies Sinclair for a significant part of the way – the predominantly rural character of the terrain, and its concern with one of England's foremost nature poets, all suggest that in *Edge of the Orison* Sinclair has shifted his focus from the marginal cultures of the urban edgelands for interests more typically identified with Middle England. As Rebecca Solnit notes, the differences between urban and rural walking involve more than a simple change of scenery: while the shady business of urban walking is never more than a misstep away from 'soliciting, cruising, promenading, shopping, rioting, protesting, skulking [or] loitering', rural walking, she observes, tends to find its 'moral imperative in the love of nature' (2001: 173–4).

Sinclair himself, however, emphasizes the continuity of the two projects, describing the Clare walk as 'unfinished business' (EO: 5). London's 'gravity', he writes, 'had to be escaped by a final unwritten chapter, a shaky attempt to place my boots in John Clare's hobbled footsteps' (EO: 5). If the *London Orbital* walk was an attempt at restitution, at restoring a sense of place to an emblematic non-place by uncovering the cultural memories erased in a landscape of amnesia, in the Clare walk the unfinished business is both a journey further into the landscape of amnesia and a return to the problem of re-presenting a past which isn't simply a product of our own needs and desires.

In this respect Clare's 'orison' stands as a figure for a general epistemological limit: as the projection of the subject's located perspective it symbolizes the interdependence of subject and object, the productive dynamic of perception and location. Clare himself is a figure who marks a variety of epistemological limits, who stands on a number of different horizons. Insofar as he is 'the one chosen out of all past and future generations of Clares ... to forge the memory system of poetry, a refinement or written version of the folksongs his father knew and played' (EO: 27) he marks the horizon that separates literary from oral culture: he marks the horizon of the written, with all that that entails. As the first Clare to become a writer he separates himself from the unrecorded generations as an individual who can be known. But individuated by his mastery of the written sign, knowable as an author, he encounters the double agency of the letter in a particularly forceful manner. His writing is strongly marked both by a sense of how his bookishness sets him apart from his family and the rest of his village and by how he is misread, as a peasant, rather than as a poet, by his urban public who desert him once the vogue for peasant poetry has passed, leaving him, literally, talking to himself.

The first Clare to become knowable he is also, as a reality effect of the sign, the first Clare to become unknowable: to discover that he has no authority over the interpretation of his words and that these words will be used to produce an endless series of Clares. This process of revision includes the epitaph inscribed on his grave: 'Poets are Born not Made' which wind, rain and lichen erode to read 'Poets are Born not Mad' – prompting Sinclair to write that '[t]here is no advantage in any man authoring his own life, predicting his future, it has already been told, warped, misappropriated by future biographers, special-interest pleaders, eco-romantics and fellow poets' (EO: 25). To become a writer, in other words, is to surrender any claim to an originary self and to become instead the subject of a series of re-readings. In thus surrendering his identity to the errancy of the sign he is the first Clare to set his identity loose on the road, to be what he will become, to construct himself through the noise of *Nachträglichkeit*.

In addition to marking the horizon that separates the (un)knowability of written culture from the oral, the memorialized from the immemorial, as a 'peasant' who saw the landscape of his childhood 'improved' by Acts of Enclosure which transformed common land into private property he occupies the horizon of modernity itself, having grown up in a world organized around relationships to property and land which, Karl Marx suggests, had been all but forgotten within two generations of his death (1990: 889). In this experience of an unalienated relation to labour and the material world, Clare thus stands as a figure too for that form of social immanence whose loss is signified by the modernity whose locus is the city.

'Who you walk with alters what you see' (EO: 6), writes Sinclair. In electing to travel up the Great North Road with Clare, Sinclair thus transforms this walk into an exploration of the themes of immanence and representation. In Clare, Sinclair aligns his concerns with reforgetting and a non-instrumentalized knowledge, with a figure – the peasant poet – who is of critical significance in wider debates about presentation and representation. The key terms of that debate have been largely determined by Gayatri Spivak's account of the subaltern (1988) which explores the ways in which radical Western intellectuals, such as Foucault and Deleuze, despite aiming to critique Western narrativizations of imperial history, effectively consolidate the position of the West as Subject. Although concerned directly with Indian history and addressing the specific problem of the contribution of peasants, tribals and women (1988: 283) to Indian nationalism, her work identifies a wider problematic of representation. Namely that representatives who speak for those who are presumed to have no voice effectively silence those on whose behalf they speak. However, identifying the unvoiced as an unknowable Other merely confirms the sovereignty of the (Western) subject against which the Other is articulated.

For Clare the problem of the subaltern is the problem of the commodity form: he struggles to be recognized as the producer of poetry rather than simply as a poetic product. Thus, when, in 1818, the Stamford bookseller Edward Drury collaborated with the progressive London publisher John Taylor, to bring out Clare's first collection, *Poems Descriptive of Rural Life and Scenery* (1821) they decided to bill Clare's work as 'the trembling and diffident efforts of a second Burns or Bloomfield' (qtd. Sales 2002: 21). To maximize their commercial success the two men agreed Clare should be branded as a ploughman poet with equal emphasis being placed upon his lowly status and his poetic genius. So great was their faith in the commercial potential not only of Clare's poetry, but the peasant-poet brand, that they took the unusual step of publishing this first volume at the publisher's risk, rather than by subscription. They took that risk because the potential of peasant poetry had already been demonstrated by the sale of 26,000 copies of Robert Bloomfield's *The Farmer's Boy* (1800) and the enduring popularity of Robert Burns, already enshrined as the national bard of Scotland. However, as Alan Vardy points out, Clare still required careful positioning if he was to appeal to a public raised on Wordsworth's precept that poetry be emotion recollected in tranquillity. This Taylor undertook in his introductory essay which echoes the 'Preface' to the *Lyrical Ballads* (1798) and presents Clare in a Wordsworthian two-for-one offer, as both 'the Poet as well as the Child of Nature' (qtd. Vardy 2000: 107). He recommends him to the reader not only for the quality of his natural description, but as himself a piece of the natural world. This doubling is necessary, Vardy suggests, because Clare's verse, while rich in the spontaneous outpouring of feeling, tends to lack the vital element of reflection which completed Wordsworth's formula.

It is the same lack of a reflective quality that disqualifies Clare from the Romantic canon which, as Spivak points out, in Marxist historiography disqualifies the peasantry from the world historical stage. Lacking consciousness of itself as a class, the peasantry must always be represented by others who speak on its behalf. Clare in other words is doubly occluded: he is denied possession of the power of self-reflection necessary to constitute himself as a subject either aesthetically or politically, either as an artist or as a peasant.

As we have seen, Sinclair clearly signals his awareness that Clare has been endlessly refashioned to meet the needs of his present readers. In one sense, however, he is repeating that process. He sets out to follow 'in the traces of the mad poet John Clare' (EO: 5). The mad poet, 'mad to shrug off the poultice of identity, to be everyone. Borderless as an inland sea' (EO: 5) is another, contemporary, version of 'the peasant poet'. Both are read as reporters from realms from which no report can come, which are beyond representation. However, as we have seen, for Sinclair, writing in the wake of R.D. Laing and the anti-psychiatry movement, madness is to be located not in the individual so much as their social context, and, for Sinclair, as a psychogeographer, in their social topography. Moreover, Sinclair does not set out to provide a biography of Clare, to know the author, but 'to follow in his traces', to cover the same terrain and thus to encounter Clare in the difference and coincidence of their walks. Secondly, it is important that Sinclair is following Clare up the Great North Road, on his path back from the capital and, as he notes at the outset of this walk,

> If you are fortunate enough to start from London, the goal of every aspiring economic or cultural migrant, then any outward expedition becomes a flight. Heading up the Great North Road, we were not advancing into a fresh narrative, a novel set of coordinates, we were running away .... (EO: 8)

To walk away from the city, back up the Great North Road is effectively to reverse the narrative of progress: it is to enter the world of the defeated, of those who could not take the city and who have failed, or turned their back on the challenge of modernity. But, Sinclair insists, it is not to travel alone: 'Quit London and you will be trampled in the stampede. Plague-dodgers. Hunted criminals .... The exhausted, the timid. The burgled, raped, assaulted. Overtaxed. Under-rewarded. Choked on thin air. Allergic to everything' (EO: 9).

To walk up the Great North Road away from London is thus in itself a form of counter-history, an avoidance of presentism, and hence of positing a non-instrumentalized relationship to the past, and Sinclair's technique for exploring that relationship is typically oblique. Neither biography nor autobiography, family history nor travel literature, *Edge of the Orison* proceeds through the resonance of the chance encounter exemplified by a 'disconcerting incident' that occurs early in the walk:

> On a long straight road coming out of Kent ... [a] stranger, dressed in the clothes Anna [Sinclair's wife, and walking companion on this stage of the journey] is wearing, a person of the same height, same length of stride, passes her, walking North. I'm slightly ahead, marching uphill towards a road sign, wanting to check if we are in the right place. I lift the camera, catch the moment. Anna split, travelling both ways at once; south towards the coast and back, alone, to London. (EO: 7)

This minor irruption of the uncanny into the narrative is illustrative of the manner in which Sinclair sets about reading Clare. Anna's doubling registers the doubling of Clare's and Sinclair's text, for the scene captured by Sinclair's camera, also captures a scene repeated, in one guise or another, throughout Clare's oeuvre: a scene which can be described as the recognition of non-recognition, or the staging of the speaker's own failure to recognize and be recognized by the object of his or her desire.

The same scene is clearly marked, for example, in Clare's title 'Lost as strangers as we pass' (Clare 1975: 333) but it is given one of its fullest poetic expressions in the lines which conclude the ballad, 'My love in dishabille':

She passed me by in silence; I passed her by the same;
I could not tell her person; I did not know her name;
But her person I love dearly, and I love her dearly still;
Though I did not know my own true love in rags & dishabille. (1975: 329)

Elsewhere the perception of strangeness as the property of the familiar provides the sentimental force in 'I am', one of Clare's most powerful asylum poems:

And e'en the dearest – that I love the best –
Are strange – nay, rather stranger than the rest. (1975: 297)[7]

Given Clare's biographical and historical circumstances this trope of misrecognition resonates at a number of levels. Professionally, it registers the Northamptonshire peasant's frustration at the public's refusal to recognize him as a poet: as the producer rather than the (picturesque) subject of his verse. Thematically it is manifest in the poetry's powerful sense of the disorientation consequent on the erasure of the landscape of his childhood after the enclosure of his home village of Helpstone which began in 1809. Seeing oneself not seeing marks the poet's sense that enclosure has not only rendered the landscape of his birth unrecognizable, but that in the loss of that world he has become unrecognizable to himself. It encodes, in other words, Clare's powerful sense of the interdependence of identity and place, of the ways in which identity is locational and as such vulnerable to those forces involved in the production and reproduction of space so powerfully evident in the processes of enclosure and agricultural improvement. As Sinclair writes:

He had to learn the difficult thing. In different places we are different people. We live in one envelope with a multitude of voices, lulling them by regular habits, of rising, labouring, eating, taking pleasure and exercise: other selves, in suspension, slumber but remain wakeful. Walking confirms identity. We are never more than an extension of the ground on which we live. (EO: 79)

---

[7]   Its structural function can be seen in the poem 'A Mouse's Nest' where the poem's narrator, having mistaken a ball of grass for a bird's nest, is shocked by the sudden appearance of an old mouse 'An old mouse bolted in the wheats/ With all her young one's hanging at her teats' (1975: 234). Only after this disorientating encounter with the grotesque has been resolved by the mouse's return to its nest does the poem pan out to provide some form of conventionally picturesque perspective in the final couplet: 'The water o'er the pebbles scarce could run/And broad old cesspools glittered in the sun' (1975: 234).

Most importantly for *Edge of the Orison* however, seeing oneself not seeing is the primary narrative situation in 'Journey out of Essex', Clare's account of his increasingly hallucinatory, eighty-mile, three-day trek from Epping Forest, and the text whose traces Sinclair sets out to follow. The difficulty of establishing an authoritative text for Clare is notorious – apart from all the editions ' "improved" or bowdlerized revisions by well-meaning meddlers and promoters' (EO: 27), and Clare's willingness to leave dealings with the 'awkward squad' of punctuation to others, 'Journey out of Essex' presents special problems. The text was written out by Clare in his Northborough cottage the day after his arrival and is based on notes he made during the walk but it is cast in the form of a journal which creates an immediate ambiguity of tense. Is it narrated on a day to day basis with no idea of the eventual outcome of the journey, or from the perspective of having reached the safety of Northborough? When, for example, Clare writes 'July 19 – Monday – Did nothing' (1983: 153), is this the 'did nothing' of somebody commenting on the nature of institutionalized life, somebody who is simply obeying the behest of the journal form to report even the fact that there is nothing to report, or is it the 'did nothing' of somebody hesitating on the verge of a desperate enterprise, caught in indecision, reporting on his failure to make the jump that will instigate his flight? The resonance of that simple entry relies on the ambiguity of the text's suspension between report and narrative. Sinclair is attentive to this ambiguity, describing the text as 'memories forged in a phantom letter … to his vanished muse' (EO: 10) and as Clare re-experiencing the journey from Epping: 'He saw himself once again, on the treadmill of the road: incidents from a fading fiction …' (EO: 10). He also notes the contrast between the confidence of Clare's handwriting striding boldly forward and the shambling progress it describes: 'Clare limps but his story pushes remorselessly towards its conclusion' (EO: 222).

What this narratological uncertainty conveys is an image of Clare as a stranger to his own words: discovering in his own hand a report from a place where he cannot remember having been: within the narrative forgetting is almost as prominent as walking.[8] The narrative itself is characterized by

---

[8] This impression is reinforced by Clare's own notes to the manuscript recording his subsequent discovery of scraps of paper in his pocket providing further details of his route: 'On searching my pockets after the above was written I found a part of a newspaper vide "Morning Chronicle" on which the following fragments were pencilled …' (1983: 156).

vivid incidents swimming up out of a general condition of uncertainty as the narrator's memory struggles and fails to fill the lacunae of his notes: 'I have but slight recollection of the journey between here and Stilton for I was knocked up and noticed little or nothing' (1983: 158). We learn of his encounter with the 'Man and the boy curled up asleep' (1983: 154); of the man in a slop frock who mistakes him for a broken down hay-maker and throws him a penny; of the drovers who were 'very saucey so [that] I begged no more of any body' (1983: 154); the civil cottagers at Potton where he called to light his pipe; the 'kind talking countryman' (1983: 156) the 'tall Gipsey... with an honest looking countenance and rather handsome' who mysteriously 'cautioned me on the way to put something in my hat to keep the crown up and said in a lower tone "you'll be noticed" but not knowing what she hinted – I took no notice and made no reply' (1983: 158).

In its overall effect this narrative, as Sinclair points out, resembles John Bunyan's *Pilgrim's Progress*, but a progress stripped of any allegorical system to enable the interpretation of encounters rendered increasingly mysterious by the pilgrim's progressive disorientation. Even physical progress is uncertain with Clare having to lie down with his head pointing North so that he will know which direction to travel when he awakes. At one point, he recalls,

> I heedlessly turned back to read [a milestone]...I then suddenly forgot which was North and South and though I narrowly examined both ways I could see no tree or bush or stone heap that I could recollect I had passed so I went on mile after mile almost convinced I was going the same way I came and these thoughts were so strong upon me that doubt and hopelessness made me turn so feeble that I was scarcely able to walk. (1983: 157)

This is a narrative which performs its author's disorientation in the starkness of its imagery and the constant confusion of narration as recollection and report. Sinclair describes it as 'one of the wonders of English prose' (EO: 10), it is also a masterpiece in the literature of alienation. It denotes not only the experience of a man who is a stranger to himself, but of a man who is alienated from the product of his labour, and in its journal format it mirrors the loss of the sense of the complete work which in Marx's account results in the alienation of the productive subject from the work through which human beings can produce themselves as fully human. Effectively it translates the notion of alienation into the loss of the 'permission to narrate' (Edward Said qtd. Spivak 1988: 283) – that Spivak identifies as the crux of the problem of representation: the knowledge that narrative implies a possession/consciousness of the whole which Clare cannot be seen to possess. Although he presents us with 'that achieved thing, a letter, never sent, to a dead woman' (EO: 5), the reader cannot possess the whole, being uncertain whether the text is reported or narrated as if reported, whether it is narration which seeks to pass as reporting, or reporting which achieves the form of a finished narrative by virtue of the completion of his walk. We do not know, in other words, whether the text is written or walked. As such Clare's narrative effectively stages its author's madness, exhaustion and total disorientation and thus performs his subaltern condition so that Clare becomes the historian of his own absence and it does so by passing back and forth over a border of the irrecoverable that it itself produces.

Inevitably, given the power of the text over which he walks, Sinclair's encounters with Clare point to his own text's impoverished experience of their shared terrain: 'He starved, tearing handfuls of grass from the side of the road. We breakfasted, full English .... He slept in a "dyke bottom", outside town where we booked ourselves into a decent pub' (EO: 10). Against Clare's wonder of English prose, his 'mere scribbles, are prompts for some unresolved future project' (EO: 10). Again the relationship is parasitic: Sinclair draws the force of his writing from the trauma of Clare's. He sees himself being seen as a figure of fun through the eyes of his family: ' "He's reading the country," they choroused: as I plunged into a thicket, across a stream, through head-high nettles. They stayed on tarmac. "Can dad fetch the car *now*?" one of them would ask before we negotiated the first incline' (EO: 261). The tranquillity of his relationship with Anna – 'the slightly dazed second courtship of that time, after the children have left home, when we sleepwalk between what is lost and what we are learning to recover' (EO: 7) – stands in pointed contrast to Clare's haunted dreams of his two 'wives' and his failure to recognize Martha and refusal to admit that Mary is dead, and that they were married only in his imagination.

Clare's text literally overpowers Sinclair's and, paradoxically, insists on its reality over and against the banality of the same landscape in Blair's Britain. Sinclair reflects this inversion by rechristening the contemporary landscape

Xanaxshire,[9] 'a sleeping country, unpeopled and overlit' (EO: 5) to reflect its general condition of narcoleptic torpor:

> Lurid sunshine on a red-grey road. No cars, no delivery vans, no people. Welcome to Middle England. Xanaxshire, in the wake of the Lloyds fiasco, the debt mountain, the Blairite establishment of urban fixers and spinners (no fox-hunting, acres of GM crops), is the home of dolour. State-sponsored clinical depression. Valium villages under the ever-present threat of imported sex-criminals and Balkan bandits; human landfill dumped in an off-highway nowhere .... (EO: 19)

In this context of 'state-sponsored clinical depression' all of Middle England resembles an asylum and Clare's flight consequently becomes a flight to reality. The condition of unreality, in other words, shifts from the individual to the collective. Specifically, Xanaxshire exists as a fiction of locality: as a local whose ultimate referent is the global, and whose principal activity is the repression of the knowledge that its meaning is always elsewhere: 'Faux rustics in monster vehicles are servicing the USAAF base at Alconbury .... Those who are left are invisible, facing up to the consequences of the good life, the glutinous subsoil of somebody else's labour; rituals of service and release, drink, madness, suicide' (EO: 19–20).

As such, the journey out of Essex becomes a journey into the global, a discovery of a landscape where a fantasy of Englishness masks the economic and political reality of England's position as a base for US military and economic ambitions and as the beneficiary of the unequal geography of global capital. If the draining of the fens and reclamation of the agricultural land in the eastern counties originally provided the impetus for the industrial revolution and Britain's rise to imperial dominion, it has now, as a natural airbase, found its economic function in assisting the space time compression that Harvey identifies as the prerequisite of global capital (1989).

However, if Xanaxshire as a fantasy of Englishness, represents the real as a non-place, a realm whose content is the repressed knowledge of its over-determination by the global, it is also the scene of a traumatic event – the

---

[9] The landscape is named after the drug Xanax a trademark of the Alprazolam 'a drug of the benzodiazapan group, used in the treatment of anxiety' (*New Oxford Dictionary of English*) but echoes of Xanadu, Coleridge's orientalist version of the Mongolian city of Shang-tu are clearly audible.

enclosure of the commons – which, according to Marx, stands at the origin of capital's reconfiguration of global space. In following in Clare's traces, Sinclair is thus walking back to the birth of capitalism and the trauma that has produced Xanaxshire. For Marx, famously, the history of enclosure deserved to be written in 'letters of blood and fire' (1990: 875). Not simply because of the human misery it caused those directly affected by dispossession, but because in creating a vast population of 'free and rightless proletarians' (1990: 895) who owned nothing other than their labour power, it provided the necessary conditions for the development of the capitalist mode of production whose subsequent exportation around the world was to play such a decisive role in the organization of space at every scale (Cosgrove 1984: 4). In its Marxist sense at least, not only does History begin in Helpstone, Helpstone constitutes the absent centre of a spatial order which defines both the global and the personal. Or as Sinclair puts it: 'Enclosure, suddenly, is a personal matter: you have been shrink-wrapped in your own skin and you can't get out. That's when the blameless horizon, that wood, those hills, begin to hurt' (EO: 19).

As such in Marx's account the crime committed in Sinclair's 'sleeping country' is ultimately ontological. It relates not simply to the amount of land expropriated from the peasantry (although Marx almost splutters with incredulity when he does the sums), but to the fact that in transforming the relations to the means of production, the enclosure of the commons erases all memory of any other possible relation: 'By the nineteenth century, the very memory of the connection between the agricultural labourer and communal property had, of course, vanished' (1990: 889). It is the restitution of this forgotten relation to the means of production and its spatial form – the commons – that provides the *telos* of Marxist history: the commons will be perfected in communism, the destruction of the English peasantry is the necessary condition for the eventual triumph of the proletariat. The landscape of enclosure is for Marx thus suffused with a significance that is theological and mythical: 'the English working class was precipitated without any transitional stages from its golden age to its iron age' (1990: 879).

It is the implications of this theological dynamic at work within the Marxist narrative that Sinclair registers in his description of Clare as another instance of the 'reforgotten' (the book is divided into six sections of which 'Reforgetting' is the penultimate). Here the familiar epithet suggests that the forgetting of

Clare is in some way necessary for narrative to proceed with the business of ordering experience as historical and for our understanding of Xanaxshire as a product of that history. As the reforgotten, Clare is both a member of Walter Benjamin's tradition of the oppressed – those to whom history must appear as a sequence of disasters – and a figure whose occlusion is a precondition of history. The destruction of the peasantry is the rupture that organizes the logic of modernity in both its temporal and spatial modalities. The reforgetting of Clare is, in other words, necessary to maintain the structures of a world where it is possible to speak of 'progressive' and 'backward' societies and the urban as the future of the rural. The world which gives direction to the Great North Road. As an emblem of that which has to be forgotten in order for a story to be told, Clare effectively constitutes a figure of narrative trauma. The subaltern cannot speak because to hear his voice would be to dissolve the fabric of the symbolic order. In Lacanian terms Clare's journey up the Great North Road might thus be termed a journey into the Real: that which cannot be assimilated within the symbolic order. In this case he disrupts the mechanisms through which narrative seeks to displace the present, the perception of the now, through anticipation (of the end which will determine the present's meaning) and towards the past through the illusion that what comes after is caused by, codified by Roland Barthes under the tag *post hoc, ergo propter hoc* (1977: 94).

In effect the peasant has the position of noise within the Marxist narrative. As Spivak notes, if the apparent noise of Indian peasant insurgencies is to be understood as signal – as a different story – rather than as irrelevancies within the narrative of Indian history, then it is necessary to posit a different receiver:

> When we come to the concomitant question of the consciousness of the subaltern the notion of what the work *cannot* say becomes important. In the semioses of the social text, elaborations of insurgency stand in the place of 'the utterance'. The sender – 'the peasant' – is marked only as a pointer to an irretrievable consciousness. As for the receiver, we must ask who is the 'real receiver' of an 'insurgency'? (1988: 82)

Jonathan Bate suggests the ways in which this logic works with respect to Clare when he notes that Clare's continued marginalization within the Romantic canon is all the more 'astonishing' given his 'centrality to two works which were seminal to the growth of late-twentieth century ideological, socially-oriented criticism of Romantic period texts' (2000: 164), namely John Barrell's *The Idea of Landscape and the Sense of Place* and Raymond Williams' *The Country and the City*. Both Barrell and Williams draw on Clare's accounts of enclosure and imaginative dispossession to demonstrate the ways in which nature was produced as a site for the symbolic resolution of the social and economic conflicts unleashed by the industrial revolution. However, despite his central role in demonstrating that, in Williams' words, 'the idea of nature contains an extraordinary amount of human history' (1975: 70) Clare, by virtue of his own attention to the detail of the natural world must himself be regarded as the victim of ideological misrecognition. As Bate notes, Clare may be the hero of Williams' and Barrell's stories, but his veneration of nature sits uncomfortably with their central thesis, 'that the bond with nature is forged in a retreat from social commitment, that it is a symptom of middle-class escapism, disillusioned apostasy or false consciousness' (2000: 164).

In this sense Clare's centrality to and absence from the cannon seems symptomatic of the problematic relationship between classic ideology critique and any concept of 'nature' which insofar as it naturalizes dominant power relations ultimately becomes that-which-must-be-historicized. It points, in other words, to the wider problem of speaking Nature within the language of critique. However, where the injunction 'always historicize' (Jameson 1986: 9), would seem to consign the proletarian nature poet to the pathos of an Althusserian *méconnaisance*, Sinclair's double-take in showing us Clare seeing himself as a man not seeing himself,[10] suggests a poet whose subject is the conditions of the recognizable, a poet marked by his awareness that the conditions of his own recognizibility are also the conditions of his objectification. Rather than a figure who is, (a) the tragic victim of a history in which he can have no agency and (b) also the victim of false consciousness who in celebrating Nature, celebrates his own ideological mystification, we glimpse a more complex figure. In the 'Journey out of Essex', Clare is neither

---

[10] A further example of Clare staging his own non-recognition occurs in his anecdote of how as a child he would present his parents with his poetry as if it had been written by somebody else, in order to get a better impression of its worth: 'My method ... was to say I had written it out of a borrowed book and that it was not my own ... and by this way I got their remarks unadulterated and without prejudice' (1983: 12).

the man who fails to recognize his own wife nor the man who recognizes that failure, but a writing subject that constitutes itself as it moves backwards and forwards across the division between report and narrative. Clare on the Great North Road is a figure who does not have the permission to narrate, who could not figure in his own narrative as narrative but who aligns narrative as a form of memory system (according to the logic of *post hoc ergo propter hoc*) with the telos of a walk to transform sequence into a signifying whole, 'that achieved thing, a letter to a dead wife' even though the home he eventually arrives at is no home.

Clare's progress up the Great North Road, in other words, is marked by its surreptitious passage between subject and object: its production of itself as the story of a man who cannot tell a story. In this it echoes his account of his birth as a poet which Sinclair narrates thus:

> An acquaintance, a Helpston weaver, owns a copy of James Thomson's poem, *The Seasons*. Young Clare's immediate and intense desire is to *possess* this wonder. Stamford on Sunday morning, bookseller's premises closed. He bribes a lad to mind the horses he has been paid to watch over. Dereliction of duty. Early return, before first light, to the market town, waiting for the shutters to be thrown open: book secured for a shilling. Clare not wanting to be observed in the act of reading, unconcerned about trespass, climbs over the wall into Burghley Park. (EO: 80)

Where, in Clare's own words, he,

> nestled in a lawn at the wall side the Scenery around me was uncommonly beautiful at that time of the year and what with reading the book and beholding the beautys of artful nature in the park I got into a strain of descriptive rhyming on my journey home this was 'the morning walk' the first thing I committed to paper. (1983: 10)

As an enactment of literature as a form of trespass by a worker who refuses to know his place it is a story which could have come straight from the pages of Rancière's study of nineteenth-century French workers, *The Nights of Labour* (1981). Like Clare the workers Rancière describes refuse to accept their designation as simply workers and, in acts of cultural production, consumption or simply aesthetic contemplation practically contest the division between manual and intellectual labour, thereby demonstrating the arbitrary nature of social division and consequently, that things could be otherwise. In becoming a consumer and a producer of poetry in virtually the same moment, Clare contests the standard Marxist constructions of 'the worker' as the subject of class history and reveals the peasant poet to be, from the moment of his birth, a subject who instigates a redistribution of the sensible: conflating production and consumption, writing and reading. The history of 'the worker', Rancière argues, is to be found not just in overtly political actions and events but in precisely the fence hopping performed by Clare.

This redistribution of the sensible is marked by the sense of the interdependence of subject and object, speaker and spoken which expresses itself in the proliferation of speaking subjects within Clare's poetry. Aware of the conditional nature of his own claim upon the status of speaking subject, it is as if there is nothing in Clare's world which cannot speak. Not only birds and brooks and bushes speak, but even, a patch of ground: 'I'm Swordy Well a patch of land/ That's fell upon the town' (Clare 2003: 211). It is the extent to which Clare's world is peopled, that is populated with speaking subjects, that gives the force to Sinclair's description of Xanaxshire in his opening sentence: 'It is a sleeping country, unpeopled and overlit' (EO: 5). The Middle England encountered by Sinclair has not only been depopulated by the historical processes of enclosure and urbanization, it is unpeopled ontologically in terms of who and what can be thought to speak.

Jonathan Bate's attempts to rescue Clare from the silence of ideology critique in the name of ecocriticism by asking 'can we conceive the possibility that a brook might actually speak, a piece of land might really feel pain? As inheritors of the Enlightenment's instrumental view of nature we cannot' (2000: 165).[11] We cannot understand Clare's nature as anything other than a form of pathetic fallacy because our thought is conditioned by the tragic gulf between subject and object, suggests Bate, before invoking the Australian

---

[11] Jonathan Bate: 'Is the voice of Round Oak Waters to be understood only as a metaphor, a traditional poetic figuration of the genius loci, or "an extreme use of the pathetic fallacy"? Or can we conceive the possibility that a brook might really speak, a piece of land might really feel pain . . . . How would the poem be read by, say, an Australian Aboriginal who has walked some of the invisible pathways which criss-cross the land, which are known to Europeans as Dreaming-tracks or Songlines and the Aboriginals themselves as Footprints of the Ancestors or the Way of the Law? "Are we to understand the sorrows of the brook as an echo of Clare's own?" asks Barrell. No, the Aboriginal reader will reply, instinct with the knowledge that the land itself is always singing. It may just be the other way round: the sorrows of Clare are an echo of the brook's own' (2000: 165–6).

Aboriginal as the prototype of a mode of perception that has escaped the conditioning of reification. However, reading Clare as a sign of narrative's struggle to contain the exclusions through which it orders experience, the lamentation of Clare's landscape need no longer be seen as gestures towards some idea of nature as unity lost to postlapsarian consciousnesses. Instead the staging of misrecognition suggests a concern with the contingencies of subjecthood – with who and what can speak, and who and what is spoken about.

In following Clare's walk up the Great North Road then, Sinclair alerts us to the presence of a Clare who is the spokesman for a world which is absent from our language. However Sinclair cannot follow him into that world, and ultimately *Edge of the Orison* can only testify to the absence of Clare while Sinclair's progress is via the connections which keep his prose moving – the fact that Lucia Joyce spent most of her life in the Northampton General Lunatic Asylum where Clare died, that although he can find no evidence of a connection between Anna and Clare, he discovers one between himself and Beckett who once played cricket against Northampton where there is a 'Beckett's Park' (EO: 231) etc. This far from London however, Sinclair too is 'out of his knowledge' and the connections and coincidences through which he weaves his narrative strands together begin to seem increasingly forced. A digression on Mary Stuart, Queen of Scots' execution at Fotheringay castle – the most melancholy place in England – for example wouldn't seem out of place in one of the texts on which Sinclair practices his parasitism, the guides to 'Clare Country' and literary England, while the fact that Anna's great-great-great-grandfather was married in 1788, 'Five years before the birth of John Clare. One year before the French Revolution' (EO: 357) suggests that Xanaxshire may have tested Sinclair's imagination to exhaustion, and once the hunt for ancestors has reached its horizon, and with the knowledge that there are now 'celebrity genealogical truffle hunts on TV' (EO: 350) it is time to head back down the Great North Road with what sounds like an admission of defeat:

> The Clare I found will not be your John Clare, nor the poet Geoffrey Hadman claimed as a relative. The track we travelled, coming from London, is no longer Clare's Great North Road. Through error, perhaps, we arrive at

a richer truth: in the telling of the tale. The trance of writing is the author's only defence against the world. He sleepwalks between assignments, between welcoming ghosts, looking out for the next prompt, the next milestone hidden in the grass. (EO: 362)

The abiding note of contemporary pastoral it seems is melancholic, and in *Edge of the Orison* Sinclair seems to discover the dependence of his text on the noise of the city. Together the two roads produce different but complementary messages about Blair's Britain. The M25 represents the transformation of the liberal ideal of mobility and personal freedom into a surveillance society – the society of total visibility implied by digital tape – the trek up the Great North Road encourages us to re-examine the relationship of country and city by problematizing the position of nature in relationship to art.

Conclusion

Ghost Milk: Calling Time on the Grand Project

In the idea of 'ghost milk' (GM: 333–8), Sinclair offers a figure of noise which condenses many of the themes worked out in earlier texts and charted above. Ghost milk, he explains, is 'CGI smears on the blue fence [surrounding the London 2012 Olympics construction site]. Real juice from a virtual host. Embalming fluid. A soup of photographic negatives. Soul food for the dead. The universal element in which we sink and swim' (GM: 338). Ghost milk as the background noise of contemporary life, and particularly urban life, becomes a figure for an idea which is increasingly prominent in his most recent work, namely, that 'the city has become an enormous argument…between the virtual and the actual' (Sinclair 2011a), that within the neoliberal city 'dramas of territory' (GM: 24) typically take the form of a contest between politicians and corporate 'imagineers' (GM: 142) who propose a succession of grand projects whose delivery is always just around the corner while the actual is experienced as a permanently suspended present of 'dirt and dust and inconvenience' (GM: 99).

With the visitation of the 2012 London Olympics on Sinclair's home in East London that argument becomes immediate and political as the CGI images of the completed park begin to drive out and even criminalize other images of the city. Photography of and on the site is forbidden for security reasons while, on the blue fence that marks London's most recent episode in the long history of enclosure, 'there [begin] to appear computer generated images of what this landscape would become that were so convincing that people are absolutely sure that it has already happened' (Sinclair 2011a).

Conceiving the city in terms of an argument between the virtual and the actual simplifies Sinclair's understanding of the nature of his own task as a writer. In the face of this 'ethically challenged fakery' (GM: 75), it is the duty of the artist simply to witness and remember. Reviewing his own options after the 'capture' of East London by the 'cardinals of capital' (GM: 64) he writes:

> I thought about leaving London for a few months, travelling around the country to investigate and record sites of collapsed lottery-funded millennium projects, ghost-milk architecture. Many of these GP disasters had been wiped from the files. They never happened. The New Labour era was about a remorseless push towards a horizon that must, of necessity, remain out of reach: the next big idea. And about mistakes of the past best handled with a blanket apology by a low ranking minister, soon to be rewarded with a joke peerage. I would also make it my business to interview surviving poets, not as unacknowledged legislators, but as witnesses. Witnesses to their own dissolution. (GM: 148)

Instead *Ghost Milk* employs the parasitic mode to find within an account of the 2012 Olympics an opportunity to discover a global within the local that takes Sinclair out from London to Beijing, Berlin and Athens, and reveals the Beijing, Berlin and Athens within London. To call time on this account, consequently, I want to note the recurrence of some of the figures of noise traced above within one of Sinclair's most recent explorations of the dimensions of neoliberal urban space.

The noise of the Olympics as a 'Grand Project' seeps into every aspect of Sinclair's life. Beyond the disruption of the urban fabric, the enclosures of common land and loss of facilities (the book is dedicated to the 'huts of the Manor Garden Allotments'), East Londoners are warned that the 'Olympics had set off a deluge of cyber crime' (GM: 92) while an expert in on-line security warns that '[t]he 2012 Games is going to attract a lot of criminal attention. There is going to be an explosion in junk mail and scams' (GM: 93). The profusion of spam in Sinclair's inbox is accompanied by a virtualization of money – 'the closer you get to the Stratford construction site, the more money, as civilians understand it, loses its meaning' (GM: 92) – which threatens to put an end to Sinclair's 'survivalist economics' as he chases payments through an increasingly bureaucratic system: 'As the postal service imploded, the old "cheque in the post" excuse became a fact of life. Nothing made it on to the mat other than junk mail [and] free council propaganda (funded from the rates)' (GM: 94). In Sinclair's account the Grand Project is, in other words, directly related to an increase in the noise of civic life which makes urban existence increasingly untenable.

Sinclair's critique of the 2012 London Olympics is developed around a number of related strands. There is the traditional, bread and circuses argument that the Olympics is simply a distraction, a 'scam of scams' (GM: 60) to promulgate the operation of international and local capital: 'The five-hooped golden handcuffs. Smoke rings behind which deals could be done for casinos and mosques and malls: with corporate sponsorship, flag-waving and infinitely elastic budgets...' (GM: 60). This is developed along with an even more sinister vision of the 'games' as a spectacle of biopolitics: 'War by other means. Warrior athletes watched, from behind dark glasses, by men in suits and uniforms. The pharmaceutical frontline. Californian chemists running their eye-popping, vein-clustered, vest-stripping androids against degendered state-laboratory freaks' (GM: 60). The Olympics, he points out, has a long history of tragedy and violence, suggesting that '[t]he neurosis of stadium building is nothing more than an unconscious desire to prepare sites for ritual sacrifice' (GM: 73). The deaths and executions associated with Berlin '36, Mexico City '68 and Munich '72, all add an apocalyptic resonance to the pre-Columbian imagery favoured by the graffiti artists decorating the site of the London 2012 Games.

More specifically, in London, the Olympics as the scam of scams is sold to a sceptical populace through the promise of 'legacy', the promise, that is, that the Games will bring about the regeneration of an area of London suffering from urban blight through the reclamation of large areas of brownfield contaminated by industry. However, the claim that the Olympics will pay for themselves purely from the increased real estate values is unlikely to come true, Sinclair contends, because the construction work has disturbed soil contaminated by Thorium used for the luminous paint on clocks and watches manufactured in the nineteenth century. Inert while buried in the ground, the thorium is activated once disturbed and is now in the Lea Valley ecosystem (GM: 70) with the result that 'regeneration' has in fact increased the toxicity of the environment at huge expense to the taxpayers. Once again, the return of the unselected is brought about by a refusal to acknowledge London's dark history, to recognize that every city needs wasteland in which to bury its secrets.

Thirdly, Sinclair seeks to show that the supposed legacy is simply providing East Londoners with facilities and opportunities that they in fact already had – sports fields and recreational land – but which were ignored by politicians focusing on the idea of urban blight. 'Everything they boasted of delivering as legacy, after the dirt and dust and inconvenience, was here already. It had always been here, but they didn't need it. They lived elsewhere' (GM: 99). Here, Sinclair contrasts the impact of the Grand Project vision of urban regeneration with the Victorian philanthropic movement – represented by the Eton and Oxford Missions to London. Despite their paternalism and imperialist mindset, Victorian philanthropists, he argues, actually produced tangible benefits in the form of common ground for the people of the East End. However, they too succumbed to the Grand Project mentality represented by the Olympics, this time in an argument over whether Eton mission funds should be used for practical programmes or the construction of a great tower (GM: 103).

His main target, however, is the impact of the Games on discursive space: on the explosion of noise that accompanies the Grand Project, and particularly its negative impact on forms of artistic production. Steve Dilworth, an old friend from his time at the Chobham Farm container depot, provides an illustration of its powers of corruption. A sculptor who worked with carrion and animal skeletons, when Sinclair first met him, he was 'the fiercest, truest to raw material sculptor/maker I had ever encountered' (GM: 123). An emblem of artistic integrity, he moved from London to live a subsistence life on the Isle of Harris producing a 'necrophile' art which was 'unexploitable' (GM: 123). However, on being 'shortlisted by Westfield to produce a suitable work of public art for the monster mall on the edge of the Olympic Park' (GM: 122), he is sucked into the noise of GP-speak where the essential literature is:

> the proposal, the bullet-point pitch, the perversion of natural language into weasel forms of not-saying. Dilworth, whose art as I understood it, was raw, impulsive and essential, was obliged to collaborate with a graphic designer on a PR document intended to flatter the inadequacies of the commissioning brief.

> **SAIL: Iconic Sculpture Proposal. Landmark Sculpture for WESTFIELD, Stratfordcity.** (GM: 125)

In Sinclair's account, Sail epitomizes the distinction elaborated in *Downriver* between different forms of public art: 'The vertical thrust of a single structure, dominating place by overlooking it', what *Downriver* terms the art of the state, that is opposed 'by horizontal energies which are always democratic, free flowing, uncontained' (D: 103). Those horizontal energies are illustrated by Stephen Gill whose *Archaeology in Reverse* I have discussed above in the Introduction along with Sinclair's essay on his work. Excluded from his beloved Hackney marshes by the erection of the blue fence around the Olympic Park, Gill becomes in *Ghost Milk* an avatar of John Clare, imaginatively dispossessed by the continuing process of enclosure.

Accompanying Sinclair on a guided tour of the Olympic site, Gill discovers that 'the first thing that goes, as [they] emerge beyond the fence, is any sense of place. There is nothing by which to navigate...' (GM: 69). His subsequent email to Sinclair quoted earlier echoes Clare's experience of enclosure: 'I had a kind of territorial feeling, everything had been taken away. I almost cried in the back of the car. It is such a political experience' (GM: 70). Like Sinclair he recognizes that in the newly narrativized landscape, the real information is always located in the unselected: 'Whenever the guide talked about removing fish, saving the newts, making homes for insects and butterflies, I always checked on the opposite side to the one he suggested, it was much more interesting' (GM: 70).

Sinclair's sense of his own position as a 'token dissident' (GM: 142) in this economy is typically ambiguous. In a passage that closely echoes his analysis in *Downriver* of the failure to 'procure an opposition' to Margaret Thatcher, discussed above, he writes:

> We have waved the disaster through, we have colluded: dozens of artists roam the perimeter fence soliciting Arts Council funding to underwrite their protests. It's so awful, such a manifest horror, we can't believe our luck. All those tragic meetings in packed café, the little movies. Blizzards of digital imagery recording edgeland signs clinging to mesh fences alongside compulsory-purchase notification: we buy gold, we sell boxes. Gold from the teeth of dying industries, cardboard boxes to bury murdered aspirations. (GM: 68)

He is aware, in other words, of the ease with which the Olympics can be turned into a platform for protest. While the front of the fence is covered with CGI images of an Olympic arcadia, 'self-sponsored galleries of opposition, occur at the back of the fence' (GM: 73). However this art of the obverse, he suggests, will itself be commercialized. The Hackney Wick graffiti artists, Sweet Toof and Cyclops use the back of the fence to develop their own language of protest drawing on Aztec iconography to allude to the apocalyptic predictions associated with 2012 but they are auditioning to 'come inside', to move off the wall and into the gallery: 'The social message is: Look at me. Admire me. Give me a show on Brick Lane' (GM: 74). Sinclair too is one of the 'weasel subversives' who enjoy 'their status as sanctioned critics corrupt enough to accept a fee for preaching disaster' (GM: 142–3).

It is in the nature of the Grand Project, he implies, that it subverts individual motives and agendas: 'the regiments of fixers, puffers, bagmen, and conceptualizers, parasitical upon the Olympics...were not bad people' (GM: 142–3); rather they are caught up in the project's chiasmic logic where everything becomes its opposite. This contradictory logic is plainly evident on the site itself where the corporations that are the most vigorous proponents of individual liberty wall themselves into heavily policed zones: 'Only by erecting secure fences, surveillance hedges, can they assert their championship of liberty. The threat of terrorism, self-inflicted, underwrites the seriousness of the measures required to repel it. Headline arrests in the Olympic hinterland followed by small print retractions' (GM: 71). Similarly, the Westfield supermall, the London Olympics' only certain legacy, actually reduces the range of goods and services available to the shopper.

But the same perverse logic is evident in his own life when the 'banning' of his book *Hackney, That Rose Red Empire* from Hackney public libraries by the Labour mayor, Jules Piper inevitably turns into a PR disaster for the council, to the delight of the Liberal Democrat opposition, and boosts his book sales: 'The "banned" book has acquired a momentum that would carry it...through six printings' (GM: 113). In this morally contaminated environment, he claims, the only ethical response is to 'bear witness. Record and remember' (GM: 144). His most condensed statement of the theme occurs in Ben Watson's accusation discussed above, that he promotes 'no values in the contemporary world beyond a belief in poetry' (GM: 145). Poets, he says, are necessary to remind him of his own '[f]ailing to fail', his failure to 'let the voices through uncensored' (GM: 147). While writing about those such as Anna Mendelssohn whose refusal to censor meant that their work never reached a wider public, his own text registers a growing sense of the danger of semantic exhaustion, of its 'failure to fail' and descent into repetition exacerbated by the media exposure attendant on the Olympics.

Responding to criticism from the public that his own work is in danger of becoming a simple denunciation of the new at a 2011 lecture in The Hague, Sinclair described his work as countering the cultural insistence on the virtual in favour of a city that is fundamentally, plural, complex and contradictory (2011a). *Ghost Milk* suggests that while he may have surrendered his traditional terrain to the 'imagineers', the eruption of a global space in his own neighbourhood has presented him with an opportunity to renew and extend that story as he finds common ground with artists from other cities who are similarly engaged in the contradictions of neoliberal space. Showing the Malaysian-born photographer Ian Teh around Hackney he writes, 'I was pushed to go beyond the story I had been peddling for so long, stones stamped flat by repetition' (GM: 109), and through Teh's eyes he learns to look at 'familiar things from a different angle … Beijing emerging out of Hackney Wick' (GM: 111). The Ian Teh section concludes with Sinclair contemplating taking up the offer of Chinese lessons from a private tutor announced in an advert in Broadway Market. The private tutor will turn out to be Yang Lian, a Beijing poet who has relocated to Hackney. From him he learns that '[t]here is no international, only different locals' (GM: 150) and to exploit the shared disaster of globalization to make intelligible the local as a site of difference. It is this lesson which prepares him to cut himself adrift from London, initially for a journey by local buses across country from Liverpool to Hull and then for trips to Berlin, Beijing, Athens, Austin and San Francisco. In the exploration of this new global space, Sinclair trusts to his ability to endow his reportage with a symbolic resonance – to turn the chronicles of the everyday into figures with the allegorical resonance of a *Pilgrim's Progress*, to make the local luminous with the global.

Ghost Milk concludes with its own noisy joke. In the 'American Smoke' section he informs us of the sale of his own ' "archive", otherwise known as skip-fillers' (GM: 392) to the Harry Ransom Humanities Research Center in

Austin, Texas. The terms in which he describes the transaction are immediately familiar from Serres:

> Forty years of scribble and grunt in eighty sacks and boxes: a still life writhing with invisible termites, micro-bugs, blisters on onion-skin paper. This material, stacked solid in Whitechapel was an insect ghetto, an unvisited Eden: until I became my own grand project and sold the memory-vault for the dollars to keep me afloat for another season. (GM: 392)

The transformation of the waste of writing – 'spiked scripts and yards of indecipherable poems' (GM: 392) – into archive signals his own transformation from witness into project. It is an act which seems to signal the termination of a narrative – '[m]any of the grey boxes had closing dates as well as dates of birth. When you are neatly sorted into chapters, you are sorted. Period. It seems rude to add another paragraph to the structure' (GM: 397). Sinclair, however, gives the lie to this attempt to sterilize the past by turning his own act of waste disposal into the activity of writing, generating thereby more waste, more food for parasites. Alongside its culture trove – 'a provocation for theses (which would themselves be acquired, catalogues, filed away, pre-forgotten)' (GM: 396) – Sinclair reports that the Harry Ransom Center also:

> stored bottles of parasites, the collateral damage of archival preservation…They were part of an unvisited museum. 'Domesticated Beetle found on a manuscript, lived in the bug jar, without food, air, or water, for 4 months.' They were already replete with the glue of Scott Fitzgerald's nightmares, fear saliva from Ford Madox Ford's moustache, wax from Soutine's inner ear, dust of Man Ray's silver gelatin. Sharers in secret sorrows. Collaborative intelligences. One consciousness splintered into sentences. (GM: 395–6)

The image echoes Serres' depiction of the Cartesian cogito as a householder who, having burned down his old home in order to drive out the rats, lies awake each night in his new residence, listening for their return (2007: 12). The Harry Ransom Center's mission to preserve and catalogue the work of living writers is undone not by the parasites on display in the museum adjacent to the words in the vaults, but by the parasitic relationship of writing and value. In cashing in his pension to fund one more road trip which will furnish one more text, Sinclair delivers his text into a new scene of writing which is articulated against a new present. Rather than the present born out of the infinite delay of the never-to-be-realized Grand Project, *Ghost Milk* opens out onto a time that is constantly reproduced in its consumption, a time where language is constantly reborn through its exhaustion. In this image of a text that produces itself through the description of its own enclosure, Sinclair also returns us to the trope of the locked room. Where the locked room of *Downriver* serves as a figure for controlling the instability of theological and enlightened perspectives, the vaults of the Harry Ransom Center for the Humanities furnish an image of a space which is opened precisely by its impossible desire of containing itself. As such, it stands as a topographic emblem of a global space where centres of learning emerge through the transformation of waste into cultural capital, and culture is produced through its productive operation upon its own waste. In this, Sinclair's parasitic trope establishes a correspondence between his own relationship to production and the general condition of precarity instituted as the global condition of labour. Post-pension, he produces a precarious writing that has sacrificed one habitus in the specificity of the local for a life on the road which is understood simultaneously in terms of the vanished locale and as a new commons where what is shared is the experience of a travel without destination.

Works Cited

Adorno, T. and Horkheimer, M. (1972), *Dialectic of Enlightenment*, London: Verso.

Alnutt, G., D'Aguiar, F., Edwards, K. and Mottram, E. (1988), *The New British Poetry*, London: Paladin.

Alvarez, A. (1973), *The New Poetry*, Harmondsworth: Penguin.

Anderson, B. (2006), *Imagined Communities: Reflections on the Origin and Spread of Nationalism*, London: Verso.

Augé, M. (1995), *Non-places: Introduction to an Anthropology of Supermodernity*, London: Verso.

Baeton, G. (2007), 'The Uses of Deprivation in the Neoliberal City', in G. Boie and M. Pauwels (eds), *Urban Politics Now: Re-imagining Democracy in the Neoliberal City*, Rotterdam: NAi: 44–57.

Baker, P. (2003), 'Psychogeography', in J. Kerr and A. Gibson (eds), *London from Punk to Blair*, London: Reaktion: 323–33.

Baker, B. (2007), *Iain Sinclair*, Manchester: Manchester University Press.

Bal, M. (1999), *Quoting Caravaggio: Contemporary Art, Preposterous History*, Chicago: The University of Chicago Press.

Ball, J.C. (2003), *Satire & the Postcolonial Novel: V.S. Naipaul, Chinua Achebe, Salman Rushdie*, New York: Routledge.

Barker, J. (2006), 'Reader Flattery – Iain Sinclair and the Colonisation of East London', *Mute Magazine: Culture and Politics after the Net*, http://www.metamute.org/en/node/8115/print [accessed 5 July 2012].

Barry, P. (2000), *Contemporary British Poetry and the City*, Manchester: Manchester University Press.

Barry, P. (2006), *Poetry Wars: British Poetry of the 1970s and the Battle of Earls Court*, Cambridge: Salt.

Barthes, R. (1977), *Image, Music, Text*, Glasgow: Fontana.

Bate, J. (2000), *Song of the Earth*, London: Picador.

Bateson, G. (1972), *Steps to an Ecology of Mind*, New York: Ballantine.

Bavidge, J. and Bond, R. (2005), *The Literary London Journal, Interdisciplinary Studies in the Representation of London* 3(2), http://www.literarylondon.org/london-journal/september2005/index.html [accessed 1 July 2014].

BAVO (2007), *Urban Politics Now: Re-imagining Democracy in the Neoliberal City*, Rotterdam: NAi.

Benjamin, W. (1969), *Illuminations*, New York: Schocken.

Benjamin, W. (2006), *One Way Street and Other Writings*, London: Verso.

Berger, J. (1989), 'Two Books and Two Notions of the Sacred', *Guardian*, 25 February 1989.

Bolter, J. and Grusin, R. (2000), *Remediation: Understanding New Media*, Cambridge, MA: M.I.T.

Bond, R. (2005), *Iain Sinclair*, Cambridge: Salt.

Bonnett, A. (2009), 'The Dilemmas of Radical Nostalgia in British Psychogeography', *Theory Culture & Society*, 26(1): 45–70.

Botting, F. (2004), 'Culture, Litterature, Information', *Critical Studies, Post-Theory, Culture, Criticism*, 35: 215–49.

Bourdieu, P. (1984), *Distinction*. Cambridge, MA: Harvard University Press.

Bourdieu, P. (1993), *The Field of Cultural Production: Essays on Art and Literature*, Cambridge: Polity.

Brooker, P. (2002), *Modernity and Metropolis: Writing, Film and Urban Formations*, Basingstoke: Palgrave.

Caddel, R. and Quartermain, P. (1999), *Other: British and Irish Poetry Since 1970*, Hanover, NH: Wesleyan University Press.

Castells, M. (1989), *The Informational City*, London: Blackwell.

Castells, M. (1996), *The Rise of the Network Society*, Vol. 1 of *The Information Age: Economy, Society and Culture*, Cambridge, MA: Blackwell.

Chambers, R. (1991), *Room for Maneuver: Reading (the) Oppositional (in) Narrative*, Chicago: University of Chicago Press.

Chambers, R. (2002), 'Strategic Constructivism? Sedgwick's Ethics of Inversion', in S.M. Barber and D.L. Clark (eds), *Regarding Sedgwick: Essays on Queer Culture and Critical Theory*, New York: Routledge: 165–80.

Chandler, J. and Gilmartin, K. (2005), *Romantic Metropolis: The Urban Scenes of British Culture, 1780–1840*, Cambridge: Cambridge University Press.

Clare, J. (1975), *Selected Poems*, London: Everyman.

Clare, J. (1983), 'Journey Out of Essex', in E. Robinson (ed), *John Clare's Autobiographical Writings*, Oxford: Oxford University Press.

Clare, J. (1985), *The Letters of John Clare*, M. Storey (ed), Oxford: Clarendon.

Clare, J. (2003), *Selected Poems*, J. Bate (ed), London: Faber.

Connell, N. (1995), 'What Happened at Miller's Court?', http://www.casebook.org/dissertations/rip-happened.html [accessed 30 September 2014].

Cooper, D. (1968), *The Dialectics of Liberation*, Harmondsworth: Penguin.

Cosgrove, D. (1984), *Social Formation and Symbolic Landscape*, Madison: University of Wisconsin.

Coverley, M. (2006), *Psychogeography*, Harpenden: Pocket Essentials.

Crozier, A. and Longville, T. (1990), *A Various Art*, London: Paladin.

De Certeau, M. (1986), *Heterologies: Discourse on the Other*, Minneapolis: University of Minnesota Press.

De Certeau, M. (1988), *The Practice of Everyday Life*, Berkeley: University of California Press.

De Quincey, T. (2009), *The Confessions of an English Opium Eater*, Peterborough, ON: Broadview.

Debord, G. (1957), 'Psychogeographical Venice', http://www.notbored.org/psychogeographical-venice.html [accessed 29 September 2014].

Debord, G. (1994), *The Society of the Spectacle*, New York: Zone.

Derrida, J. (1976), *Of Grammatology*, Baltimore: The Johns Hopkins University Press.

Derrida, J. (1978), *Writing and Difference*, London: Routledge.

Derrida, J. (1994), *Spectres of Marx: The State of the Debt, The Work of Mourning and the New International*, London: Routledge.

Derrida, J. (1996), *Archive Fever: A Freudian Impression*, Chicago: University of Chicago Press.

Descartes, R. (1972), *Philosophical Writings*, London: Nelson.

Descartes, R. (1991), *The Writings of René Descartes*, Vol. III, Cambridge: Cambridge University Press.

Diepeveen, L. (2003), *The Difficulties of Modernism*, New York and London: Routledge.

Dorn, E. (1967), *North Atlantic Turbine*, London: Fulcrum.

Eliot, T.S. (1984), *Selected Prose of T.S. Eliot*, London: Faber.

Emilsson, W. (2002), 'Ian [sic] Sinclair's Unsound Detectives', *Critique*, 43(3): 271–88.

Erlich, V. (1980), *Russian Formalism: History Doctrine*, New York: Walter de Gruyter.

Evans, E.J. (1997), *Thatcher and Thatcherism*, London: Routledge.

Fenton, J. (1991), 'Keeping up with Salman Rushdie', *New York Review of Books*, 28 March 1991: 31–3.

Fisher, A. (2005), *Place*, London: Reality Street.

Fisher, M. (2009), *Capitalist Realism: Is There No Alternative?* Winchester: Zero Books.

Florida, R. (2003), 'Cities and the Creative Class', *City & Community*, 2(1): 3–19.

Foster, H. (1985), *Recodings: Art, Spectacle, Cultural Politics*, Port Townsend, WA: Bay Press.

Foucault, M. (1991), *The Order of Things: An Archaeology of the Human Sciences*, London: Routledge.

Freud, S. (1960), *The Psychopathology of Everyday Life*, London: Hogarth.

Friedland, M.L. (1984), *The Trials of Israel Lipski: A True Story of a Victorian Murder in the East End of London*, New York: Beaufort.

Fuentes, C. (1989), 'Words Apart', *Guardian*, 24 February 1989.

Fukuyama, F. (1989), 'The End of History', *National Interest*, http://www.wesjones
.com/eoh.htm [accessed 26 June 2014].

Galloway, G. and Thacker, A. (2007), *The Exploit: A Theory of Networks*, Minneapolis,
MN: University of Minnesota Press.

Gibbons, F. (2001), 'Does This Painting by Walter Sickert Reveal the Identity of
Jack the Ripper?', *Guardian*, 8 December 2001, http://www.guardian.co.uk/
artanddesign/2001/dec/08/art.artsfeatures [accessed 14 July 2011].

Grant, C. (2007), *Uncertainty and Communication*, Basingstoke: Palgrave.

Greer, G. (2006), 'Reality Bites', *Guardian*, 24 July 2006.

Guilhamet, L. (1987), *Satire and the Transformations of Genre*, Philadelphia, PA:
University of Pennsylvania Press.

Habermas, J. (1989), *The Structural Transformation of the Public Sphere*, Cambridge:
Polity.

Hall, S. (1988), *The Hard Road to Renewal: Thatcherism and the Crisis of the Left*,
London: Verso.

Hardt, M. and Negri, A. (2000), *Empire*, Cambridge, MA: Harvard University Press.

Hardt, M. and Negri, A. (2009), *Commonwealth*, Cambridge, MA: Belknap.

Harvey, D. (1989), *The Condition of Postmodernity*, Cambridge, MA: Blackwell.

Harvey, D. (1989a), 'From Managerialism to Entrepreneurialism: The Transformation
of Urban Governance in Late Capitalism', *Geografisker Annaler* 71(1): 3–17.

Harvey, D. (2005), *A Brief History of Neoliberalism*, Oxford: Oxford University Press.

Hayek, F. (1978), 'The Atavism of Social Justice', in *New Studies in Philosophy, Politics,
Economics and the History of Ideas*, Chicago: The University of Chicago Press: 57–68.

Hayles, N.K. (1990), *Chaos Bound: Orderly Disorder in Contemporary Literature and
Science*, Ithaca: Cornell University Press.

Hayles, N.K. (1991), *Chaos and Order: Complex Dynamics in Literature and Science*,
Chicago: Chicago University Press.

Head, D. (2008), *The State of the Novel: Britain and Beyond*, Chichester: Blackwell.

Heartfield, J. (ND), 'Londonostalgia', http://www.heartfield.org/Londonostalgia.htm
[accessed 20 October 2014].

Heartfield, J. (2006), 'Will Self's Mockery of the Mockneys', *Spiked*, 26 July 2006,
http://www.spiked-online.com/newsite/article/1293#.VETHKL4xEcg [accessed
20 October 2014].

Hillis-Miller, J. (1995), *Topographies*, Stanford: Stanford University Press.

Hopkins, B. (1997), 'Modernism and the Collage Aesthetic', *New England Review*,
18(2): 5–12.

Horovitz, M. (1969), *Children of Albion: Poetry of the 'Underground' in Britain*,
Harmondsworth: Penguin.

Hungerford, A. (2005), 'Postmodern Supernaturalism: Ginsberg and the Search for a Supernatural Language', *The Yale Journal of Criticism*, 18(5): 269–98.

Hunt, L. and McNamara, P. (2007), *Liberalism, Conservativism and Hayek's Idea of Spontaneous Order*, London: Palgrave.

Hutcheon, L. (1988), *A Poetics of Postmodernism: History, Theory, Fiction*, London: Routledge.

Huyssen, A. (1995), *Twilight Memories: Marking Time in a Culture of Amnesia*, New York and London: Routledge.

Huyssen, A. (2003), *Present Pasts: Urban Palimpsests and the Politics of Memory*, Stanford: Stanford University Press.

Jackson, K. and Sinclair, I. (2003), *The Verbals*, Tonbridge: Worple.

Jameson, F. (1986), *The Political Unconscious: Narrative as a Socially Symbolic Act*, London: Methuen.

Jameson, F. (1993), *The Postmodern Condition: Or the Cultural Logic of Late Capitalism*, London: Verso.

Jannowitz, A. (2005), 'The Artifactual Sublime: Making London Poetry', in J. Chandler and K. Gilmartin (eds), *Romantic Metropolis: The Urban Scene of British Culture, 1780-1840*, Cambridge: Cambridge University Press: 246–59.

Jeffries, S. (2004), 'On the Road', *Guardian*, 24 April 2004, http://www.guardian.co.uk/books/2004/apr/24/featuresreviews.guardianreview14 [accessed 24 April 2014].

Johnson, S. (1997), *Interface Culture: How New Technology Transforms the Way We Create and Communicate*, San Francisco: Harper.

Kellner, D. (2005), 'Radical Politics, Marcuse, and the New Left', in H. Marcuse (ed), *The New Left and the 1960s: Collected Papers of Herbert Marcuse*, Vol. 3, London and New York: Routledge.

King, A.D. (1991), *Global Cities: Post-Imperialism and the Internationalization of London*, London: Routledge.

Kley, R. (1994), *Hayek's Social and Political Thought*, Oxford: Clarendon.

Knabb, K. (1994), *Situationist International Anthology*, Berkeley: Bureau of Public Secrets.

Kujundzic, D. (2003), 'Archigraphia: On the Future of Testimony and the Archive to Come', *Discourse* 25(1&2): 168–88.

Lefebvre, H. (1991), *The Production of Space*, Oxford: Blackwell.

Lefebvre, H. (2003), *The Urban Revolution*, Minneapolis: University of Minnesota Press.

Lichtenstein, R. and Sinclair, I. (2000), *Rodinsky's Room*, London: Granta.

Link, A. (2004), ' "The Capitol of Darknesse": Gothic Spatialities in the London of Peter Ackroyd's *Hawksmoor*', *Contemporary Literature* 45(3): 516–37.

Liu, A. (2002), 'Literary Studies in Cyberspace: Texts, Contexts, and Criticism', Modern Languages Association Annual Convention, New York, 29 December 2002.

Lotman, J. (1977), *The Structure of Artistic Texts*, Ann Arbor, MI: University of Michigan Press.

Luckhurst, R. (2002), 'The Contemporary London Gothic and the Limits of the "Spectral Turn"', *Textual Practice* 16(3): 527–46.

Luckhurst, R. (2003), 'Occult London', in J. Kerr and A. Gibson (eds), *London from Punk to Blair*, London: Reaktion.

Lukács, G. (1971), *The Theory of the Novel*, Cambridge, MA: M.I.T.

Lynch, K. (1960), *The Image of the City*, Cambridge, MA: M.I.T.

Lyotard, J. (1984), *The Postmodern Condition: A Report on Knowledge*, Minneapolis, MI: University of Minneapolis Press.

MacFarlane, R. (2005), 'A Road of One's Own', *Times Literary Supplement*, 7 October, 2005: 3.

MacKay, D. (1969), *Information, Mechanism and Meaning*, Cambridge: MIT Press.

Mackenzie, A. (1997), 'The Mortality of the Virtual: Real-Time, Archive and Dead-Time in Information Networks', *Convergence* 3(2): 59–71.

Marcuse, H. (2005), *The New Left and the 1960s: Collected Papers of Herbert Marcuse*, Vol. 3, London and New York: Routledge.

Marshall, A. (2001), 'Order from Chaos and the "Economy-Ecology Analogy": A Re-reading of "Postmodern Science"', *Yearbook 2001 of the Institute for Advanced Studies on Science, Technology and Society*, http://www.ifz.tugraz.at/ias/IAS-STS/Publications/Yearbook-2001 [accessed 25 August 2014].

Marx, K. (1977), *The Eighteenth Brumaire of Louis Bonaparte*, Moscow: Progress.

Marx, K. (1990), *Capital: A Critique of Political Economy*, Vol. 1, Harmondsworth: Penguin.

Mayr, O. (1986), *Authority, Liberty and Automatic Machinery in Early Modern Europe*, Baltimore, MD: Johns Hopkins University Press.

McHale, B. (1989), *Postmodernist Fiction*, London: Routledge.

McKay, G. (1996), *Senseless Acts of Beauty: Cultures of Resistance*, London: Verso.

Meacher, C. (2005), 'Breaking the Skin of Things: Iain Sinclair Talks to Colette Meacher About Joycean Epiphany, Being Held at Gunpoint, the Trashed Sublime, Narrative Leaps, Writing Things into Being, and Punk Transcendence', *Literary London Journal, Interdisciplinary Studies in the Representation of London*, 3(2), http://www.literarylondon.org/londonjournal/september2005/interview.html [accessed 1 October 2014].

Merivale, P. (2010), 'Postmodern and Metaphysical Detection', in C.J. Rzepka and L. Horsley (eds), *A Companion to Crime Fiction*, Oxford: Blackwell: 308–20.

Merivale, P. and Sweeney, S.E. (1999), *Detecting Texts: The Metaphysical Detective Story from Poe to Postmodernism*, Philadelphia: University of Pennsylvania Press.

Mink, L.O. (1987), *Historical Understanding*, Ithaca: Cornell University Press.

Moran, J. (2005), *Reading the Everyday*, London: Routledge.

Morrison, B. and Motion, A. (1982), *The Penguin Book of Contemporary Poetry*, Harmondsworth: Penguin.

Morton, T. (2009), *Ecology Without Nature: Rethinking Environmental Aesthetics*, Cambridge, MA: Harvard University Press.

Mottram, E. (1972), *Allen Ginsberg in the Sixties*, Brighton/Seattle: Unicorn Bookshop.

Nancy, J.L. (1991), *The Inoperative Community*, Minneapolis: University of Minnesota Press.

Nava, M. (2007), *Visceral Cosmopolitanism: Gender, Culture and the Normalisation of Difference*, Oxford: Berg.

Nora, P. (1996), *Realms of Memory: Rethinking the French Past*, Vol. 1, New York: Columbia University Press.

Nunes, M. (2011), *Error: Glitch, Noise and Jam in New Media Cultures*, New York and London: Continuum.

Nuttall, J. (1970), *Bomb Culture*, London: Paladin.

Olson, C. (1987), *Charles Olson & Robert Creeley: The Complete Correspondence*, Vol. 8, Boston: David R. Godine Publisher.

Olson, C. (1994), 'Projective Verse', in P. Hoover (ed), *Postmodern American Poetry: A Norton Anthology*, New York: Norton.

Oudenampsen, M. (2007), 'Amsterdam TM, the City as a Business', in BAVO (G. Boie and M. Pauwels) (eds), *Urban Politics Now: Re-imagining Democracy in the Neoliberal City*, Rotterdam: NAi: 110–27.

Panagia, D. and Rancière, J. (2000), 'Dissenting Words: A Conversation with Jacques Rancière', *Diacritics*, 30(2): 113–26.

Paulson, W. (1988), *The Noise of Culture: Literary Texts in a World of Information*, Ithaca: Cornell University Press.

Paulson, W. (1991), 'Literature, Complexity, Interdisciplinarity', in N.K. Hayles (ed), *Chaos and Order: Complex Dynamics in Literature and Science*, Chicago: Chicago University Press.

Petit, C. and Sinclair, I. (2004), *London Orbital*, Illuminations, DVD.

Petit, C. and Sinclair, I. (2004a), 'Interview with the Film-Makers', *London Orbital*. Illuminations, DVD.

Pilkington, M. and Baker, P. (2002), 'City Brain: A Meeting with the Pioneer Psychogeographer', *Fortean Times*, April 2002, http://www.forteantimes.com/features/interviews/37/iain_sinclair.html [accessed 27 November 2014].

Potter, R. (1994), 'Culture Vulture: The Testimony of Iain Sinclair's *Downriver*', *Parataxis*, 5: 40–8.

Rancière, J. (1989), *Nights of Labour: The Worker's Dream in Nineteenth-Century France*, Philadelphia: Temple University Press.

Rancière, J. (1999), *Disagreement: Politics and Philosophy*, Minneapolis: University of Minnesota Press.

Rancière, J. (2009), *The Politics of Aesthetics: The Distribution of the Sensible*, London and New York: Continuum.

Rancière, J. (2010), *Dissensus: On Politics and Aesthetics*, London: Continuum.

Royle, N. (2003), *The Uncanny*, Manchester: Manchester University Press.

Sales, R. (2002), *John Clare: A Literary Life*, Basingstoke: Macmillan.

Samuels, R. (1992), 'Mrs. Thatcher's Return to Victorian Values', *Proceedings of the British Academy*, 78: 9–29. Online at http://www.proc.britac.ac.uk/cgi-bin/somsid. cgi?page=volumes/pba78 [accessed 20 July 2011].

Sassen, S. (2001), *The Global City: London, New York, Tokyo*, Princeton: Princeton University Press.

Sassen, S. (2005), 'The Global City: Introducing a Concept', *The Brown Journal of World Affairs*, 11(2): 27–43.

Sassen, S. (2006), *Cities in a World Economy*, Thousand Oaks, CA: Pine Forge.

Scheick, W.J. (1997), ' "Murder in My Soul": Genre and Ethos in Zangwill's, *The Big Bow Mystery*', *English Literature in Transition, 1880–1920*, 40(1): 23–33.

Schirato, T. and Webb, J. (2003), *Understanding Globalization*, London: Sage.

Seale, K. (2008), 'Textual Refuse: Iain Sinclair's Politics and Poetics of Refusal', unpublished Ph.D thesis, University of Sydney.

Sears, J. (2005), 'Walking in the Literary Necropolis: Iain Sinclair's Overwritings of the Dead', *Interculture*, Vol. 2, http://www.fsu.edu/~proghum/interculture/ Walking%20in%20The%20Literary%20Necropolis.htm [accessed 1 June 2009].

Serres, M. (1982), *Hermes: Literature, Science and Philosophy*, Baltimore: Johns Hopkins University Press.

Serres, M. (1995), *Genesis*, Ann Arbor: University of Michigan Press.

Serres, M. (2007), *The Parasite*, Minneapolis: University of Minnesota Press.

Sheppard, R. (2005), *The Poetry of Saying: British Poetry and Its Discontents 1950-2000*, Liverpool: Liverpool University Press.

Sheppard, R. (2005a), 'Iain Sinclair's *Lud Heat*', http://robertsheppard.blogspot. com/2005/11/robert-sheppard-iain-sinclairs-lud.html [accessed 23 October 2014].

Sheppard, R. (2006), 'Poets Behaving Badly', *Jacket*, 31, http://jacketmagazine.com/31/ sheppard-barry.html [accessed 16 September 2014].

Sheppard, R. (2007), *Iain Sinclair*, Tavistock: Northcote House.

Shannon, C. (1948), 'A Mathematical Theory of Communication', *Bell System Technical Journal*, 27: 379–423; 623–56, http://cm.bell-labs.com/cm/ms/what/shannonday/paper.html [accessed 23 June 2010].

Sinclair, I. (1971), *The Kodak Mantra Diaries*, London: Albion Village Press.

Sinclair, I. (1991), *Downriver: (Or, the Vessels of Wrath), a Narrative in Twelve Tales*, London: Paladin.

Sinclair, I. (1994), *Radon Daughters: A Voyage, Between Art and Terror, from the Mound of Whitechapel to the Limestone Pavements of the Burren*, London: Cape.

Sinclair, I. (1995), *White Chappell, Scarlet Tracings*, London: Vintage.

Sinclair, I. (1996), *Conductors of Chaos: A Poetry Anthology*, London: Picador.

Sinclair, I. (1997), *Lights Out for the Territory: 9 Excursions in the Secret History of London*, London: Granta.

Sinclair, I. (1998), *Lud Heat and Suicide Bridge*, London: Granta.

Sinclair, I. (1999), *Sorry Meniscus*, London: Profile Books.

Sinclair, I. (2001), *Landor's Tower: or The Imaginary Conversations*, London: Granta.

Sinclair, I. (2001a), 'Introduction', in A. Baron (ed), *The Lowlife*, London: Harvill.

Sinclair, I. (2002), *White Goods*, Uppingham: Goldmark.

Sinclair, I. (2002a), *London Orbital: A Walk around the M25*, London: Granta.

Sinclair, I. (2004), *Dining on Stones: (or The Middle Ground)*, London: Hamish Hamilton.

Sinclair, I. (2005), *Edge of the Orison: In the Traces of John Clare's 'Journey Out of Essex'*, London: Penguin.

Sinclair, I. (2006), *London City of Disappearances*, London: Hamish Hamilton.

Sinclair, I. (2007), *Debriefing*, The Picture Press, DVD.

Sinclair, I. (2007a), 'Diving Into Dirt', in S. Gill, (ed) *Archaeology in Reverse*, London: Nobody in Association with the Archive of Modern Conflict.

Sinclair, I. (2009), *Hackney, That Rose-Red Empire: A Confidential Report*, London: Hamish Hamilton.

Sinclair, I. (2009a), 'My House', http://www.independent.co.uk/property/house-and-home/my-house-iain-sinclairs-40year-love-affair-1652507.html

Sinclair, I. (2011), *Ghost Milk: Calling Time on the Grand Project*, London: Hamish Hamilton.

Sinclair, I. (2011a), 'Hague', recording of lecture: The Knight's Move, at KABK (Royal Academy of Art) The Hague. 19 January 2011, author's personal recording.

Sinclair, I. (2013), *Silenic Drift*, London: Strange Attractors.

Sinclair, I. (2013a), *Austerlitz & After: Tracking Sebald*, London: Test Centre.

Sinclair, I. and Boal, I. (2011), 'Orbiting London: A Conversation with Iain Sinclair', 21 March 2011, Recording at http://www.bbk.ac.uk/bih/news/sinclair

Sinclair, I. and Klinkert, R. (2007), *Ah! Sunflower*, The Picture Press, DVD.

Sinclair, I. and Petit, C. (2002), *London Orbital*, Illuminations, DVD.

Sinclair, I. and Petit, C. (2002a), 'Interview', in I. Sinclair and C. Petit (eds), *London Orbital*, Illuminations, DVD.

Sinclair, I. and Self, W. (2008), 'Psychogeography: Will Self and Iain Sinclair in Conversation with Kevin Jackson', http://www.literarylondon.org/london-journal/march2008/sinclair-self.html [accessed 31 October 2014].

Sloterdijk, P. (2010), *Critique of Cynical Reason*, Minneapolis: University of Minnesota Press.

Solnit, R. (2001), *Wanderlust: A History of Walking*, Harmondsworth: Penguin.

Spivak, G. (1976), 'Translator's Preface', in J. Derrida (ed), *Of Grammatology*, Baltimore and London: The Johns Hopkins University Press.

Spivak, G. (1988), 'Can the Subaltern Speak?' in C. Nelson and L. Grossberg (eds), *Marxism and the Interpretation of Culture*, Urbana: University of Illinois Press: 271–315.

Standing, G. (2011), *The Precariat: The New Dangerous Class*, London: Bloomsbury.

Swyngedouw, E. (2007), 'The Post-Political City', in BAVO (G. Boie and M. Pauwels) (eds), *Urban Politics Now: Re-imagining Democracy in the Neoliberal City*, Rotterdam: NAi: 58–77.

Vardy, A. (2000), 'Viewing and Reviewing Clare', in J. Goodridge and S. Kövesi (eds), *John Clare New Approaches*, Peterborough: The John Clare Society.

Walkowitz, R.L. (2006), *Immigrant Fictions: Contemporary Literature in an Age of Globalization*, Madison: University of Wisconsin Press.

Watson, B. (2005), 'Iain Sinclair: Revolutionary Novelist or Revolting Nihilist', http://www.militantesthetix.co.uk/critlit/SINCLAIR.htm [accessed 23 September 2013].

Weller, P. (2009), *A Mirror for Our Times: 'The Rushdie Affair' and the Future of Multiculturalism*, London: Continuum.

White, H. (1975), *Metahistory*, Baltimore, MD: Johns Hopkins University Press.

Wiener, N. (1954), *The Human Use of Human Beings*, London: Eyre and Spottiswoode.

Williams, R. (1975), *The Country and the City*, St. Albans: Paladin.

Wilson, E. (1992), *The Sphinx in the City: Urban Life, the Control of Disorder and Women*, Berkeley: University of California Press.

Wolfreys, J. (1998), *Writing London: The Trace of the Urban Text From Blake to Dickens*, London: Macmillan.

Wolfreys, J. (2004), *Writing London: Materiality, Memory, Spectrality*, Vol. 2, London: Palgrave.

Wright, P. (1993), *A Journey Through Ruins: A Keyhole Portrait of British Postwar Life and Culture*, London: Flamingo.

Wright, P. (1996), Iain Sinclair in conversation with Patrick Wright in *Walk*. BBC Radio 3, broadcast 5 January 1996.

Zangwill, I. *The Big Bow Mystery*, http://www.gutenberg.org/ebooks/28164 [accessed 1 November 2014].

Žižek S. (1992), *Looking Awry: An Introduction to Lacan Through Popular Culture*, Cambridge, MA: M.I.T.

Žižek S. (2008), *The Sublime Object of Ideology*, London: Verso.

Žižek S. (2008a), 'Tolerance as an Ideological Category', *Critical Inquiry* 34: 660–82.

Žižek S. (2008b), *Violence*, London: Profile.

Žižek S. (2008c), *Violence: Six Sideways Reflections*, New York: Picador.

Index

absolute space
    abstract space *vs.* 74, 79–80
    city as *imago mundi* 75
    'From Camberwell to Golgotha'
        (essay) 75
    heterotopical position 75
    in *Lud Heat* 73, 76–7
    in *The Production of Space* (Lefebvre)
        73–4
abstract labour 79
Act of Seeing With One's Own Eyes, The
    (Brakhage's film) 75
Adorno, T. 23, 44, 48, 132, 136, 139, 140
Ah! Sunflower (AS) 29, 31, 34
Albion Village Press 3
"Alice in the Train" (Tenniel) 113–14
Alice through the Looking-Glass
    (Carroll) 113
Alnutt, G. 62
Alvarez, A. 61, 62
Amis, M. 91
Anderson, B. 51
Angry Brigade 23, 46–7, 49, 51–2
anti-road protest 54
artistic production 27
Augé, M. 148, 149

Baker, B. 23, 28, 49, 50, 102, 105, 143
Baker, P. 72 n.4
Bal, M. 116
Ball, J. C. 116
Baroque cycle (Stephenson) 60
Barry, P. 61, 64
Barthes, R. 172
Bate, J. 172, 173, 175
Bateson, G. 8, 10, 29
Bavidge, J. 3, 4
BBC Radio 4 3
beautiful soul – or *belle ame* (Hegel) 49
Benjamin, W. 48, 95
Benn T. (Postmaster General) 30

Berger, J. 107
Big Bow Mystery, The (1892) 98
Black Mountain Poets 2
Bleeding London (Nicholson) 60
Boal, I. 49
Bolter, J. 148
Bond, R. 3, 4, 135
Bonnett, A. 28
Botting, F. 14
Brakhage, S. 75–6
British Museum 68
British poetry
    alternative tradition 24
    city as topic 64
    contemporary 61–2
    exclusive communalism 86
    experimental 60
    Lud Heat 61–2
    Olson's effect 66
    post-war 62
British Poetry Revival 60–2, 86.
    See also Lud Heat (LH)
British Socialist Worker's Party 27
Brooker, P. 98, 105, 106
Burroughs, W. 40, 52, 88
Byatt, A. S. 91

Camberwell Art School 75
Cantos, The 83
Caretaker (Pinter) 137
Carmichael, Stokely 28–9, 32, 34–5
Castells, M. 12
Catling, B. (sculptor) 75–6
Chambers, R. 101–2
Channel Tunnel 150
city as encounter. *See also* London
    motorway extension 56
    public and private space 54–7
    type of space 54
City of Glass (Auster) 42
Clare, J. 25, 26, 47, 143, 161–76, 183

Clash, The 111
class conflict 110
Cold War 88, 104, 107
collage
    disenfranchised authors 45
    Hopkins view 37–8
    Modernist technique 37
    walk as spatial 54–7
Conductors of Chaos (1996) 62
Congress on the Dialectics of Liberation
    28–9, 33
Connell, N. 98
Conservative Party 109, 116
Cooper, D. 33, 35
Cosgrove, D. 171
cosmopolitanism 7, 108
Coverley, M. 38, 39
Crozier, A. 62
cultural capital 27
cultural resistance 111, 118
cybernetic hypothesis 36

Daily Telegraph 28, 144
Dark Lanthorns (1999) 124, 138
De Quincey, T. 70
Debord, G. 31, 40
Debriefing (DB) 29, 36–7
Derrida, J. 16, 18, 27 n.1, 125, 126, 127, 129
Descartes, R. 11
detective fiction 99–101
Dining on Stones (DS) 5, 16, 91 n.1, 124,
    133, 138, 143
Director's Cut (Royle) 60
Diving Into Dirt (DD) 21
Dorn, E. 66
Downriver (1991)
    cultural and aesthetic space 108
    cultural cynicism 92
    dual status of narrative 91
    female characters 93, 119
    form of opposition 109
    locked room mystery 92, 95, 97–102,
        104, 187
    narratological questions 89, 92
    nature of labour conditions in 87–8
    Penguin edition 87
    post-historical context 24, 88–9,
        106, 109
    post-modernism 88, 107, 112

publishing process 87
revision of Rushdie's name 104
structure of the text 102
Thatcherism, satires of 110, 117
TV-pitch language 90
vessels of wrath 89–90, 116–20
victim's role 94–5
Victorian values 116

economic radicalism 1990s 51
Edge of the Orison (EO) 25–6, 47, 160–1,
    165, 167, 177
Edwards, K. 60
Eliot, T. S. 37, 61, 72, 84
Emilsson, W. 17, 18
Enlightenment 100, 102, 105, 112–13, 119,
    125, 175
Erlich, V. 13
Evans, E. J. 92

Farmer's Boy, The (1800) 164
Fenton, J. 106–7
Fisher, A. 52, 59–60, 65–7
Fisher, M. 65, 110
Florida, R. 5
Fordism 49, 52
Foster, H. 6
Foucault, M. 113, 114 n.7, 163
Freud Museum (London) 125
Freud, S. 15, 16
Friedland, M. L. 99
From Hell (1991–8, 1999, graphic serial) 60
Fuentes, C. 106
Fukuyama, F. 24, 88

'George Davis is Innocent' 46
Ghost Milk (GM) 4, 26, 179–87. *See also*
    London Olympics 2012
Gibbons, F. 115 n.8
Ginsberg, A. 28–36
    address to cameras 29
    non-violent resistance 34
    revealing moments of *The Kodak
        Mantra Diaries* 31–4
    on revolutionary transformation 28
    TV programmes on 32
globalization 2, 7, 21, 25–6, 46, 118, 185
The Golem 123
Grand Project. *See* London Olympics 2012

Grant, C. 10
Granta 3, 72
Great Bow Mystery (Zangwill) 102
Grusin, R. 149
Guardian, The 106, 124
Guilhamet, L. 119

Habermas, J. 153
habitus 105, 149, 187
Hackney, That Rose-Red Empire (HRE) 3
Hamish Hamilton 3
Hardt, M. 11, 12, 20, 44, 45, 52, 53
Harvey, D. 2, 4, 12, 144, 150 n.4, 170
Hawksmoor (Ackroyd) 60
Hawksmoor, N.
    occult significance 2
    sense of dread 76
    Sinclair's quotes on 81, 85
    skyline signals 80–1, 86
    spiritual and secular topographies 78
Hayek, F. 2, 141
Head, D. 108 n.5, 110
Heart of Darkness (Conrad) 102, 112
Heartfield, J. 28, 144
Hillis-Miller, J. 129
Holocaust 123, 125, 131, 136
Holy War 105
Hopkins, B. 37–8
Horkheimer, M. 132, 136, 138–40
Horovitz, M. 61
How the Dead Live (Self) 60
Howl (1956) 29
Hungerford, A. 29
Hunt, L. 141
Huntington, S. 107
Hutcheon, L. 88
Huyssen, A. 125, 158

Icarus (university literary magazine) 2
immigrants 46
In the Red House (Roberts) 60
industrial revolution 30
Internationale Situationist # 1, 1957 38
'Isle of Doges (PLC) Vat City' section 111, 118

Jack the Ripper 18, 24, 70, 89, 92, 94–5, 115
Jackson, K. 2, 3, 8, 39, 39 n.2, 68 n.3

James Tait Black Memorial Prize 3
Jameson, F. 88, 110–12, 116, 173
Jeffries, S. 39, 41
Johnson, S. 64
Joyce, J. 12, 37, 72, 88

King Rat (Miéville) 60
Klinkert, R. 29–32
Knabb, K. 40
Kodak Mantra Diaries, The (KMD) 31–2, 34, 36
Koran 107
Kujundzic, D. 125, 130, 131

Laing, R. D. 29, 42, 164
Landor's Tower 91 n.1
Lefebvre, H. 23, 73–6, 135
liberalism 26, 107, 142
Lichtenstein, R. (Rodinsky's room) 25, 121–5, 127–32, 136–40
    'colourful characters' 123
    darkness of twentieth-century 136
    industrialization of mourning 132
    lamed vavnik, legend form 128
    logic of archive 127, 130, 137, 139
    London legend 140
    noise as *lieu de mémoire* 123–4
    about Poland 130–3
    pre-Hasidic myth 128
    textual cohabitation 122
    theological and epistemological combination 129
    urban topography 125
Lights out for the Territory: 9 Excursions in the Secret History of London (1997) 39, 47, 124
Liu, A. 126
London
    bombings July 2007 158
    cityscape in 1990s 47
    contemporary 72
    ethnic diversity 108
    expansion in 1986 50
    heterotopic geography 76
    Millennial 1
    mythologization 82
    new buildings 30
    pre-classical architecture 81
    topography 68–9, 85, 133

London City of Disappearances 50
London Fields (Rushdie) 91
London Olympics 2012 21, 179, 181, 184
London Orbital (LO) 6, 143, 150, 154–5
London Orbital (LOf). *See also* M25 walks
   'acoustic footstep' 149
   background noise 154
   effect of consciousness 156
   location-based identities 151
   neoliberalism 152
London Review of Books 3, 91, 143
'Londonostalgia' 28, 144
Londonostalgics 28
Lotman, J. 13
Luckhurst, R. 60
Lud Heat (LH)
   absolute space 73, 76–7, 85
   American inheritance in 67
   British Poetry Revival 62
   construction of place in 62, 64
   Fisher's review 59–60, 84
   funerary rituals 85
   generic mutation 68, 82, 86
   kinds of space in 73
   London's topography 85–6
   Modernist paradigm 64–5, 71–2
   mythic method 84
   narrator's exclusion 78
   notions of community as blood-land 85
   occult topography 83, 85
   Olsonian project 61, 65–8, 76
   prose sections 75
   resemblance with *Künstlerroman* 67
   spatial language 83
   ubiquitous in the representation of
      London 60–1
   welfare state, depiction 85
Lukács, G. 88, 93, 94, 97
Lyotard, J. 125
Lyrical Ballads (1798) 164

M25 walks 2, 25–6, 143, 149–57, 160–1,
   177
MacFarlane, R. 28, 144
MacKay, D. 14
Mackenzie, A. 126
Manpower Commission 49
Marcuse, H. 29, 35
Marshall, A. 141

Marx, K. 163, 164, 168, 171
McHale, B. 88, 99, 100
McKay, G. 57 n.6
McNamara, P. 141
Meacher, C. 158, 158 n.6, 159, 160
Merivale, P. 99
middle-class 51, 63, 98, 117, 173
Mink, L. O. 91, 91 n.2, 92
Moran, J. 150 n.3, 151, 151 n.5
Morrison, B. 61
Morton, T. 49
Mother London (Moorcock) 60
Motion, A. 61
Mottram, E. 31, 60, 62
multiculturalism 108
Murders in the Rue Morgue (1841) 99

Nancy, J. L. 85
Nava, M. 107
Negri, A. 11, 12, 20, 44, 45, 52, 53
neoliberalism 2, 9–10, 18–19, 21–2, 25,
   27, 46, 48, 50, 52, 57, 109, 117, 118,
   142, 144–7, 148–50, 150–2, 153,
   160, 179–80, 185
New Labour 2, 109, 144, 151, 180
New Left Review, The 110
New York Times 32
nihilism 27
Nora, P. 123–8, 134
Nunes, M. 10

Olson, C. 61, 65–8, 67 n.2, 76
omniscience 89, 98–102, 104, 121
Oudenampsen, M. 21, 146

Paladin (publishing house) 3
Panagia, D. 20
Parks Department Manual, The 79
Paulson, W. 13, 71
Penguin 87, 155
*Penguin Book of Contemporary British
   Poetry, The* (1982) 61
Performance (Roeg and Cammell) 137
Petit, C. 154–7, 160
Pilkington, M. 72 n.4
Poe, E. A. 99, 102
poetry. *See also* British poetry
   abstract labour and space 79–80
   British tradition 24

Clare's 163, 175
communicative function 63
experimental 60–1
linguistic noise 12–13
Mendelson's 49
Modernist paradigm 63, 72
myth and 84
Olson's binary oppositions 65–7
open 76
political value of 19
ragbag approach 65
small press production 13, 48
speech-based 76
urban space and 4, 68
Wordsworth's perception 164
as workplace 77
political radicalism 1970s 51
postmodernism
    in *Downriver* 24, 88, 103, 106–7,
        110–12, 116
    'Economy-Ecology' 141
    neoliberalism 151
    orthodoxy 106–7
    in *Rodinsky's Room* 125
    poetics 72
'Postmodernism, Or, The Cultural Logic
    of Late Capitalism' (Jameson's
    essay) 110
Potter, R. 92
powerlessness 54, 56
Prima Donna's tale 89, 95–8, 103
private space *vs.* public space 52, 54–7
Production of Space, The (Lefebvre) 73
Protestantism 118

radicalism
    1960s 11, 48
    1970s 48, 51
    1990s 48, 52
    British 47, 49
    economic 51
    enterprise culture 51–2
    homelessness 46
    nostalgic 27–8
    political 51
Radon Daughters (RD) 42
Rancière, J. 13, 19–21, 56, 148, 174, 175
reforgetting forms
    historiography 51

private and public space. 52
production process. 52–3
radicalism 51–2
structures of exclusion 53
revolutionary situations
    qualitative 35–6
    quantitative 35–6
revolutionary transformation 29–30
Rhys, J. 88
Rodinsky's Room (RR)
    anti-Semitism 132
    fictional and historical ontologies
        136
    Ghost storage 138–40
    'locked room mystery,' 121
    logic of redemption 139
    metaphorical aspect 136
    narrative topography of London
        133
    narrative *vs.* archive 137
    occult fabulation 133
    Polish immigrants, 123
    prominence of the archive 125–7
    Sinclair's description 122–4
    Spitalfields 122, 124, 134–5
    urban narratives 122, 125
romanticism 27–8
Royal Observatory (Greenwich) 68
Royle, N. 60, 100
Rushdie, S.
    fatwa on 26, 92, 104
    freedom of expression 107–8
    Sinclair on 104–5
    thematic comparison with Sinclair's
        novels 91

Sales, R. 163
Samuels, R. 116
Sassen, S. 1, 12, 145
Schirato, T. 12
scientific socialism 28
Seale, K. 4, 5
Sears, J. 137, 138
Self, W. 39, 60
Serres, M. 8, 11, 18, 35, 36, 82, 149, 152,
        153, 154, 186
Shannon, C. 8, 10, 14
Sheppard, R. 21, 61–3, 65, 66, 68, 89
Silenic Drift (SD) 6

Sinclair, I.
  2012 London Olympics 179, 181, 184
  artistic practice 37
  career change 142
  cartographic perspectives 42
  depiction of the walk 27
  dérive, notion of 40–1
  dériviste's role 41
  description of Xanaxshire 175–6
  first description of Rodinsky's room
    121, 124
  on Grand Project (Olympics) 180–1
  idea of mobility 160–1
  imagination power 119
  on *The Kodak Mantra Diaries* 36
  MacFarlane on 28
  mythic topography 85
  on neoliberal urban space 144, 180
  'nostalgic radicalism' 28
  on objective violence 35
  political assessment 28
  power of imagination 28, 112, 119–20,
    137, 176
  proprietorial promptings 156
  psychogeography 23, 29, 38–42, 57,
    153
  on revolutionary transformation 29
  satire 18, 109–10, 116–18 (*see also*
    Thatcherism)
  twitchy net-curtain syndrome 51
  on urban walking 38–42, 44, 46, 54,
    56–7
  vision of the Dome 143, 145
  Watson's expression 27
Situationist International 29
Sloterdijk, P. 112, 118, 119
small-press
  publications 47–8
  radical politics 47–51
social conflict 106–7
socialism 28, 109
Solnit, R. 161
Sorry Meniscus (SM) 143, 145
space
  absolute 73–6, 80
  abstract 72–4, 76–7, 80, 85
  bureaucratization 139
  contemporary perceptions 126
  dissensual 23–5, 121

  global 7, 104–5, 171, 185, 187
  instrumentalization 139
  public 52, 54–6, 69, 78, 105,
    146, 150
  types in cities 145
  urban 2, 4, 15, 23, 28, 41, 45, 50, 65, 68,
    74, 122, 145, 180
  waste 14, 22
Spivak, G. 163, 164, 169, 172
Standing, G. 5
Stevenson, R. L. 81
Still Life with Chair Caning (Picasso) 37
Stravinsky, I. 37
Swyngedouw, E. 21

tagging 43–5
Teh, I. 185
'Territories' (Twain) 47
Thatcherism 10, 18, 52, 89, 92, 109–10,
  117, 119–20, 125, 133. *See also*
  Downriver
tiers exclu 35–6
Trinity College, Dublin 2
'TV was a Baby Crawling Towards That
  Death Chamber,' (Ginsberg's poem)
  29

Ulysses (Joyce) 37, 83
urban theory 29

V-shaped walk 41–2
Vardy, A. 164
Vatican 112, 118
Victorian novelists 86
Victorian values 108, 116–17
violence, forms of 33–5

walk
  M25 2, 25–6, 143, 149–57, 160–1,
    177
  Sinclair's depiction 27
  spatial 54–7
  urban 38–42, 44, 46, 54, 56–7
  V-shaped 41–2
Walkowitz, R. L. 108
Waste Land, The (Eliot) 37, 83
Watson, B. 18, 19, 28, 184
Weller, P. 113
West Deutsche Radiofunk (WDR) 32, 36

White Chappell, Scarlet Tracings (WST)
  critique of the Dome 143–5, 147–8
  culture of waiting 146
  description of book dealers 143
  Millennium Experience 144, 147–8
  structural and ideological changes
      (British economy) 142
  symbolic function of the road 141–2
White Goods (WG) 14
White, H. 92
Wiener, N. 8, 10

Williams, R. 173
Wilson, E. 19
Wolfreys, J. 113
Woman in White, The (Collins) 103
working-class 27 n.1, 109, 117, 134
Wright, F. L. 38
Wright, P. 92, 124

Xanaxshire 170–2, 175–6

Zangwill, I. 98–9
Žižek, S. 34–45

Lightning Source UK Ltd.
Milton Keynes UK
UKOW05f2058180517
301449UK00001B/60/P